Partners All:

A HISTORY OF BROOME COUNTY, NEW YORK

VISIONS FEDERAL CREDIT UNION

*is pleased to make available this book
on the history of Broome County, New York,
to the Greater Binghamton community.*

OFFERING A WIDE VARIETY OF QUALITY financial products and services, Visions Federal Credit Union has been serving the financial needs of its members in the Greater Binghamton area since 1965. Today, forty years later, we are a premier community credit union continuing to provide financial services to families and businesses throughout Greater Binghamton. We are committed to the credit union philosophy of "People Helping People" and to being an active, involved part of the communities we serve.

We are proud to be a part of *Partners All: A History of Broome County, New York* and prouder yet to be a part of this wonderful community we live in. It is our privilege to join with the Broome County Historical Society in a project that will help the Society maintain its tradition of protecting the history of this great community, one that will honor the history represented by the images inside these pages.

Special thanks to the author Gerald R. Smith and his assistant Charles J. Browne. Their documentation has preserved our history into something that will benefit each of us, as well as future generations.

Frank E. Berrish
President/CEO

PARTNERS ALL:
A History of Broome County, New York

BY GERALD R. SMITH

THE
DONNING COMPANY
PUBLISHERS

Copyright © 2006 by Gerald R. Smith

All rights reserved, including the right to reproduce this work in any form whatsoever without permission in writing from the publisher, except for brief passages in connection with a review.

For information, please write:

The Donning Company Publishers
184 Business Park Drive, Suite 206
Virginia Beach, VA 23462

Steve Mull, General Manager
Barbara Buchanan, Office Manager
Pamela Koch, Editor
Amanda D. Guilmain, Graphic Designer
Amy Thomann, Imaging Artist
Susan Adams, Project Research Coordinator
Scott Rule, Director of Marketing
Stephanie Linneman, Marketing Coordinator

Mary Taylor, Project Director

Library of Congress Cataloging-in-Publication Data

Smith, Gerald R., 1954-
  Partners all : a history of Broome County, New York / by Gerald R. Smith.
    p. cm.
  Includes bibliographical references and index.
  ISBN-13: 978-1-57864-339-4 (hardcover : alk. paper)
  ISBN-10: 1-57864-339-2 (hardcover : alk. paper)
  1. Broome County (N.Y.)—History. 2. Broome County (N.Y.)—History—Pictorial works. I. Title.
  F127.B8S59 2006
  974.7'75—dc22
                           2005029396

Printed in the United States of America at Walsworth Publishing Company

On cover and title page: *View of Binghamton from Mt. Prospect*, 1852 by Edward Beyer.
Courtesy Roberson Museum & Science Center

Dedication

To my wife, Kathy, and my daughters,
Amelia and Abigail—
for their patience and endurance
in good and bad times.
Their faith in me and their love fulfills my life.

	Preface	8
	Introduction	9
	Timelines	10
section one—OUR HISTORY		12
1	LAND OF THE LONGHOUSE	14
2	THE AMERICAN REVOLUTION AND THE IROQUOIS	26
3	A NEW LAND FOR SETTLEMENT	36
4	A COUNTY IS BORN	50
5	CANAL FEVER	66
6	THE ARRIVAL OF THE IRON HORSE	78
7	IMMIGRATION AND INDUSTRY	96
8	A GOOD FIVE-CENT CIGAR	120
9	WHICH WAY EJ?	146
10	THE RISE OF IBM	176
11	THE VALLEY THAT CAME IN FROM THE COLD	196
12	THE DECLINE OF INDUSTRY	216
13	THE NEW MILLENNIUM	232

table of CONTENTS

section two—OUR COMMUNITIES — 242

14	THE CITY OF BINGHAMTON	244
15	THE TOWN OF BARKER	252
16	THE TOWN OF BINGHAMTON	258
17	THE TOWN OF CHENANGO	264
18	THE TOWN OF COLESVILLE	270
19	THE TOWN OF CONKLIN	278
20	THE TOWN OF DICKINSON	284
21	THE TOWN OF FENTON	292
22	THE TOWN OF KIRKWOOD	300
23	THE TOWN OF LISLE	306
24	THE TOWN OF MAINE	312
25	THE TOWN OF NANTICOKE	320
26	THE TOWN OF SANFORD	326
27	THE TOWN OF TRIANGLE	332
28	THE TOWN OF UNION	338
29	THE TOWN OF VESTAL	346
30	THE TOWN OF WINDSOR	354
31	THE VILLAGE OF DEPOSIT	362
32	THE VILLAGE OF ENDICOTT	368
33	THE VILLAGE OF JOHNSON CITY	376
34	THE VILLAGE OF LISLE	386
35	THE VILLAGE OF PORT DICKINSON	392
36	THE VILLAGE OF WHITNEY POINT	398
37	THE VILLAGE OF WINDSOR	404

Bibliography	410
Index	412
About the Author	416

Preface

OVER THE LAST EIGHTEEN YEARS since my first book, *The Valley of Opportunity: A Pictorial History of the Greater Binghamton Area* (Donning Co., 1988), was published, I have felt great satisfaction that I produced something that is still found in numerous homes and used in classrooms. But there was a lingering urge to move beyond just the events and history of what was often called the Triple Cities of Binghamton, Johnson City, and Endicott.

There was a need to relate the history of all of Broome County. Although numerous shorter histories and pictorial works had been published, there was no full-scale history since William Seward edited a three-volume work in 1924. Often, researchers had to blow the dust off those tomes only to find that the twentieth century got shortchanged in the work. Broome County's bicentennial in 2006 gave me just such an opportunity.

Much has changed over the eight decades since that last history. We have also had time to reflect upon the aspects of history often left out of the earlier works—the role of women, immigrants, and children. How has industry and technology affected our lives in Broome County?

A work of this size does not happen with the efforts of just one person. I am forever indebted to many people for their expertise and, often, patience during the creation process. The work and assistance of the historians of Broome County has been invaluable. They are: Town of Barker—Christine Gillette; Town of Binghamton—Judy Zurenda; Town of Chenango—Alice Ruby; Town of Colesville—Val LaClair; Town of Conklin—Bob Barber; Town of Dickinson & Village of Port Dickinson—Bob Blakeslee; Town of Fenton—Alice Deanjou; Town of Kirkwood—Sam Borruso; Town of Lisle & Village of Lisle—Eleanor Ticknor; Town of Maine—Nancy Rutkowski; Town of Nanticoke—Joann Costley; Town of Sanford—Ann Parsons; Town of Triangle—Alice Mesceda; Town of Union—Suzanne Meredith; Town of Vestal—Elizabeth Bartlow; Town of Windsor—Helen Osborne; Village of Deposit—Mary Cable; Village of Endicott—Lavonne Hausamann; Village of Johnson City—Janet Ottman; Village of Whitney Point—Juanita Aleba; and Village of Windsor—Charles English.

I want to offer my thanks to the staff at the Broome County Local History & Genealogy Center including Monica Buckley and Michael Cimaomo (who never said "run away," only an occasional "nee"), the volunteers of the Broome County Historical Society who have made the Local History & Genealogy Center such a success. My thanks to Donna Reigel, director of the Broome County Public Library; David Dixon, president, and the other members of the board of the Broome County Historical Society for their faith in my work; Eve Daniels of the Roberson Museum & Science Center for her assistance in finding artifacts; Mark Secoolish for bearing up during nearly forty years of friendship; and my family, including Kathy, Amelia, Abigail, and my father, Robert.

Finally, I offer my unending thanks to Charles Browne for being my assistant in this work and for serving as deputy county historian with constant support and help. Without his guidance and patience, this work would never have been completed.

Introduction

IT IS HARD TO DESCRIBE what makes Broome County, New York, such a great place to live. Those who have lived here all of their lives certainly do not count on a sunny, warm environment as enticement to stay. Maybe it is the many hills and valleys that make up this county. Perhaps it is our streams, brooks, and rivers flowing to the Chenango and Susquehanna Rivers that have their confluence in the city of Binghamton. These geographic elements offer magnificent views and picturesque autumns, but these alone are not enough to keep people here.

In earlier times, it could be said that it was the opportunity for employment and a new life working for paternalistic companies such as Endicott Johnson or IBM that made life here enticing. But much of this stable economic environment has disappeared or greatly changed. So why is Broome County still considered a great place to live? It is because there is a partnership that continues to live and grow in this county. It is a partnership between white collar and blue collar, between farmer and industrialist, between urban and rural, between government and private sector, and between the young and the aged. These partnerships have been built on trust and the knowledge that each needs the other to survive.

For more than two centuries, these partnerships have evolved and endured in times of plenty and in times of scarcity. It is this constancy that promotes a feeling of warmth and quality of life that is Broome County. It is because we are *Partners All*.

broome county timeline

1500 BC–c.1780	Iroquois Settlement
1779	Sullivan-Clinton Campaign
1790	William Bingham purchased land of present-day Binghamton
1798	Joshua Whitney (1773–1845) became land agent for William Bingham
1805	Wooden bridge constructed across Chenango River at Court Street
1806	Broome County created, named in honor of Lt. Col. John Broome
1834	Binghamton incorporated as a village
1837	Chenango Canal opens
1848	Erie Railroad opens line through area; others follow between 1853 and 1869
1854	Christ Church constructed by James Stewart Wells; Lester Brothers Boot & Shoe Company founded
1858	First cigar factory in Binghamton; New York State Inebriate Asylum constructed
1867	Binghamton incorporated as a city
1870	Population increases with influx of 1,920 immigrants from Eastern Europe
1877	Chenango Canal closed and filled to become State Street
1889	Bundy Manufacturing founded
1890	Fifty cigar factories operating, major strike; Henry B. Endicott takes control of Lester Brothers, keeping George F. Johnson (1857–1948) as superintendent
1892	Lestershire incorporated as a village
1899	Endicott Johnson Corporation founded
c.1900	Bundy Manufacturing renamed International Time Recording Company
1906	Endicott incorporated
1914	Thomas Watson (1874–1956) hired to run Computing-Tabulating-Recording Company (formerly ITR) in Endicott
1916	Lestershire renamed Johnson City

international timeline

1688	"Glorious Revolution"; constitutional monarchy in England
1776	Declaration of Independence
1783	Treaty of Paris; Britain recognized American Independence
1787	Constitutional Convention
1789	French Revolution began
1790	First US Census
1804–05	Lewis & Clark Expedition
1812–15	War of 1812
1814	Emperor Napoleon Bonaparte abdicated
1821	Electric motor & generator invented by M. Faraday
1825	Erie Canal opened
1831	Steam locomotive
1848	California Gold Rush; first US women's rights convention in Seneca Falls, NY; *Communist Manifesto* written by Marx & Engels
1861–65	American Civil War
1876	Telephone patented by Bell
1888	First successful overhead electric trolley model built by Frank Sprague of Richmond, VA
1898	Spanish-American War
1903	Wright Brothers flight
1912	Fox trot, inspired by ragtime music, hit the ballrooms
1914	Panama Canal opened

timelines

1924	Computing-Tabulating-Recording Company renamed International Business Machines
1935–36	Two major floods hit area
1942	Local firms involved in war effort; Agfa-Ansco seized by federal government because of ties to Germany
1946	Triple Cities College created in Endicott as part of Syracuse University
1947	Broome Community College started in Binghamton
1949	First local television station, WNBF, began broadcasting
c.1950s	Population moved from urban center; EJ began decline
1954	Roberson Museum opened
1964	Urban renewal began in Binghamton
1965	Newly named State University of New York at Binghamton located on Vestal Parkway
1968	EJ sold to outside firm; Route 17 expanded; Interstate 81 completed
1975	Oakdale Mall opened
1981	Fire in state office building closed facility for thirteen years
1992	NYSEG stadium opened, home to Binghamton Mets
1995–96	Link sold to Hughes Aircraft; last EJ shoe store closed
1998	Tornado hits area, killing three people
1999	Population of Broome County falls below 200,000
2005	Major flood reaches level of 1936 flood
2006	Broome County celebrates bicentennial

1914–18	World War I
1929	Black Tuesday precipitated Great Depression
1934–38	New Deal
1935	Monopoly board game introduced
1936	Spanish Civil War
1939–45	World War II
1941	Pearl Harbor attack by Japanese; US enters war
1945	United Nations created
1946	First electronic computer
1948	State of Israel created
1950–53	Korean War
1954	Rock 'n' roll music began
1955	Disneyland opened
1961	First men in space
1963	John F. Kennedy assassinated
1967	First heart transplant
1969	First man walked on the moon
1975	Vietnam War ended; personal computer created
1979	Compact disc invented
1990	Reunification of Germany
1991	Dissolution of the Soviet Union
2000	Millennium
2001	Terrorist attacks on US; World Trade Center destroyed; Global War on Terror begins

CHAPTER 1
Land of the Longhouse
PREHISTORY TO 1768

This painting by Foster Disinger depicts the thirteenth-century Owasco culture village that existed near present-day Castle Creek in the town of Chenango. The inhabitants lived in longhouses rather than the structures shown in the painting. (Courtesy Broome County Historical Society)

This is an illustration of the bark house used by the Iroquois nations for their longhouses. The Native American groups that inhabited this area used the longhouse as their home. (From *League of the Iroquois* by Lewis Henry Morgan, 1851)

IT IS HARD TO IMAGINE THE LAND that is Broome County covered with hundreds of feet of thick ice. Twelve thousand years ago, that was the sight that one would see upon looking over our county. Slowly, but surely, temperatures rose. The glaciers of the last Ice Age began to melt and recede from the future New York State. Around 10,000 BC, the fingers of the glaciers pushed the soil down creating the valleys that ring Broome County.

Tons of rock and stone were picked up and deposited throughout the region. As the ice melted, the water ran through the valley bed, creating channels. New streams, creeks, brooks, and rivers were formed that enriched the soil. The climate was still relatively cool, with enough moisture to support the growth of trees such as pine, spruce, and birch.

Animal life was found throughout the area. Mastodons and mammoths roamed the land. Their bones would later be found in places such as Lisle. Smaller animals such as bison, caribou, beavers, and wolves found a home in this valley. Cold-weather plants grew in what can only be described as a tundra-like environment.

Around 8,000 BC, the climate began to warm. Many of the colder plants and animal life moved northward. New species of flora and fauna began to flourish. This climatic change became significant somewhere between 5,000 BC and 3,000 BC. The warmer and drier weather began to support deciduous, nut-bearing trees. Rich soil and more plant life aided in supporting a more varied and larger animal population.

By the time of the mastodons and mammoths, the region's first people had arrived. They were prehistoric nomadic hunters who relied on the meat of the big game for their diet. These people—men, women and children—roamed the area looking for food. They also used plant life to supplant their diet. Little archaeological evidence remains of their time in our valley. The hunters used crude tools such as bone spear points and knives to hunt and prepare their food. The prehistoric hunter groups moved out of the area along with their prey as the climate warmed.

By 1,500 BC, the climate of the region was much more temperate. Rich and varied vegetation grew throughout the region. Many species of animal life made this their home, and it was also home to the people of the Late Archaic period. They lived together in groups of twenty-five to thirty individuals. They hunted, fished, and used the abundant plant life to enjoy a more diverse diet than that of their prehistoric predecessors. Rather than move with the large game, they would track them when they moved through the valley, and they relied on smaller game as well as nuts and other food when they were in season.

Above: This is an example of the pottery found at the Castle Creek excavations of the Native American inhabitation of that site. It is representative of beaded pottery. (Photograph by Foster Disinger, courtesy Broome County Historical Society)

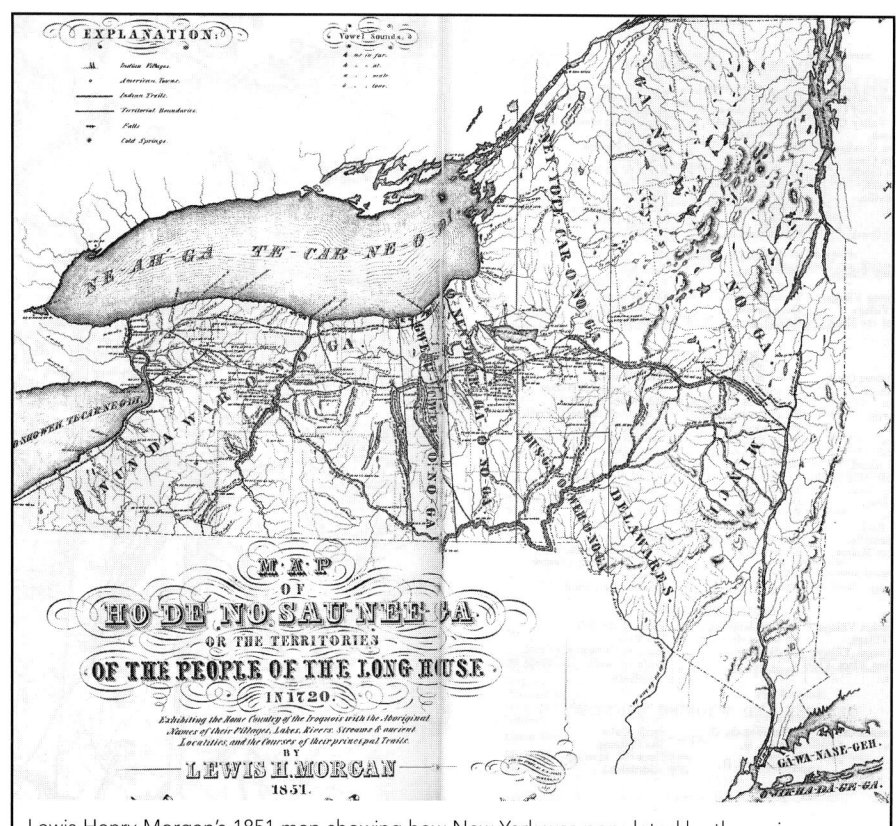

Lewis Henry Morgan's 1851 map showing how New York was populated by the various nations of the Iroquois Confederacy. Mainly Onondaga and Oneida populated the area that is now Broome County. (From *League of the Iroquois*, 1851)

They had more tools to harvest and catch their food. They lived together as a group in small settlements. Smaller groups of hunters would be sent out to procure the food rather than moving the entire group. They would move but only to other seasonal encampments. These settlements were separated by geography—hills, valleys, and rivers. The groups began to adopt cultural traits that distinguished themselves from other groups.

From 1,500 BC to 1,000 BC, the region entered the Transitional Period. New types of implements were introduced into the lives of our area's inhabitants. Items such as stone bowls and clay pots became part of the culture.

It is still unsure whether the local people traded with people from more southerly regions who had already developed the technology of pots made from fired clay, or if the local inhabitants lived farther northward, allowing for the southern groups to move into the region.

By 1,000 BC, the region had entered the Woodland Period. There are few sites that support archaeological evidence of the Early Woodland Period. Digs have found evidence that fired pottery was much more commonplace. The people continued to hunt, fish, and gather but were more focused on certain types of plant life for sustenance. They used plants such as goosefoot seed for flour and others to provide essential vitamins in their diet.

Some of the groups living throughout the region began to trade with others living in the Ohio Valley. The effort at trade continued to expand during the Middle and Late Woodland Period. New traditions began to emerge. Burial ceremonies and items of trade such as shell necklaces entered into the world of our early inhabitants.

Decoration of clay pots began to appear during the Middle Woodland Period. Similar to the decoration styles of later southwestern Native Americans, some of the designs were probably tied to clans or particular groups. Burial mounds were common during this period. Items of high value were often buried with the deceased, not unlike the burial customs of the pharaohs in Ancient Egypt. Unfortunately, many of the mounds have entirely disappeared with the constant plowing of fields and the expansion of settlements in the area. Some of these mounds were noted by early settlers of the eighteenth century and on early maps of the region.

The clans of people moved seasonally from one area to another but would still stay in the local region. Patterns of settlement began to emerge. The first archaeological discovery of agriculture in the eastern United States was at the Round Top site in the town of Union in Broome County. This important site dates to 1,000 AD. The archaeological evidence

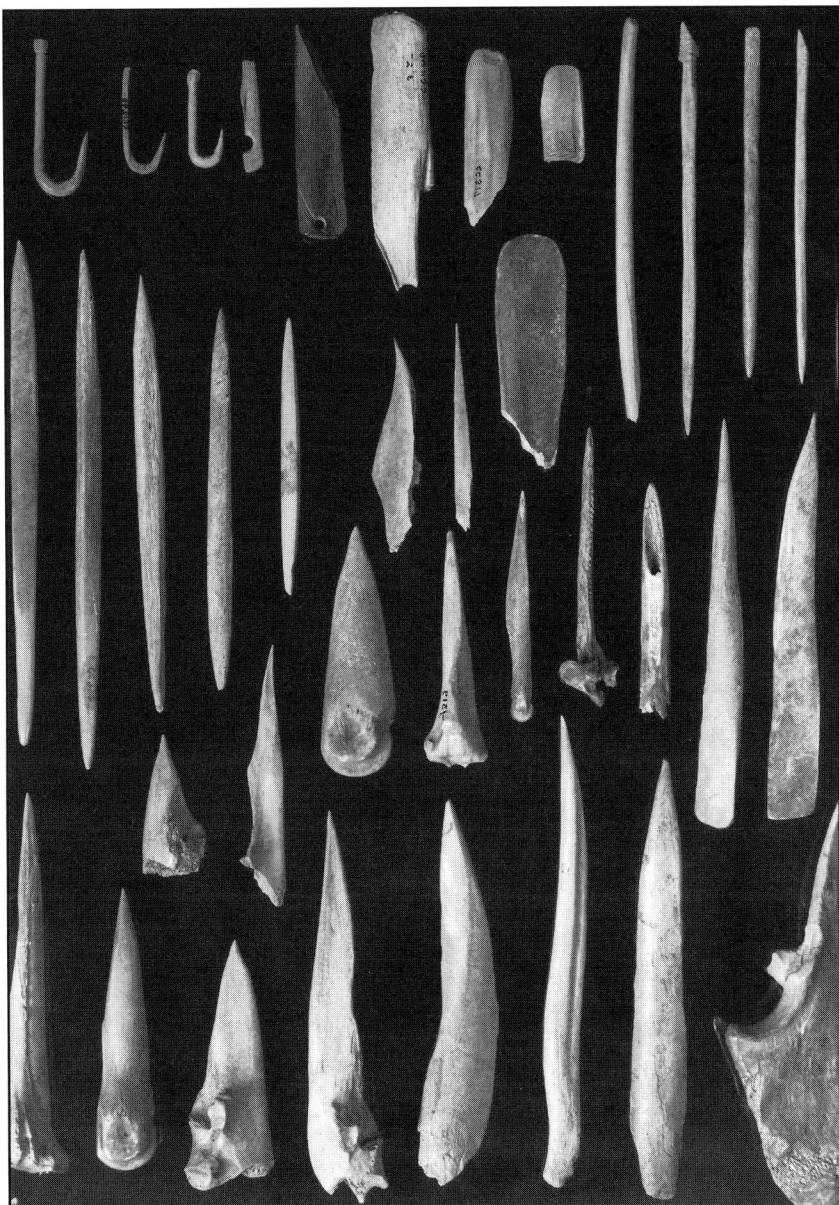

This photograph shows a sample of the variety of bone tools that were discovered during the excavations of the Castle Creek archeological site. These tools would also have been used at Native American sites throughout this area. (Courtesy Broome County Historical Society)

indicated that the settlement had grown corn, beans, and squash as part of their diet. This combination of vegetables was prevalent in the later Iroquois cultures when the vegetables were known as the "three sisters" (Versaggi, *Hunter to Farmer*).

CHAPTER 1: LAND OF THE LONGHOUSE   19

The Castle Creek site as it looked during the excavations in 1972. This view is looking northeast toward the Chenango River and shows the cemetery knoll and the remains of the "moat" around the former village. (Courtesy Broome County Historical Society)

The advent of agriculture changed the lifestyles of the local populations. Rather than moving on a seasonal basis, permanent villages began to evolve. The inhabitants would cultivate food near their villages, and hunters would move in a much closer area to their homes. Customs and cultures developed that were unique to the new villages. Migrating groups invaded the villages, resulting in warfare among the people. Settlements such as the Castle Creek site in the town of Chenango, dating to about 1200 AD and inhabited by Owasco Native Americans, were protected by stockades. These stockades kept the warring groups out and the local inhabitants safe from harm.

Most of these groups spoke the Algonquian language (Ellis, *A History of New York State*). Many of these people would form the core of the Iroquois. A subgroup of the Algonquians called the Lenni-Lenape or Delaware were mainly in the area of present-day Pennsylvania but also migrated into the eastern portion of the future Broome County and the foothills

This diorama was created by Foster Disinger and depicts the arrival of missionary Gideon Hawley at Onaquaga on June 4, 1753. Hawley came with interpreters and guides from Massachusetts. He would stay at the village for several years. (Courtesy Broome County Historical Society)

of the Catskill Mountains. Other groups from the mid-Mississippi Valley began migrating in search of new areas in which to hunt.

The Seneca moved through the Ohio and Allegheny Rivers and into present-day New York State. Moving south from Lake Erie, the Erie and the Susquehannock entered into the region. The Onondaga carved out a region in the area west of Cazenovia Lake and south to the Otseningo area. The Mohawk moved into the region in the sixteenth century. A subgroup of the Mohawk, the Oneida, settled between the Mohawk and the Onondaga. The new Iroquoian groups warred with the Algonquian, and many Algonquian were killed, left the region permanently, or assimilated into the new Native American nations.

The Iroquoian groups who settled in this valley were matriarchal in nature. They lived in longhouses, and in some areas, these longhouses would form a village that would be protected from outsiders by a stockade. In those longhouses, both immediate and extended families would coexist. Families consisted of parents and children, as well as grandparents, aunts, uncles, and cousins. Property belonged to the women. Children took the name of their mother. The groups were made up of several families banded together as clans. Each clan was governed by a council that consisted of males nominated by the matriarchs of privileged clans. These clan councils would select representatives to the tribal council. Chiefs remained in power only as long as the residents of the Native American nation supported them.

The origin of the Iroquois Confederacy is masked in the mists of time. Legend tells of Hiawatha, a member of the Onondaga Nation who was converted to the belief in the Great Spirit by Deganawidah, a Huron. Deganawidah brought Hiawatha a message of peace and power. Hiawatha agreed to spread the message among the Iroquois and had soon received the agreement of what was now called the League of Five Nations—Onondaga, Oneida, Cayuga, Seneca, and Mohawk.

In 1715, the Tuscaroras left the Carolinas and moved northward, settling in the area of what is now eastern Broome County and the Catskills. The Tuscarora joined the League, and, henceforth, the Iroquois Confederacy consisted of six nations. It was an important period in Native American history. Independent bands of people joined forces for common peace and prosperity. A central government consisted of fifty sachems that met each year to find answers to problems among the Native American nations. It was truly a representative government that, according to some evidence, was influential in visions of a new American government among Founding Fathers such as Thomas Jefferson.

The Confederacy became much more important when forced to confront the increasing problem of contact with white settlers. In the future Broome County, two main settlements arose by the early eighteenth century. Onaquaga was the larger of the two and was located near present-day Windsor in eastern Broome County. It was not a focused single point of habitation, but like many Native American settlements in this region, it consisted of a number of small villages that were spread along the Susquehanna River. It was an important base of operations for some of the Iroquois because of its close proximity to the Delaware River and the more frequent contacts it had with the white traders and missionaries making their way through the area. It deservedly earned its nickname as "the southern door of the Iroquois longhouse." Its population was made up of members of the Oneida, Tuscarora, and Delaware Nations.

Along a fourteen-mile stretch of the Chenango River between the Tioughnioga River and the location of present-day Binghamton stood Otseningo. It was also a collection of villages that was comprised of residents from the Onondaga, Nanticoke, Shawnee, and other nations. It played the role of a strategic protector at the confluence of the Susquehanna and Chenango Rivers. The name Chenango is a derivation of the word Otseningo (which has at least forty different spellings).

A smaller settlement, Chugnut, was located at the mouth of the Choconut Creek (a derivation of Chugnut) in the present-day town of Vestal and may have spread across to the northern side of the Susquehanna River in the town of Union. The Nanticoke group arrived in 1753 and settled near the Otseningo villages (Hinman, *Onaquaga, Hub of the Border Wars*). At various times, other small groups of Native Americans such as the Mahickanders made their way through the valley.

Sir William Johnson (1715–1774) was an Englishman who came to the Mohawk Valley in 1738. He was the major force interceding between Great Britain and the Iroquois and helped create the Fort Stanwix Treaty of 1768. (Painting circa 1765, from *The Papers of Sir William Johnson*, 1921, v. 3)

Indian agent and interpreter. He stayed at Otseningo while on his way to Onondaga. In his writings, he described the settlement as one consisting of a starving people who had existed off maple sugar for the previous month.

Moravian missionaries also made their way to this valley. In 1753, David Zeisberger and Henry Frey visited with the people at Otseningo in the company of the migrating Nanticokes. The Nanticokes were allowed several miles to settle along with the other members of Otseningo. This influx of new groups into the traditional villages along the Susquehanna and Chenango Rivers was a deliberate attempt on the part of the Iroquois Confederacy to populate the southern borders of its reach and protect itself from

The first contact with Europeans was with Etienne Brulé, an interpreter and explorer who followed the route of the Susquehanna River for Samuel de Champlain in 1615. He traveled the river through to its mouth in the Chesapeake Bay. The first written account of this area dates to 1737 and the diary of Conrad Weiser, an

burgeoning British settlement (Bothwell, *Broome County Heritage*).

One of the Moravians, Reverend Gideon Hawley, was a missionary who had made significant contact with the occupants of Onaquaga. He lived at the settlement from

CHAPTER 1: LAND OF THE LONGHOUSE   23

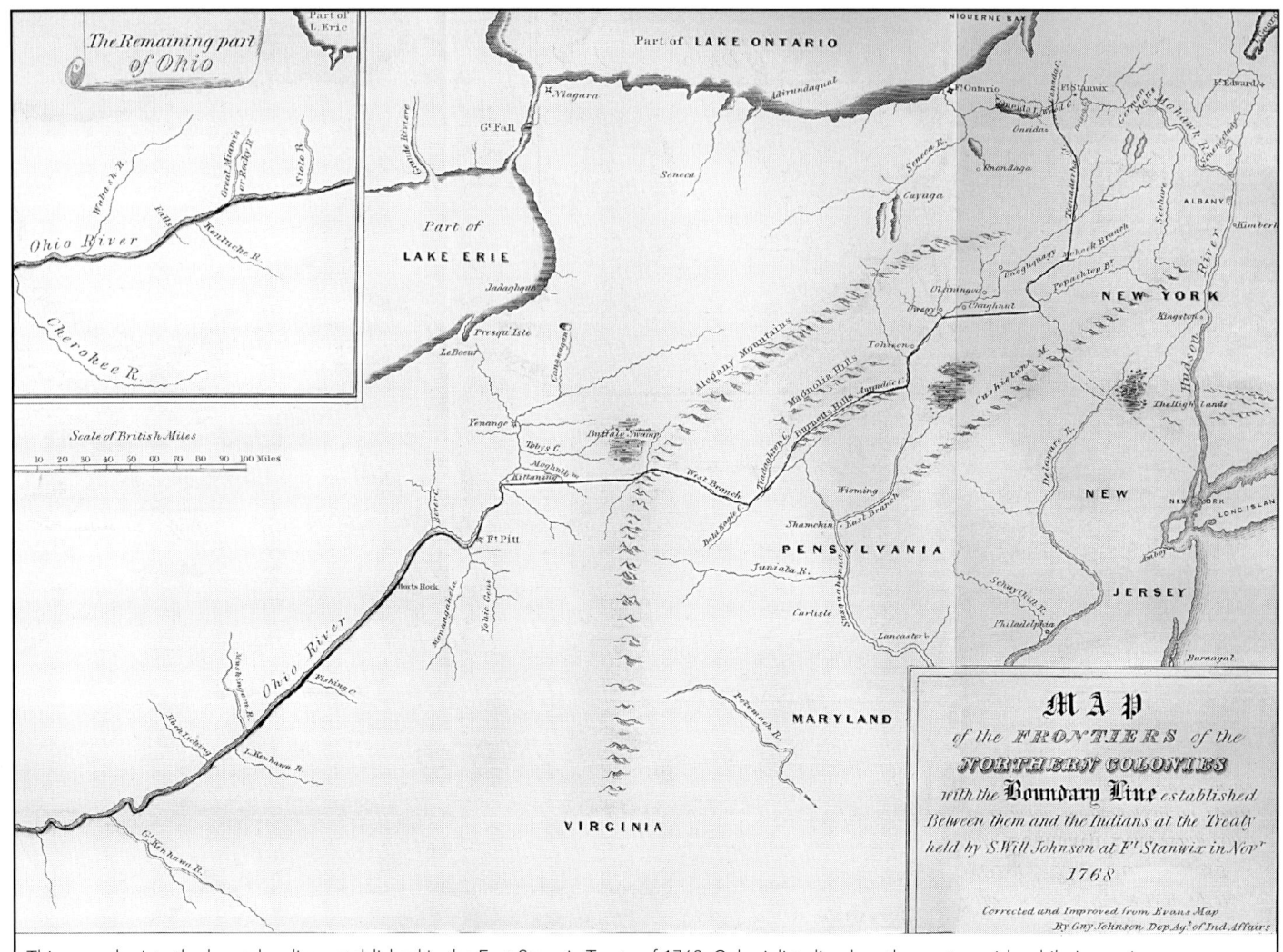

This map depicts the boundary line established in the Fort Stanwix Treaty of 1768. Colonialists lived on the eastern side while Iroquois were confined to the western region. A portion of the line forms part of Broome County's eastern boundary. (From *Documentary History of the State of New-York*, 1849)

1753 to 1757 and was able to persuade the Native Americans living there to construct a fort at the settlement to protect themselves during the French and Indian War (Seward, *Binghamton and Broome County: A History*). Increasing contact with white settlers and traders added to the tensions between the settlers and the various Native American settlements.

The British government recognized the need to alleviate the strain while protecting the white settlers. Sir William Johnson (1715–1774) was appointed Superintendent of Indian Affairs. Johnson, born in Ireland, had arrived in the Mohawk Valley in 1738. By the mid-eighteenth century, he had established a trading post at Onaquaga. The rapport that Johnson developed with the Native American

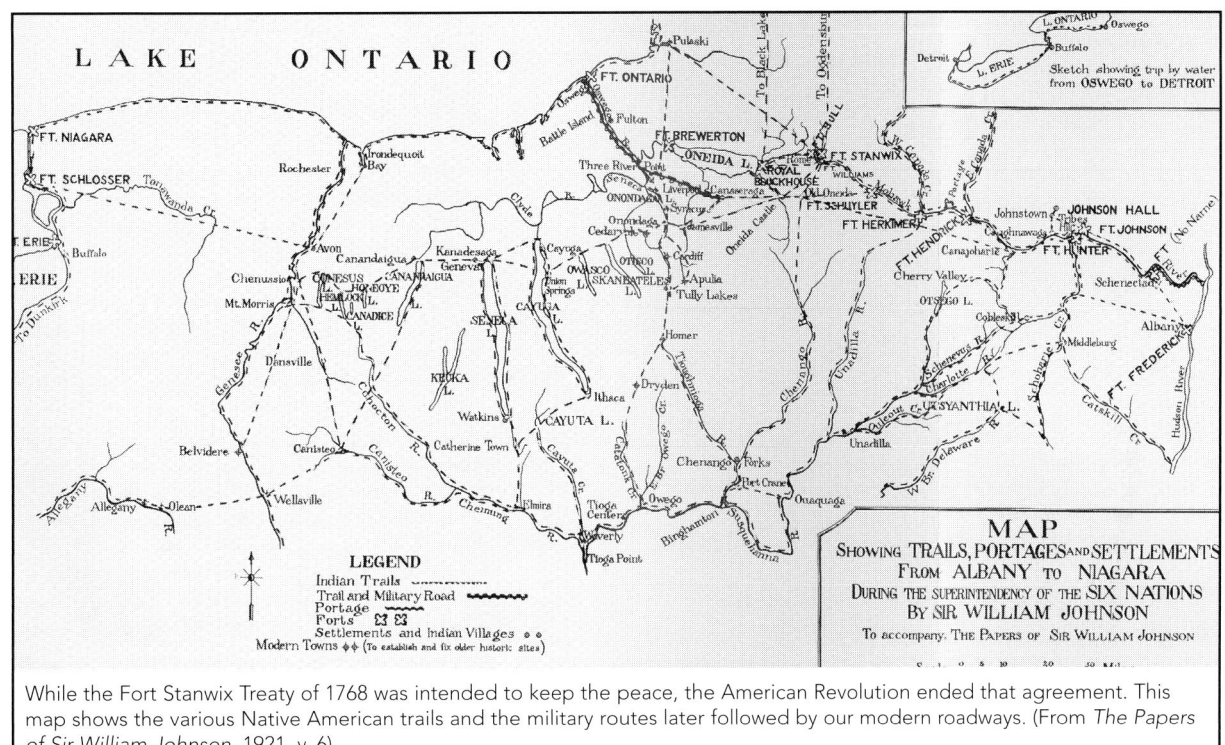

While the Fort Stanwix Treaty of 1768 was intended to keep the peace, the American Revolution ended that agreement. This map shows the various Native American trails and the military routes later followed by our modern roadways. (From *The Papers of Sir William Johnson*, 1921, v. 6)

inhabitants was used to quell some of the tensions between the rights of this area's original settlers and incoming British settlers.

The conflict between the British and the French during the French and Indian Wars did not allay the fears of the Native Americans. Johnson soon realized that a formal arrangement would be the only solution to the problem. In 1768, he arranged to have representatives of the Iroquois Confederacy and of the British government meet at Fort Stanwix (present-day Rome, New York). The result of that meeting was the Fort Stanwix Treaty—it called for settlers to remain east of a line drawn southward from Fort Stanwix and followed the route of the Delaware River. Native American groups were to reside in the portion to the west of the line.

It seemed a simple solution that could bring peace and calm in the colony of New York. It made Sir William Johnson an integral player in the development of the expanding colonial government. The peace that all parties had hoped would last for generations would all but evaporate seven years later with the distant shots of muskets at Lexington and Concord.

CHAPTER 2
The American Revolution and the Iroquois
1768 TO 1783

This print by Donna Westerman depicts the forces of the Sullivan-Clinton Campaign burning the fields and villages near Newtown (Elmira). They had already destroyed or found destroyed both Onaquaga and Otseningo. (From *1776–1976, New York State Bicentennial Prints*, Marine Midland Bank, 1976)

PEACE HAD COME TO AN END, and war took its place. The problems that had resulted in the Fort Stanwix Treaty were not the only tensions in colonial New York. The tactics of the British throne and the royal government toward the colonialists raised the ire of many of the residents of the colonies. There was increasing talk of a need for a split with the British Crown. Oppressive acts by the British government to retain control over the ports and trade of the colonies only fueled the flames of independence.

As the tensions increased between the two sides, so did the need to assure each party of its favor with the members of the Iroquois Confederacy. The leader of the Confederacy was Joseph Brant (1742–1807), whose Mohawk name was Thayendanegea. Brant became a favorite with Sir William Johnson when Brant's sister, Molly Brant, became Johnson's traveling companion after the death of his wife.

Joseph Brant accompanied Sir William Johnson in the Lake George campaign against the French in 1755. In 1761, Johnson sent Brant to Eleazar Wheelock's Indian Charity School in Lebanon, Connecticut. The school was the forerunner of the modern-day Dartmouth College. Brant studied a number of subjects and was converted to the teachings of the Anglican Church. He spent two years at the school and became an interpreter with the Reverend Charles Jeffrey Smith. Smith now

Eleazar Wheelock (1711–1779) operated the Moor's Indian Charity School in Lebanon, Connecticut. The school was part of the Indian missionary efforts of the mid-eighteenth century and helped educate Joseph Brant. It was the forerunner of Dartmouth College. (From *The Papers of Sir William Johnson*, 1921, v. 3)

ran the mission at Onaquaga. Brant met his first wife, the daughter of an Oneida chief, at Onaquaga. He would later marry her half-sister after his first wife's death.

Brant became close to the inhabitants of Onaquaga. As Brant later wrote,

At Oghwago [Onaquaga] I owned another farm with a comfortable house of square logs, a flourishing orchard of apple, pear, and peach

This is an illustration of the Wyoming Massacre that occurred on July 3, 1778. Joseph Brant and his followers participated in the raid with British forces under the control of Major John Butler. The Sullivan-Clinton Expedition was in response to this raid and others like it. (From *Life of Joseph Brant*, William L. Stone, 1838)

trees, fifty acres of cleared land, and fifteen to twenty head of livestock. Also I owned a small island in the river on which improvements were begun. (Bothwell)

He also became increasingly close to the British during this period. Brant became the secretary of Sir William Johnson's son-in-law, Guy Johnson, in 1774. Brant and Guy Johnson worked closely to ensure that the British remained close to the Iroquois, and they worked equally close to ensure that the Native American groups over whom they had power and influence would remain tied to the British.

Members of some of the Iroquois groups, especially the Oneida and Tuscarora, were more supportive of the colonialists' movements toward independence. But Brant was persuasive, and the largest portion of the Native American groups in New York backed the British. Brant and Guy Johnson went to England in 1776 to ask for continued support of the Iroquois. The British government agreed to settle all grievances after it restored peace to the colonies.

The British could promise continued trade with the Iroquois, an important factor in bringing most of the Native American groups

General John Sullivan (1740–1795) began his career as an attorney but was selected by General George Washington to lead his forces in an effort to wipe out the Native American threat to the colonialists' frontier settlements. (From *Journals of the Military Expedition of Major General John Sullivan...*, Frederick Cook, 1887)

into the British fold. Joseph Brant was given a commission in the British army as a captain in 1776. In that same year, Brant returned to America and participated in the Battle of Long Island in August. He quickly became convinced that the British would defeat the colonialists and began the trek back to Onaquaga to recruit Native American forces to aid the British.

In May 1777, Joseph Brant arrived back at Onaquaga and found seven hundred warriors already at the settlement ready to side with the British. More would be arriving shortly, and Brant took the momentum of the moment to move against the patriot families located at Old Unadilla. He successfully drove the families off their lands and claimed the area as a Tory outpost for the British. Only a few weeks later, Brant and his forces intervened in the Battle of Oriskany and stopped General Nicholas Herkimer from aiding Fort Stanwix. But despite his victory during the battle, the win was bittersweet. It was the first time that the nations of the Iroquois Confederacy took opposing sides during the battle. The peace that had been their hallmark was now gone forever.

On September 3, 1777, the Committee of Safety (the group within the Continental Congress that oversaw war risks, spies, and other wartime movements) declared that the Iroquois living at Onaquaga would be considered enemies of the patriot forces. Brant continued to use Onaquaga as a base of operations. He raided patriot settlements, took prisoners, and burned buildings. Onaquaga quickly became a target for destruction by the patriot forces. Governor George Clinton sent an urgent message to Colonel John Cantine in 1778 to strongly urge the elimination of the Iroquois settlement. Before Cantine could act on the order from Clinton, Colonel William Butler took action.

In fall of 1778, Butler was stationed at Schoharie and began an expedition to Onaquaga. In his journals, Butler describes his trip:

I cross'd the River and took Possession of the Town about 11 o'clock at night without interruption; the Enemy having that day left the Town, in the greatest Confusion & at least 2,000 bush'ls of Corn, a Number of Horses, Poultry, their Dogs, household furniture, etc. etc. It was the finest Indian town I ever saw; on both sides the River; there was about 40 good houses, Square logs, Shingles & stone Chimneys, good floor, glass windows, etc. etc. (Bothwell)

Despite Butler's admiration for the beauty of Onaquaga, his forces destroyed the town in less than one day.

Brant had already moved his troops to nearby Koo-Koose (present-day Deposit) and established it as a new base of operations. The destruction of Onaquaga changed the tone of Brant's actions. He had been highly defensive of the rights of the Native American groups and their lands as promised in the Fort Stanwix Treaty of 1768. After the destruction of his home at Onaquaga, he sought revenge

Joseph Brant (1742–1807) was the last major leader of the Iroquois Confederacy. He used Onaquaga as a base of operations during the American Revolution. It was there that he met his first wife and also her half-sister, who later became his second wife. (From *The Papers of Sir William Johnson*, 1921, v. 7)

on the patriot forces. He led a raid against the inhabitants of Cherry Valley in November 1778. It was a particularly harsh action, with the destruction of the property of many innocent settlers. The severity and, as some reports have described it, the savagery of this "massacre" of the lives of these people incited George Washington to take action.

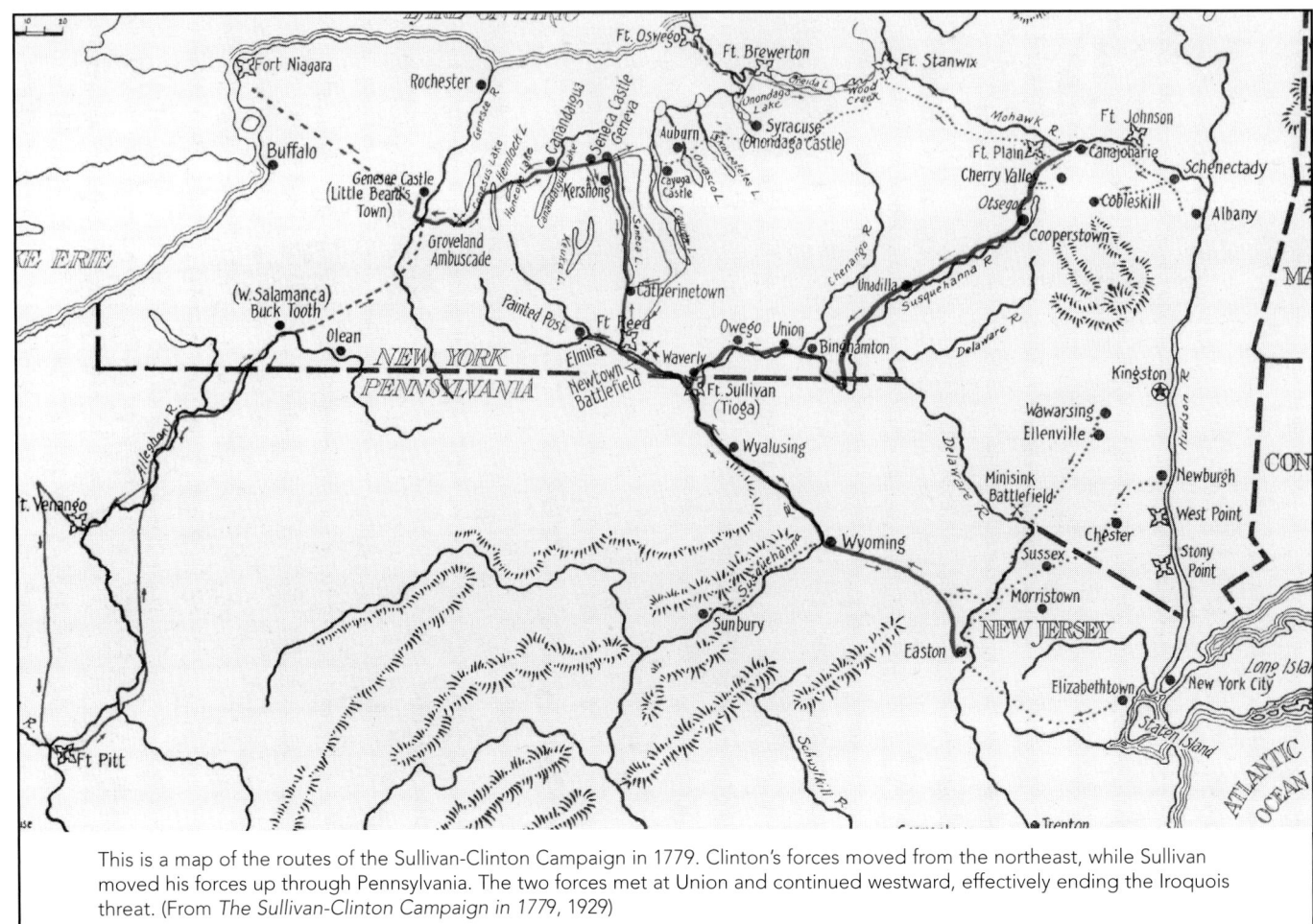

This is a map of the routes of the Sullivan-Clinton Campaign in 1779. Clinton's forces moved from the northeast, while Sullivan moved his forces up through Pennsylvania. The two forces met at Union and continued westward, effectively ending the Iroquois threat. (From *The Sullivan-Clinton Campaign in 1779*, 1929)

In the spring of 1779, Washington came to the conclusion that the threat to the patriot cause from the Native American groups must be ended. He ordered General John Sullivan (1740–1795) and Brigadier General James Clinton (1733–1812), the brother of George Clinton, to take up this cause. His order stated that,

The immediate objects are the total destruction of the hostile tribes of the Six Nations and the devastation of their settlements and the capture of as many prisoners of every age and sex as possible.

He also ordered Sullivan to "lay waste the settlements around so that the country may not only be overrun but destroyed…and [to push] the Indians to the greatest practicable distance from our settlement and our frontiers; to throw them wholly on the British enemy."

Sullivan and his forces moved westward from Easton, Pennsylvania, toward the Susquehanna River to Tioga Point (present-day Athens), Pennsylvania. There, the force under the command of Clinton would move southwest from the Cherry Valley area along the Susquehanna River and meet Sullivan's forces in the southern border area of New York where they would combine to move westward in a search-and-destroy mission. The campaign began on April 18, 1779, when forces under Colonel Goose Van Schaick moved across

Onondaga Lake and destroyed the traditional capital of the Iroquois Confederacy.

Clinton began his campaign at Otsego Lake in present-day Cooperstown. The lake served as the start of the Susquehanna River. The lake was dammed and flooded so that Clinton could move two hundred flat-bottom boats across the lake and down the river toward the Native American settlements. In addition to the boats, Clinton had an additional 1,500 troops on land to clear the area of the Indian threat. Butler's forces had already destroyed Onaquaga the year before, so they set their goal as Otseningo.

When the troops arrived, they found the village already in flames, destroyed by the residents before the arrival of the patriot troops. One of the few things found in the burning village was a powder horn. It had been carved in high style as a presentation piece to the Native Americans during the French and Indian War. John LaGrange, who would be one of the few soldiers of the campaign to return to this area after the war's conclusion, picked it up. The powder horn remained in his family for the next two hundred years and is now in the possession of the Broome County Historical Society.

With the threat of both Onaquaga and Otseningo removed, Clinton rested his army at the confluence of the Chenango and Susquehanna Rivers. The next day, he moved

Brigadier General James Clinton (1733–1812) was the brother of Governor George Clinton. He brought his forces from the northeast toward Onaquaga and met Sullivan's troops at Union before marching west to the Battle of Newtown. (From *Journals of the Military Expedition of Major General John Sullivan…*, Frederick Cook, 1887)

toward the west to destroy the last remaining settlement, Chugnut, which was located on the banks of the Susquehanna River. Near Round Top Hill, the inhabitants of the settlement ambushed Clinton's army. In a stroke of good timing, Clinton's forces were reinforced by a detachment under the command of General Enoch Poor. Together they were able to put

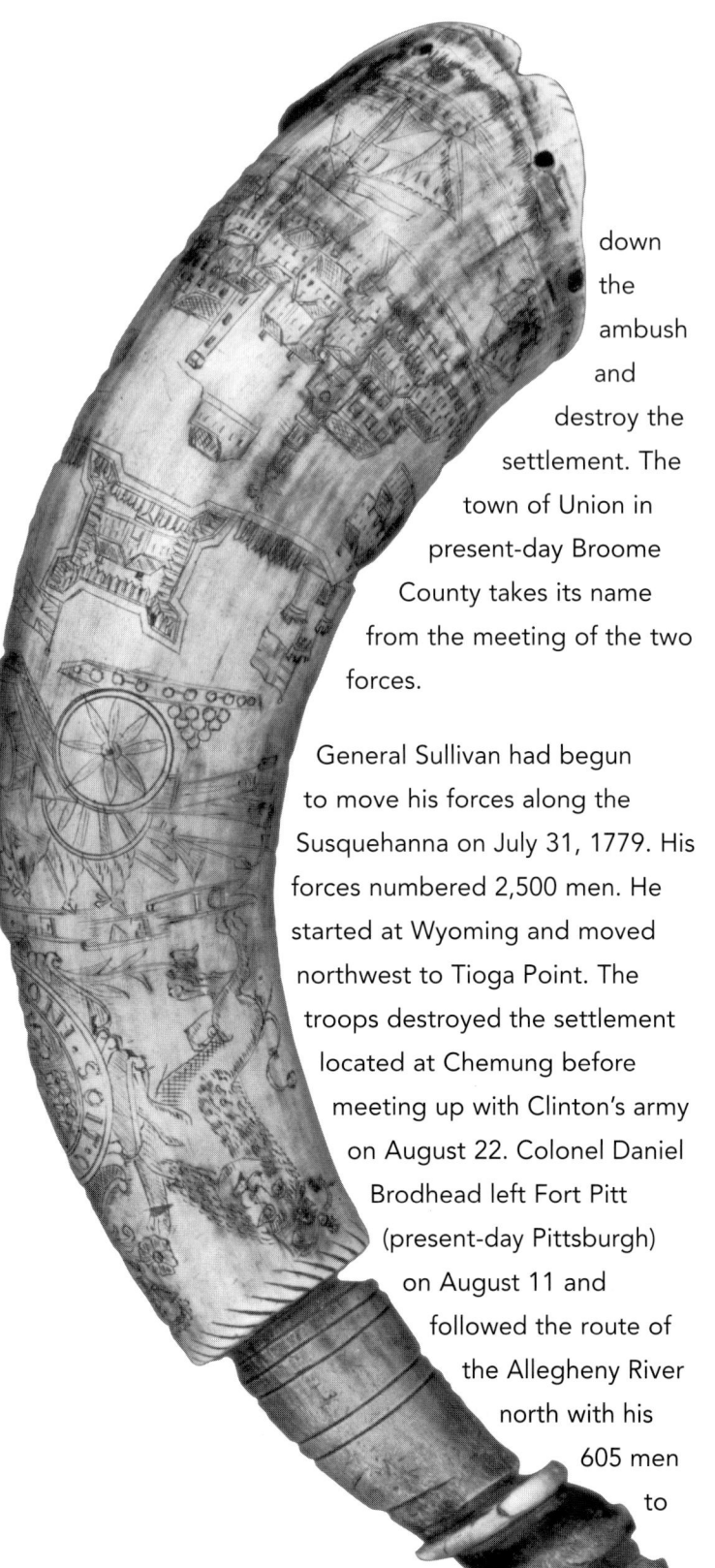

down the ambush and destroy the settlement. The town of Union in present-day Broome County takes its name from the meeting of the two forces.

General Sullivan had begun to move his forces along the Susquehanna on July 31, 1779. His forces numbered 2,500 men. He started at Wyoming and moved northwest to Tioga Point. The troops destroyed the settlement located at Chemung before meeting up with Clinton's army on August 22. Colonel Daniel Brodhead left Fort Pitt (present-day Pittsburgh) on August 11 and followed the route of the Allegheny River north with his 605 men to destroy any settlement in the western New York area. His efforts were very successful, with a large number of houses burned and about five hundred acres of crops destroyed.

With the union of Sullivan's and Clinton's armies, they moved toward the west. They reached the settlement of Newtown (present-day Elmira) on August 29, 1779. Here, the forces under the control of Joseph Brant and Tory forces under Walter Butler made their only stand during the entire campaign. The Native American and British forces were greatly outnumbered and finally ceded control of the site to the American armies. Many of the soldiers from Sullivan's and Clinton's forces spent the next day destroying crops. Others were occupied in less honorable duties. Reports indicate that one party was sent to find dead Native Americans. At least two bodies were skinned, with one skin given to a major and the other to a lieutenant (Bothwell).

This Sullivan-Clinton Campaign was concluded on October 17, 1779, with the return of the army to Easton, Pennsylvania. By military standards, the campaign did not accomplish its goal. If the end result was only to destroy the settlements of the Native Americans, then the campaign was successful. But Washington had wanted the total destruction of the ability of the Indian population to pose any threat. In this, the campaign failed. It made the war an intense personal affront to the Native American groups, especially for those who had sided with the American forces prior to the outbreak of war. Thousands of Native Americans from all nations were left starving and homeless.

The British did offer shelter to the homeless members of the Iroquois Confederacy at Fort Niagara. By November 1779, over 2,900 refugees had arrived there with little food and a harsh winter ahead of them. Joseph Brant did not leave his home base willingly. He continued to use Onaquaga to launch raids throughout the region. War parties numbering at least sixty per year would leave the Fort Niagara area to attack both Americans and members of the Oneida and Tuscarora who had sided with the Americans. This was the end of the strength of the Iroquois Confederacy, split apart by the forces of the war.

General Cornwallis surrendered the British forces to the Americans at Yorktown on October 19, 1781. The fighting of the American Revolution had come to a conclusion, the problem of the remaining Native Americans had not. Brant petitioned the British government for land in Canada to resettle those still loyal to him. In 1784, the Canadian government offered land in the Grand River Basin for a home to the thousands who had nowhere to live. Beginning in 1785 and continuing over the next few years, the Native Americans migrated across the border. A second Fort Stanwix Treaty in 1784 declared the entire state of New York to be sovereign over all land formerly held by the Iroquois. New York established the first Indian reservation.

Joseph Brant spent the remaining years of his life in Canada—a leader of a Confederacy that no longer existed. It was destroyed by the Revolution and by the split in the very loyalties that had long held it together. The Treaty of Paris in 1783 ended the Revolution and left New York a new state, open for the expansion of settlers across the entire land that the first Fort Stanwix Treaty had hoped to stop. Without the treaty and without the Native Americans, the western half of New York was ripe for new growth.

Opposite page: John LaGrange was a member of the forces under the control of General Clinton when he found this powder horn in the burning ruins of Osteningo. A presentation horn from the French & Indian Wars, it remained in the LaGrange family for two centuries. (Courtesy Broome County Historical Society)

CHAPTER 3
A New Land for Settlement
1783–1806

The area's abundant timber was cleared to make way for the growing homes and farmsteads. The lumber that was not used for building was formed into rafts and floated downriver to be sold at other markets. *(Rafting on the Susquehanna*, by Linton Park. Courtesy Broome County Historical Society)

THE END OF THE AMERICAN

Revolution left the southern tier of New York open for speculators and settlers to assume control of the former Native American lands. But a problem remained. Where exactly were the boundaries of New York? Royal grant claims from both Massachusetts and Connecticut clouded the locations of the borders of both New York and Pennsylvania. A royal grant to the Plymouth Colony in 1620 had given Massachusetts an early claim to New York. A settlement in 1786 between Massachusetts and New York gave New York the control over the land but Massachusetts the first option to purchase the land from the Native Americans. Finally, an agreement was reached where Massachusetts would end its claim with control over six million acres in western New York and an area comprised of 230,400 acres located between the Chenango and Owego Rivers and north of the Susquehanna River.

This smaller area was given to sixty proprietors in 1789 at the cost of 12½ cents per acre. The area was called the Boston Purchase (or alternatively, the Boston Ten Towns). Some of the new owners relocated to this region, but many others sold their claims for profit. This still left another five million acres of land open for sale by New York State. The government quickly moved to sell this to raise money and help settle its war debt. The regions were divided into townships, and large tracts of land called patents were sold to individuals or companies intent on making a profit off the land.

Well-known individuals speculated in the growth of the country. The future Broome County had no less than twelve signers of the Declaration of Independence as partial owners of its lands at one time or another. This included Robert Morris, who obtained thirty thousand acres of land in southern and eastern Broome County, only to lose them through bankruptcy. Many speculators would never travel to these new lands. They hired surveyors and land agents to do the work of finding new settlers to purchase smaller parcels from these patents.

The area surrounding the confluence of the Susquehanna and Chenango Rivers was a prime location for settlement. The rivers offered water to sustain life and to provide transportation. The land was rich for the growth of crops. Former Native American trails provided rudimentary roads on which the new settler could travel. In 1786, two land patents were granted. One grant went to Colonel Robert Hooper of New Jersey and the other to William Bingham and James Wilson of Philadelphia. Judge James Wilson was another

These illustrations of the four stages of homesteading first appeared in the *Pioneer History of the Holland Purchase* by A. Turner. They show the development of communities from log cabins to the "civilized" Greek Revival homes on cultivated farms. (Courtesy Broome County Historical Society)

signer of the Declaration of Independence to purchase land in Broome County. Wilson had been buying land along the route of the Delaware River but needed an influx of money to complete the purchases. He turned to William Bingham (1752–1804), a wealthy financier of the American Revolution. Together they formed the Canaan Company.

CHAPTER 3: A NEW LAND FOR SETTLEMENT

William Bingham (1752–1804) was a wealthy Philadelphia banker who wanted to create a model town at the meeting of the Susquehanna and Chenango Rivers. He was a financier of the Revolutionary War. This painting is in the National Portrait Gallery. (Courtesy Broome County Historical Society)

with Hooper receiving a portion of the land in the western part of the patent, Wilson receiving the central part of the patent, and Bingham receiving the portion surrounding the confluence of the two rivers. The ten thousand-plus acres proved to be the prime location for the creation of a new village, and Bingham had plans for his new acquisition.

Bingham served the American Revolution as an agent of the Continental Congress in the West Indies, but his most important contribution was as a financier. Through the war, Bingham played an important role in the West Indies and assisted

Colonel Hooper had been one of the soldiers in the Sullivan-Clinton Campaign who came back to the area to settle. He had hoped to own the land between Great Bend and Tioga Point along the Susquehanna River. The conflict over the two opposing claims was settled in 1790 with the trade necessary to continue the war effort. He also made a fortune during the war. Bingham married Anne Willing, the daughter of Thomas Willing of Philadelphia, in 1780.

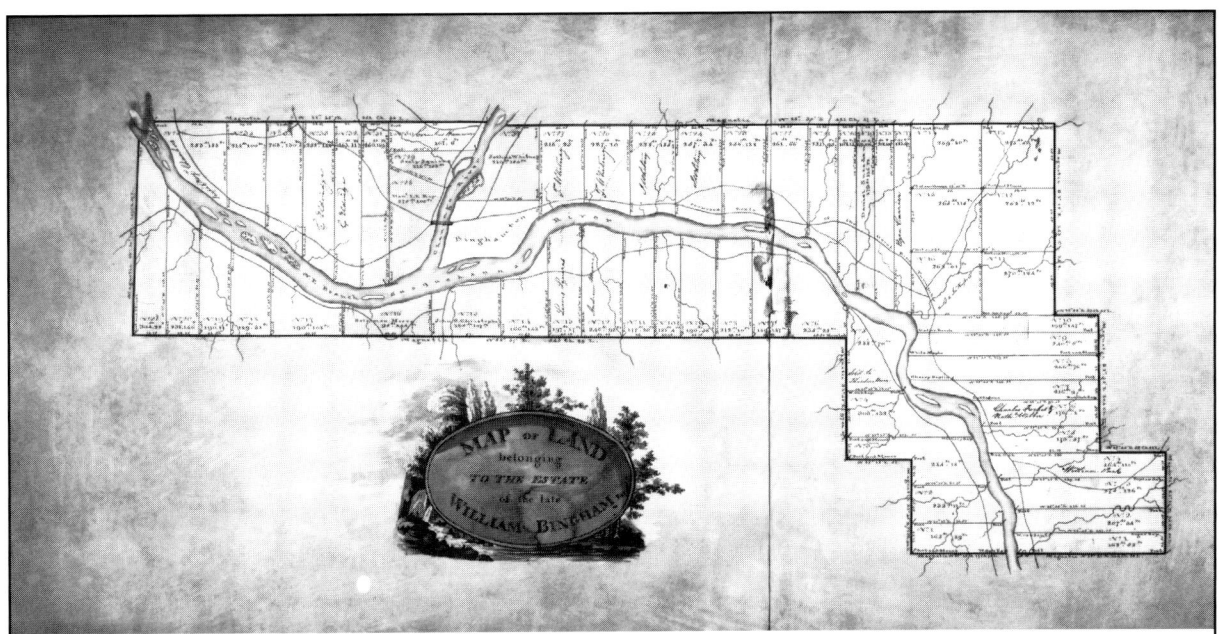
This map dates from circa 1800 and shows William Bingham's land patent of about ten thousand acres at the meeting of two rivers. The patent comprised much of the city of Binghamton and parts of the towns of Conklin, Kirkwood, and Vestal. (Courtesy Broome County Historical Society)

Bingham had been involved in an early bank venture called the Bank of Pennsylvania in 1780, but it did not last long despite the investment of many wealthy landowners. In 1782, Bingham became a director of the Bank of North America, of which his father-in-law, Willing, was president. This fiscal institution was more successful and made Bingham a very wealthy man. By 1791, Bingham had also become a director in the Bank of the United States.

Anne Willing Bingham (1764–1801) was the epitome of class and a favorite among the social circles of the time. She became friends with the Jeffersons and the Madisons. She was an acquaintance of Martha Washington and a friend of Abigail Adams. Adams and Anne Bingham became especially close after they spent time in Paris together in 1785 before Bingham went to London. Her diaries and correspondence illustrate the growth of the upper crust of American society.

Bingham adored his wife. He wanted to surprise her by having the entire family portrait painted by Gilbert Stuart. Stuart was one of the premier portrait painters now working in Europe. Stuart hated to paint children, and during the sessions, he put down his brushes and the portrait was never finished. Eventually, Stuart did paint Bingham's portrait, and the Binghams purchased Stuart's "Lansdowne" portrait of George Washington, which is now world-famous. (Alberts, *The Golden Voyage: The Life and Times of William Bingham, 1752–1804*). The well-known British portraitist, Sir Joshua Reynolds, painted Anne Bingham's likeness.

Bingham had quickly become one of the largest land speculators in the new nation. Aside from his land in this area, Bingham owned nearly three hundred thousand acres of land in his home state of Pennsylvania and over three million acres of land in the state of Maine. Despite the relatively small size of his holdings in New York, Bingham did not ignore its potential. He recognized the richness of the land and its proximity to two rivers as an excellent place to create a model town, a town that he hoped to develop.

There has been a long dispute over who was the first white settler of present-day Broome County. Early histories mentioned Captain Joseph Leonard, a veteran of Bunker Hill, as the first permanent settler. But there were others who were here prior to Leonard's arrival in 1787. Leonard heard about this spot from Amos Draper, a trader with the Native Americans. By this time, Leonard was living in the Wyoming Valley in Pennsylvania. He was determined to bring his young wife, two children, and hired hand to live in the newly opened area.

Leonard settled on the west bank of the Chenango River about three miles to the north of present-day Binghamton and across from what would become Broome Community College. Despite Leonard's claims to be the first settler, he had been ferried across the Chenango River by James Lyons. Lyons ran a ferry operation just north of the confluence of the Chenango and Susquehanna Rivers. It later became the site for the Ferry Street Bridge and the current East Clinton Street Bridge.

A few months after Leonard's arrival, Colonel William Rose and his brother, Solomon, settled near him in an area called Goosetown. It is today called Nimmonsburg and hugs the borders of the towns of Chenango and Dickinson. Leonard had made a lease agreement with the remaining Native Americans still living on their ancestral home. The lease called for a term of ninety-nine years for a one-square-mile parcel along the Chenango River. Leonard's partner was Amos Draper, but he had quickly sold his interests off to the Rose brothers (Lawyer, *Binghamton: Its Settlement, Growth and Development*). Other arrivals made their way to the valley in 1787. Joshua and William Whitney arrived and settled about two miles north of the confluence of the two rivers in an area called Whitney's Flats. In this same area, Ebenezer Greene made his home.

By 1798, a number of transplanted New Englanders, Pennsylvanians, and settlers from northern New Jersey had moved along the banks of the two main rivers. A crude but expanding town known as Chenango

Village was developing near Goosetown. It had a meetinghouse, Whitney's mercantile establishment, and the Lewis Keeler tavern, along with a few other structures. It seemed ripe for growth into a new town, except for one thing—nearly all of the settlers of the town were squatters.

These particular squatters were on the lands of the owners of the Boston Township, but those landowners were not alone in their problem. William Bingham had the same issue on his lands. Like almost all other land speculators of that time, Bingham did not visit the holdings in person. He relied on the work of others living or working in those areas. He needed to hire a land agent whose responsibility would be to devise a plan to entice new settlers to the land and to create plans for roads and bridges to make travel easier for the incoming new inhabitants. The land agent also had to arrive at a settlement with the squatters.

By 1786, Thomas Harding was employed as the land agent for Bingham, James Wilson, and Robert Hooper. Several early plots were sold prior to the formal legal settlement between the patentees. In mid-1794, Bingham hired Balthazar DeHaert as the overseer of his land. DeHaert was from New Jersey and used the title "Judge" (Hinman, *Bingham's Land, Whitney's Town*). DeHaert had to overcome the obstacle of the squatters. He worked on this problem from 1795 through March 1798.

Finally, an agreement was reached with thirty-seven of the squatters. There were some who refused to acknowledge Bingham's claim on the land.

Ebenezer Park, who may have been Bingham's first land agent, took the petition signed by the squatters to Bingham in Philadelphia in spring of 1798. The petition read:

To the honorable Wm. Bingham:
A petition from the inhabitants and settlers on said Bingham's Patent, on Susquehanna River in the towns of Union and Chenango, County of Tioga, and State of New York, humbly prayeth:

That, whereas we, your petitioners, having been to considerable expense in moving on said land and making improvements, we pray your honor would grant us three lives lease, and we will pay an annual rent for the same; otherwise, let us know on what terms we can have the land, and you petitioners, as dutiful tenants, shall ever comply.

Chenango, Feb. 15, 1798 (Wilkinson, *The Annals of Binghamton of 1840*)

It was signed by [alphabetical order added]: Levin Bennett; Samuel Bevier; William Brink; John Carr; Abraham Carsaw; Judge Chamberlain; David and Joseph Compton; Andrew and Thomas Cooper; Daniel Delano; Jonathan Dunham; James Ford; Robert Foster; Silas Hall; Roswell Jay; Ezra and Ira

Keeler; Joseph Lemerick; James Lyon; Arthur and William Miller; Silas and Zebulon Moore; Ebenezer Park; Walter Sluyter; Abraham, Abraham Jr., and Daniel Sneden; Zachariah, James, and Asa Squires; Nathaniel Taggert; Amos Towsley; Asher Wickham; and Barnabus and Solomon Wixon.

By the time William Bingham received the petition in early 1798, he realized that he had to have a permanent land agent to manage the lands in New York State. Bingham had apparently already used the talents of Joshua Whitney's son, Joshua, to show the surveyor and overseer around Bingham's holdings. Joshua Whitney, the father, realized the potential for growth and power if he could handle the management. He began negotiations for the position of land agent for Bingham. He left his store and home in Chenango Village with official papers in his pocket to go to Philadelphia and consummate the deal. He told his twenty-five-year-old son, Joshua, to meet him at Wilkes-Barre, Pennsylvania, with a Durham boat to move goods to Philadelphia.

As the elder Joshua Whitney reached the town of Wind Gap, Pennsylvania, he fell deathly ill with yellow fever. He was confined to a bedroom in a tavern and managed to send word to his son to hurry to him. Young Joshua Whitney arrived barely in time but was forbidden to enter his father's room at first because of the contagion. Young Whitney went in anyway and was there when his father died on September 26, 1798. It was a double blow for young Whitney. His mother had died just a month prior to this, and now he was an orphan with two brothers and two sisters that needed tending.

Young Joshua Whitney (1773–1845) took charge of the situation. He continued the trek to Philadelphia and negotiated a position as Bingham's land agent. There had been an earlier plan to develop the land around the meeting of the two rivers, but it had been abandoned. Whitney saw the place as a more desirable location for growth than Chenango Village. Chenango Point, as the location at the confluence came to be called, had all the trappings for growth except for a bridge to make travel easier than relying on ferries across the rivers.

Despite the fact that Whitney would not receive power of attorney over the lands until 1802, he took it upon himself to begin the development of Chenango Point. In 1800, he learned that Lucas Elmendorf had received a charter to construct a bridge across the Chenango River. Movement to build the bridge went nowhere, but this did not dissuade Whitney. He simply took it upon himself to make it happen. He marched into Lewis Keeler's tavern in Chenango Village and announced the news of the new bridge to be built. The next day, Whitney and five others set out with axes to clear the spot

Joshua Whitney (1773–1845) became the land agent for William Bingham after the death of his father in 1798. Whitney was responsible for the founding of Binghamton, especially after the death of Bingham in 1804. This three-hundred-pound "General" was the area's first state representative. (Courtesy Broome County Historical Society)

a more advantageous location than the older Chenango Village to the north. In 1800, the New York State Legislature passed a post road bill that allowed for the construction of a road from the Hudson River through the Catskills to Unadilla and then down to Chenango Point. In March 1801, the court for the eastern district of Tioga County determined that a new house should be built for court. Since 1793, it had been held in Joshua Whitney's home in Chenango Village, but both distance to travel and amount of legal business made it necessary to formally create a second courthouse within the boundaries of Tioga County.

Lewis Keeler decided to move to Chenango Point and build a new tavern and hotel business. Several owners of structures in Chenango Village actually dismantled their buildings to rebuild them in Chenango Point. A new town was being carved out of the

for the bridge. It was Whitney who took the lead and announced that the bridge would be built at a spot marked on either side of the river by an elm tree. He also cleared an acre of land on the east side of the Chenango River for the construction of a new home.

The "twin elms" episode was the culmination of several events that made Chenango Point

CHAPTER 3: A NEW LAND FOR SETTLEMENT   45

John LaGrange (1771–1858) and Hannah Halsey LaGrange (1774–1838) were early settlers of the town of Vestal. John LaGrange had first come through as part of the Sullivan-Clinton Campaign, and he later became president of the Binghamton Bank. Both were originally from New Jersey. (Courtesy Broome County Historical Society)

wilderness. There was a movement to rename the town in honor of him on whose land it stood. But there was also opposition from some to renaming the village Binghamton. Whitney and his allies pushed the issue with some maps showing the new name as early as the first decade of the 1800s. However, the formal name change would not take effect for another three decades.

Despite the advancement of Chenango Point, Whitney's plan to move ahead with Bingham's vision for a new town hit a major hurdle. On May 1, 1801, Anne Willing Bingham died suddenly in Bermuda. When William was not in session in Congress (where he served from 1795 to 1801 as senator for Pennsylvania), the Binghams had been spending a great deal of time on the island. Her death hit Bingham especially hard, and he had little energy for dealing with land development. He left the West Indies en route for Britain where he settled in Bath, England.

In England, Bingham tried to settle into some type of new life, but it was never satisfying. Late in 1803, he became ill and went under a doctor's care. From the description of the symptoms, it appears that he had suffered some type of stroke. It became clear by January 1804 that Bingham was not going to recover from the illness. He made a final will during that month. By the end of January, the children and other family members gathered at his home in Bath. He made arrangements for portions of his fortune to be distributed to various family members. On February 6, 1804, William Bingham breathed his last. The notice of his death was carried in the *London Sun* four days later. It merely mentioned that he had been a United States senator. He was buried in Bath Abbey, and a monument was erected at the site of his burial. After word finally reached America of his demise, Dr. Benjamin Rush of Philadelphia wrote of his death in common book, *Died at Bath, Wm. Bingham of this city. He left an estate valued at three million dollars, half a million of which was in stock, of different kinds. He was pleasant in his manners, amiable in his temper, liberal but said [to] be charitable....He acquired his immense estate by his own ingenuity....In all his money speculations he was fortunate.* (Alberts)

William Bingham died never having seen the land that would later bear his name. His death left Joshua Whitney with the problem of having to deal with the attorneys for Bingham's estate. It was a tense relationship at best and one that would make it very difficult for Whitney until the 1820s. Whitney had other developments that would occupy his time. By the death of William Bingham, more and more settlers were moving into the region. Some of these controlled both land and money resources at locations away from the burgeoning Chenango Point.

Robert Harpur (1733–1825) was born in Ireland of Scottish parents and educated at Glasgow University. In 1761, he was appointed

Above: William Macclure was a surveyor hired to map the patents of several landowners during the 1790s. Macclure Settlement in the town of Sanford was home to "Castle William," and his globe is now in the possession of the Old Onaquaga Historical Society. (Courtesy Broome County Historical Society)

professor of mathematics at King's College (now Columbia University). Harpur left active teaching after a few years amidst rumors of a scandal involving a young woman and continued as librarian. He also speculated in land in New York and eventually became secretary of the state's land board. It is Harpur that many give credit for classical place names that are found across the Mohawk Valley and central New York. In 1790, he purchased thirty thousand acres of land along the Susquehanna River near the borders of the future Broome and Chenango Counties. At Harpur Manor, Robert Harpur watched as Harpursville grew around his lands.

In the opposite end of the future county, Joshua Mersereau (1734–1804) became the leading power on that portion of the Susquehanna River. He was descended from French Huguenots who had moved to America in 1685. Joshua and four of his brothers served in the American Revolution. Joshua became the quartermaster general of the New York troops and was eventually appointed deputy commissary general on the staff of George Washington. Mersereau and his family were forced to flee their home on Staten Island after the British seized control of that area. He and his family moved into the area in 1784. Joshua Mersereau became the agent and surveyor for Robert Hooper's and James

Wilson's lands. He and his brother John first lived on the south side of the Susquehanna (present-day Vestal) but quickly moved across to the north side of the river to Union. Joshua was appointed one of the first judges of the eastern portion of Tioga County in 1781 (Bothwell).

By 1806, the eastern portion of Tioga County was still very much a pioneer area with few residents. But the groundwork for growth had already been laid.

Joshua Whitney and others saw this region as having great potential for growth. Settlers from surrounding states found the valley surrounding the Chenango and Susquehanna Rivers as an excellent place to put down roots and begin a new life. Crude log cabins were still plentiful, but here and there new homes exhibiting grace and elegance were being built, such as Washingtonian Hall (1799) in Union. Broome County entered the next phase of its history ready for expansion.

Job Mersereau (1801–1882, opposite page) and Major David Mersereau (1801–1885, this page) were the grandsons of settler John Mersereau of the town of Union. Job ran a farm and sawmill while David began the Major House, a hotel and tavern in the village of Union. (From *History of Broome County*, H. P. Smith, 1885)

CHAPTER 3: A NEW LAND FOR SETTLEMENT

CHAPTER 4

A County Is Born

1806–1834

The ample supply of virgin wood provided the beginnings of a lumbering industry and the creation of new settlements in the young Broome County. This photograph dates from 1899 but shows that the techniques had not changed much from the early 1800s. (Courtesy Broome County Historical Society)

BY THE EARLY 1800s, it was apparent that the eastern portion of Tioga County was evolving into a new region. New York State was already experiencing growing pains. Thousands of new settlers were pouring to the lands formerly held by the Native Americans. As a result, the state took upon itself the task of dividing the large counties into smaller, more manageable areas. The rule of thumb was that the counties and their county seats should be no more than one day's ride from anyplace within the jurisdiction. In 1798, Chenango County was formed from the town of Jericho (present-day Bainbridge) and a portion of Herkimer County. The excessively large town of Union, which had been formed when Tioga County was created in 1791, was cut into three portions. In 1800, the town of Tioga was broken off the western portion, and in 1801, the town of Lisle was created from the northeast portion.

Finally, it was apparent that a new county was necessary for the convenience of its residents. On March 28, 1806, four townships—Chenango, Union, Lisle, and Tioga—were split off from Tioga County to form a new county. New counties had previously been named for the nearby rivers such as Chenango; Susquehanna had been used for the county across the border into Pennsylvania. The state had also been naming counties after recent governors, but all already had a county named after them. This time, the honor went to the

Lieutenant Governor John Broome (1738–1810) served as a lieutenant colonel during the American Revolution before entering politics. He resided on Broome Street in New York City when not in Albany. When the new county was formed from Tioga County, it was named for Broome. (Courtesy Broome County Historical Society)

then-current lieutenant governor of the state, John Broome (1738–1810).

Broome had come from the New York City area and had been a leader of the Sons of Liberty and served as a lieutenant colonel in the Revolutionary War. Broome, like other speculators at the time, had land holdings in many areas. He purchased two lots in the

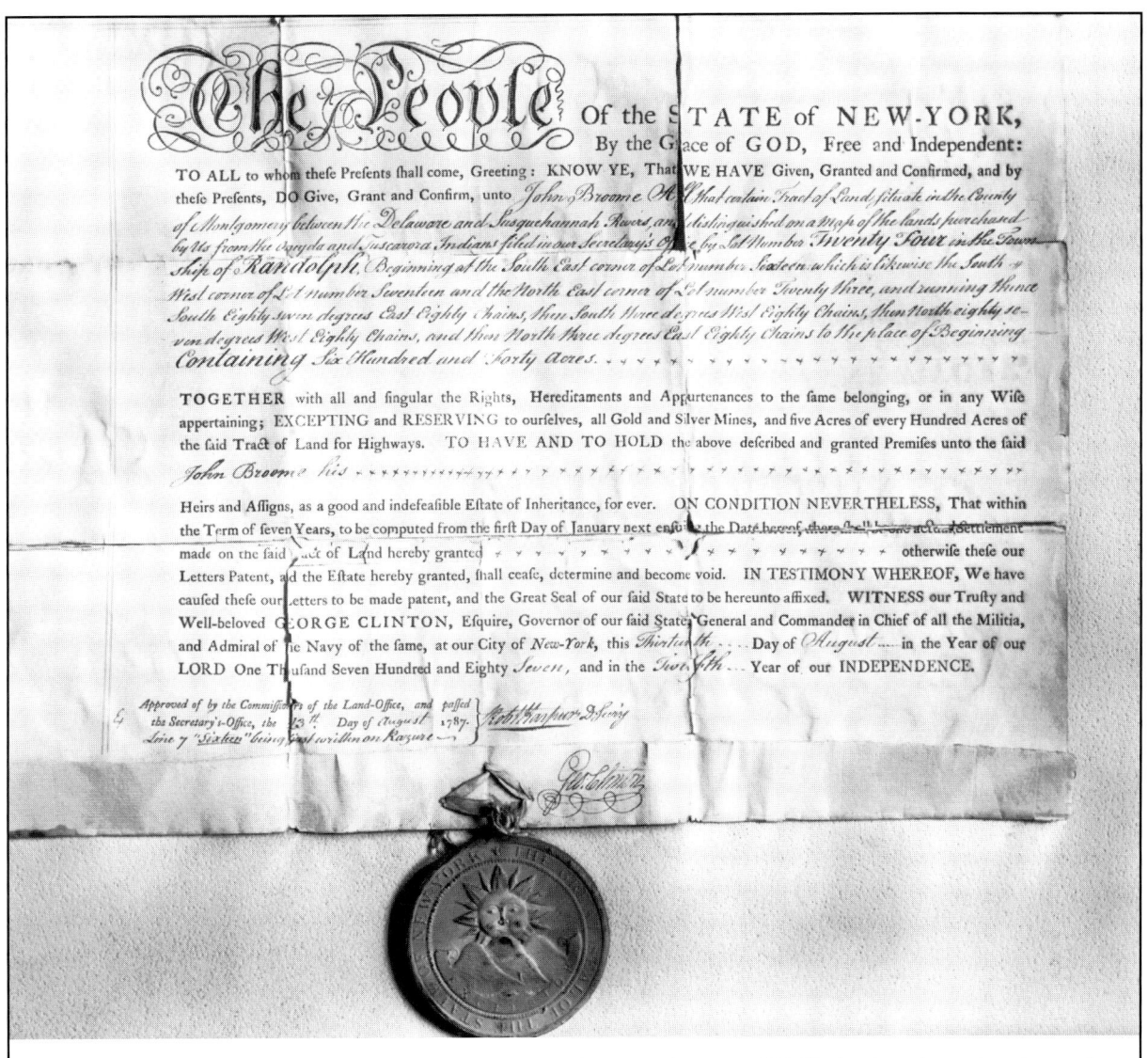
This is the land grant given to John Broome after the creation of Broome County in 1806. The land was located on the south side of the hamlet of Chenango Point (Binghamton) on Mill Street. Later generations of his family would live there. (Courtesy Broome County Historical Society)

present-day town of Windsor. His family was also granted a parcel of land on the south side of the Susquehanna River near Mill Street in the present-day city of Binghamton. Among the honors that came with having the county named after him, Broome was able to design the official seal for the new county. He used the Broome family coat of arms incorporating the image of the blindfolded Justice. He never did live on the lands either purchased or granted to him. He died and is buried in the New York City area. However, some of his family members did live in Broome County. They stayed on the lands on Mill Hill in Binghamton where the entrance to the drive to the family estate was denoted by markers bearing the Broome coat of arms.

With the creation of Broome County, Chenango Point was chosen as the county seat. Although

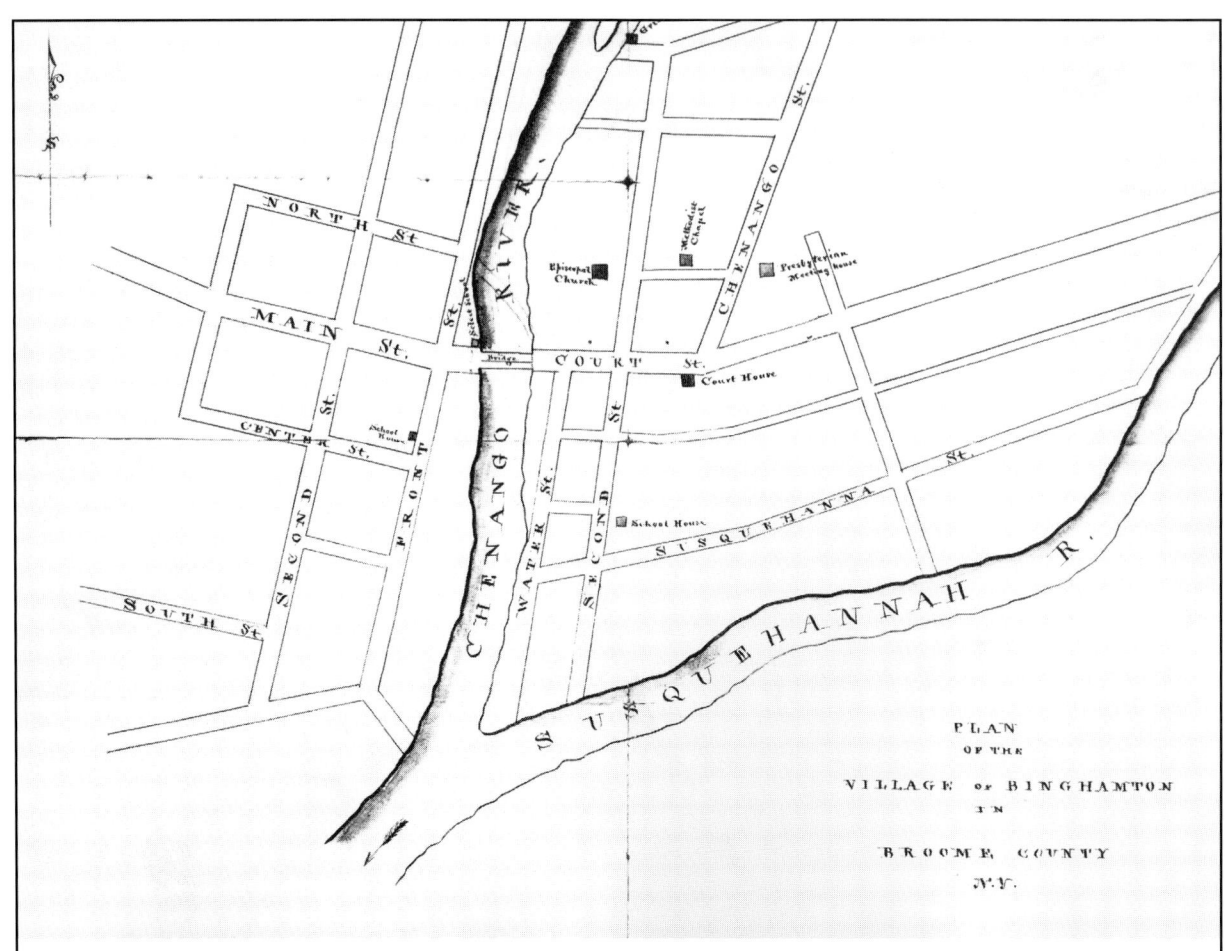

This map dates from about 1822 and shows the early street plan for the village of Binghamton. Joshua Whitney designed the first plan with an area set aside for a courthouse. Many of the early churches are already established by this date. (Courtesy Broome County Historical Society)

it was not yet an official village, Chenango Point, or Binghamton as many residents had taken to calling the town, had grown significantly. Joshua Whitney continued as land agent for the William Bingham estate. Although he was restricted in selling only the lands he himself had purchased from the estate, he continued on the path of developing a model village. He laid out the original street plan, including Court Street, First and Second Streets (now Water Street and Washington Street, respectively), and Chenango Street.

In 1808, six years after Whitney had walked into the Keeler Tavern and announced the construction of a bridge, one was finally constructed. Lucas Elmendorf had finally applied to the state for permission to construct the bridge in 1805, but it took another two full years for the bridge to open. Constructed by Marshall Lewis, it was a covered bridge that spanned six hundred feet of the Chenango River where the two elms had grown. It, like most other bridges of the time, was a toll bridge. Users of the span had to pay fees regulated by New York State. Drivers with four-wheel carriages and two horses paid 25¢, one horse two-wheel carriages paid $1.25, and the fee structure varied for livestock brought across.

Many new visitors to the growing town of Chenango Point would traverse one of the six turnpikes in the region that the state authorized between 1806 and 1816 along the major rivers of the region. Many used the routes carved out by the Iroquois prior to the American Revolution. While new settlers kept arriving, this area was still sparsely populated. There were 2,730 residents in 1800—six years before it was a county. Ten years later, in 1810, the population stood at 6,481. William Lawyer estimated that there were between 250 and 300 residents of Chenango Point by 1812. Some of these residents bought property from Joshua Whitney but many more leased the land. They paid the leases to Joshua Whitney, as the official collector for the Bingham estate. While it generated funds for the estate, it also made the incidence of movement off the lands by the tenants far more frequent than Whitney would have preferred.

While Chenango Point was the center of activity of the new county, it was certainly not the only hamlet to thrive during the first quarter of the nineteenth century. The township of Tioga was ceded back to Tioga County in 1822, but by then the hamlet of Union was growing along the northern bank of the Susquehanna River. The arrival of people like the Mersereau brothers, Amos Patterson, and others helped to settle the western portion of the county. In the north, Lisle was growing, along with the township of the same name. Created in 1801, the town was originally called Mudlick. During a visit by General Lafayette, he commented that the region reminded him of his own home in Lisle, France. The name was changed shortly thereafter.

General John Patterson arrived in the area in 1792 and settled at the meeting of the Otselic and Tioughnioga Rivers in what would become the township of Triangle. David Seymour followed him in 1792. In 1802, Thomas Whitney, the brother of Joshua Whitney, arrived in the community. He quickly became a leader with the early settlers, and the name of the hamlet soon became Whitney's Corners, now Whitney Point. Maine grew on the approximate midpoint between Union and Whitney Point. Robert Harpur was already settled in Harpursville, and to the east was Windsor near the site of Onaquaga. It was separated from the old town of Chenango as an independent township in 1807. The settlement near its center quickly evolved into a viable hamlet.

Smaller settlements formed at crossroads throughout the county by the early 1800s. Many were based on the waterpower of the streams, brooks, and rivers that powered the sawmills that sprang up in the first two decades

Agriculture was the mainstay in the first half of the nineteenth century. Farmers raised sheep, cattle, and horses and grew a variety of crops to feed their own families and to sell the surplus to people in the growing hamlets. C. Fred Harris took these photographs. (Courtesy Broome County Historical Society)

of the nineteenth century. The extensive virgin timber that ringed the river valleys provided the lumber necessary to help build new homes, bridges, churches, and other structures, helping to make these communities grow and thrive. Trees of oak, pine, maple, birch, elm, and other species provided ample wood to fill the needs of the growing county. Besides lumber for structures, the wood was used to build furniture and to construct pens, sheds, and outbuildings. Many farmers used the trees and stumps from cleared fields to make potash, and they sold it to those who needed the substance to enrich their soil and grow better crops.

Besides the gristmills, sawmills, and small stores located in the growing hamlets in Broome County, most of the inhabitants were occupied with farming. For most of the first half of the nineteenth century, the major "industry" of Broome County was agriculture. Most of settlers who came in the first few decades sought land on which to build a farm. Some had what has been called "itchy feet syndrome." They settled in an area for a few years, and then, when the population came too close to them, or boredom set in, they moved farther west. Other families that settled on the farmland in the early 1800s have descendants

that can still be found within a few miles of the ancestral home.

The terrain of Broome County offered farmers both opportunity and a test of patience. Along the river valleys, the soil was rich and flat—good for the growing of crops and the grazing of livestock. The problem with these areas was the frequency of springtime flooding that limited their use. However, most of Broome County was not located in the bottom of those valleys but among the hills that encircle the area. The hills cannot be said to offer easy land for farming. One publication about neighboring Delaware County calls this type of terrain "two stones for every dirt." The same can be said for much of Broome County.

Despite this, family after family acquired land in these regions and developed the skills to cultivate a substantial farming economy from that land. The women of the households played roles as important as those of the men. Many of them helped clear the land, plant seeds, and take care of the livestock. They gave birth to large families, hoping enough children would live to adulthood to help perpetuate the family farm. Many women also died during childbirth or shortly thereafter. Although an exact study has not been done, the mortality of females of childbearing age was fairly high, and it was not unusual to see a man wed at least twice.

Many of the early settlers were Revolutionary War veterans who used what pension or allocation of land they had been given to settle the new frontier. It has been estimated that as many as four hundred veterans may have made their way to Broome County. However, less than a handful of these had served in the Sullivan-Clinton Campaign. The settlers of the early villages and the farmers who surrounded them were not our only residents. Despite the success of the Sullivan-Clinton Campaign during the American Revolution, not all of the Iroquois left Broome County. As J. B. Wilkinson wrote in his *Annals of Binghamton of 1840*:

The Indians in their treaty with the New England commissioners, reserved to themselves the right of hunting upon the lands they had sold, for the term of seven years; and also made a reserve of one-half mile square, as their own possession. This reserve was situated near the mouth of Castle Creek, and went by the name of the Castle Farm. Upon this reserve the Indians of the neighborhood who did not remove to New Stockbridge, or Oneida, resided. Their number on the farm is said to have been about twenty families.

The families were led by Chief "Squire" Antonio, an Onondaga who was much respected by both the members of the farm and by those living in the Castle Creek area of the town of Chenango. The residents of the reservation were peaceable and interacted well with the white settlers of the area. How long the farm was used by the remaining Iroquois is unsure. But the residents were unscrupulously removed from their lands sometime before 1812.

There was one more type of resident to be found in the newly formed Broome County—African Americans. Many came to the area as slaves of the wealthier landowners of the time. Slavery was legal in most states in 1790, but many northern states had begun to take steps to end the bonds of involuntary servitude. New York was the northern state with the largest number of slaves in 1790, but the weakness of the system and the strength of the abolition movement forced an end to slavery within the state. In 1799, the New York State Legislature passed a statute that provided that children of slaves born after July 4, 1799, should have the status of bondservant and would acquire freedom (males at age twenty-eight and females at age twenty-five). This act was strengthened in 1817 when it declared, "every

Another early occupation found in the growing Broome County was that of blacksmithing. Whether one needed horseshoes or objects for the home, the village blacksmith was a valuable member of the community. This photograph dates from the early 1900s. (Courtesy Broome County Historical Society)

Daniel LeRoy arrived in Binghamton in 1801 and was one of the most prominent attorneys in the new village. He partnered with John Collier and owned a large tract of land where Front Street ends at the Susquehanna River. He left the area in 1817. (Courtesy Broome County Historical Society)

negro...born before the 4th day of July, 1799, shall, from and after the 4th day of July, 1827, be free" (Ellis, *A History of New York State*).

There were over thirty-one thousand African Americans in New York State in 1800, but Broome County's population was far smaller. There were somewhat less than one hundred African Americans in 1825. Most were slaves or former slaves of well-known families such as Joshua Whitney's and Oliver Crocker's.

Some had traveled with the families as they settled here from New England. Others were purchased after the families had settled in Broome County. Joshua Whitney purchased James Peterson from Philadelphia as his body servant. He also purchased George and Phoebe Dorsey from the Honorable Dugald Cameron of Bath in Steuben County. Descendants of the Dorseys still reside in Broome County. Unlike the southern system, the northern system did not differentiate between domestic and fieldwork. The slaves held mainly menial jobs. Despite the small number of slaves in Broome County prior to its demise, advertisements and broadsides for the sale of slaves have been found to indicate that the trade was still active in the first two decades of the nineteenth century. There were also free African Americans who resided in Broome County. Some had been here interacting with the Native American population prior to the Revolutionary War while others came here to live and work. The scarcity of material relating to their stories leaves little evidence of their lives in the county.

As the number of residents grew in each of the hamlets and evolving villages, so did the number of professions. The first known physician to live in Broome County was Ozias Crampton. He came to Windsor in 1791 from Montpelier, Vermont. He was trained and had worked in that state before moving to Broome County. He died suddenly in 1797 while on a trip to Pennsylvania. Daniel A. Wheeler moved to just north of Binghamton in 1793 and relocated to Whitney Point in 1797. He practiced there until his death in 1823. He also built the first gristmill in Lisle. By 1800, there were eight doctors practicing in what would become Broome County (Seward).

Some of the physicians had lengthy medical practices. Dr. Tracy Robinson (1778–1855) arrived in Binghamton in 1810 and took over the practice of Dr. Phinehas Bartholomew. Robinson was a descendant of the Reverend John Robinson, the religious leader of the Pilgrims. Robinson was a partner for a brief time with Dr. Ammi Doubleday (1790–1867) before setting up his own practice in 1822. He participated in early temperance movements and later became the chapter president of the American Colonization Society. Dr. Doubleday was a cousin of the dubious founder of baseball, Abner Doubleday. He came to Binghamton in 1812 and set up a successful practice on Court Street. He suddenly stopped his medical practice in 1829 to pursue other interests such as railroads and banking. Despite these arrivals, the number of doctors practicing in 1810 was the same as it was ten years before.

A number of early residents served as judges in the first decade of the 1800s. These included General John Patterson and James Stoddard of Lisle, Amos Patterson of Union, and Daniel Hudson of Chenango (Seward). Others also served but were not licensed as attorneys. William Stewart most likely holds the honor of being our first licensed attorney. He settled in this region in 1802 and served on the Court of Common Pleas. Another well-known early lawyer was Daniel LeRoy. LeRoy owned much of the Front Street area in Binghamton and was interested in land development. He left the area in 1817 but not before selling his interest to his partner, John A. Collier.

Collier and LeRoy were competitors against Joshua Whitney. They wanted to develop their own area for settlers and persisted in being a constant irritation to Whitney. Collier had a distinguished career in law in Binghamton. He served as district attorney from 1818 to 1822, a member of Congress in 1830, state comptroller in 1841, elector-at-large in 1848, and president of the Electoral College (Seward). When Millard Fillmore succeeded to the presidency upon the death of Zachary Taylor in 1850, he wanted to reward well-known Whig supporters. Collier was in line for a plush political appointment until some of his very vocal detractors strongly urged Fillmore not to appoint Collier. Apparently, Collier had been arrested in Albany for exposing himself from a hotel lobby window to young ladies passing by in the streets. Fillmore was eventually persuaded to pass Collier by, and his political career was at an end.

Aside from medicine and the law, another major segment of society to arrive in the early 1800s was organized religion. Just as it had been in the development of the New England states, religion played an important role in the development of Broome County. Aside from the missionaries who had ministered during the time of the Iroquois, a Baptist minister named Howe performed the first known religious service as early as 1789. The service was held on the west side of the Chenango River near where Front and Prospect Streets meet in the city of Binghamton. This small society never had many members and quickly disbanded. A Dutch Reformed Church missionary named Finley held services near Binghamton in 1798, but his attempts also faded rapidly.

As in many instances of early religion in the northeastern United States, it was the itinerant clergymen who helped establish regular religious services in the area. The Reverend Seth Williston was a Congregational missionary who used Lisle as his base of travels beginning in 1797. He traveled over a large area, including Union and Onaquaga. His journals are particularly noteworthy for his many stops at local residents' homes and his constant attempts at bringing Christianity to all he met. Similar itinerant clergy could be found in the Methodist and Episcopal faiths as well.

The first established congregation was under the control of the Reverend Daniel Nash who started the Episcopal Church of Chenango and Union in 1810 in Binghamton. Most of the major leaders of the Binghamton region were members of this church, including Joshua Whitney, Dr. Tracy Robinson, Daniel LeRoy, Lewis Keeler, and Mason Whiting. The first services were held in a room in the courthouse, but the congregation soon moved into a small wooden structure on Academy, now Washington, Street. The new church took the name Christ Church, and a larger structure was built in 1822. The original building was moved offsite to Henry Street and was sold to the Methodist Episcopal Society.

In 1814, the first Methodist Episcopal Society was founded in Broome County. They also met in the courthouse for a few years and had less than ten members. In order to survive, the society expanded in 1819 into the First Methodist Church in the towns of Union and Chenango, in the county of Broome (Seward). The name was changed to the First Society of the Methodist Episcopal Church in Binghamton in 1821. Several other changes and expansion led to the creation of a church located on Henry Street in 1822. The building had been relocated to the site from Academy Street on land donated by General Joshua Whitney. Another group called the M.E. Protestant Church of Binghamton opened up a church at the corner of Court and Carroll Streets in Binghamton in 1840. The building was used as a church by this group for only about a decade

The first Broome County Courthouse was on the north side of Court Street. This brick building became the second courthouse. It faced west on Court Street and was used until 1858. Its design showed the growing importance of Binghamton in the area. (Courtesy Broome County Historical Society)

when it was taken over by a splinter group of the Henry Street church. They, too, did not last long, and the church was closed, although the structure remained standing for another century.

In 1789, a small band of residents held a Baptist service at a local home located on the west side of the Chenango. This group was not very well organized until 1829 when

Peterson's Tavern was located on the corner of Front and Main Streets in Binghamton. A popular stagecoach stop, in 1834 it was used as the meeting hall for the newly incorporated village of Binghamton. First Congregational Church now stands on the site. (Courtesy Broome County Historical Society)

a meeting at the courthouse allowed for the formal incorporation of this group called the Chenango First Baptist Church. The first structure was completed on Chenango Street in 1831 with Michael Frederick serving as pastor of the church.

The growth of Broome County, in particular the area around Binghamton, was limited by the means of transportation into and out of the area. New York State's post road bill had begun the process to encourage the construction of major roads throughout the state and had led to the development of the bridge across the Chenango River at Binghamton. But in many ways, Broome County was largely isolated from the rest of the state. Despite having both the Chenango and the Susquehanna Rivers as the core of its waterway system, neither river was truly navigable. The depth of the water ranged from inadequate for boating to merely adequate. At times in the summer months, one could walk across the Susquehanna River in spots and have no fear of drowning. Rafting was often the only way to move any goods from one point to another. In Deposit in eastern Broome County, rafting on the Delaware River was the method of choice for moving the lumber being shipped down the river to the Philadelphia area. In the next few years, several events were about to happen that would forever change the direction and development of Broome County.

The small number of residents in Broome County in the early 1820s had been partially the result of the obtuse method of selling the lands of William Bingham. His estate lawyers had held up the sale of lands and forced Joshua Whitney to either sell his own plots or to hold a complex series of leases on the lands. Finally, in 1826, the lawyers conceded to the sale of the lands, with Joshua Whitney receiving a compensation of 5 percent. This would lead to the prospect of increasing the population of the fledgling Binghamton. Whitney took advantage of the situation. He used his new ability to sell the property and converted many of the leased properties that he had held for many years into parcels to be sold to the tenants or new settlers.

In 1817, New York State authorized the construction of a canal to cross the state from Albany to Buffalo. The monumental task of completing this project was celebrated with the opening of the Erie Canal in 1825. For the first time, a reliable system of transportation allowed people and goods to effectively move from New York City and the Hudson River across the entire state. The Erie Canal was able to shorten by two-thirds the time it took to move goods, and it reduced the cost by as much as 90 percent (Bothwell). The canal was very successful and spurred other areas to see the opportunity of improving their own place in New York by being connected to the Erie Canal.

As early as 1825, politicians from many areas of the state took aim at the state's leaders, and in the Omnibus Canal Bill of that same year, they obtained the right for surveys to be taken toward the possibility of constructing seventeen lateral canals that would connect to the Erie. One area that was surveyed was the Chenango River valley. Teams of engineers had to walk the entire length of the valley to see if it was possible to move packet boats across many changes in elevation and overcome problems such as the constant feeding of water into the canal. Efforts to develop a canal from the Erie to Binghamton continued for the next eight years. Those who pushed for the completion of such a canal realized that its construction would open a new chapter in the development of Broome County.

CHAPTER 5
Canal Fever
1834–1848

Binghamton pushed for the construction of the Chenango Canal, which opened in 1837. This 1858 painting depicts a packet boat near the site of the former North Presbyterian Church. (Painting on loan to Roberson Museum from the Canal Society of New York State, courtesy Broome County Historical Society)

This stereographic view shows the crossover bridge over the Chenango Canal at Lewis Street in Binghamton. The small Greek Revival home still stands in the rear of the Lewis Street buildings. The canal helped promote the growth of Binghamton. (Original owned by Robert Connelly, courtesy Broome County Historical Society)

CANAL FEVER! It caught on like wildfire. Everyone had to have his own canal, and the state seemed to take notice. The approval of the survey of seventeen areas was only the first step in the long process toward additional canals in New York State. In February 1833, the state authorized the construction of a canal that would follow the route of the Chenango River. The greatest initial fight was not over the sufficiency of water for the canal or over the number of locks necessary to move the packet boats through the canal. It was the location of the northern terminus of the canal. The most direct route would be to have Binghamton as the southern terminus and Whitesboro as the northern terminus where the canal would connect to the Erie Canal.

But a political fight ensued over the northern terminus. The leaders of Utica wanted the canal to run through their town. They realized that the canal would bring both people and revenue to their growing city. Despite the logic of the Whitesboro route, which would have required fewer locks, the Utica contingent won the battle, and the route was relocated through that city. The new canal required a ninety-five-mile route with a four-hundred-foot change in elevation from one terminus to the other. The canal would require 116 locks, 1 guard lock, 19 aqueducts, 52 culverts, 21 waste weirs, 56 road bridges, 106 farm bridges, 53 feeder bridges, 12 dams, and 11 lockhouses (McFee, *Limestone Locks and Overgrowth: The Rise and Descent of the Chenango Canal*).

John B. Jervis was selected as the chief engineer, who would be faced with the monumental task of completing the canal through Oneida, Madison, Chenango, and Broome Counties. Workers had to be hired to dig the canal bed—forty-two feet wide at the top and twenty-six feet wide at the bottom. On either side of the canal bed was a bank two feet higher than the four feet of water required to move the packet boats.

A towpath was constructed with a width of ten feet that was adequate to hold the horses or mules used to pull the boats along the canal. In some areas, wood would be used to brace sections of the canal bed. Certain sections of the bed had stone bottoms although much of the construction used dirt as the basis for the sides and bottom of the bed. Stonework and wood were reserved for the construction of the gates. The gates were a simple pressure-based system of leveling the water from one lock to another to allow the boats to pass through. Each set required two people to operate. Many of the construction workers were local residents hired to work on the project although a greater and greater number of Irish immigrants eventually found employment in the canal construction and in its maintenance.

Hotels were among the first businesses to cluster near the canal. The Exchange Hotel was located on Court Street. It opened as the Phoenix Hotel in 1838 and later became offices before being demolished in 1949 to make way for Woolworth's (now Family Dollar). (Courtesy Broome County Historical Society)

The canal opened new markets for traditional industries such as lumbering and finished goods. This is a 1900 photograph of the Bartlett & Blanchard Lumber Company, which operated next to the canal. It is now the site of the Government Plaza. (Courtesy Broome County Historical Society)

accomplished something that even Joshua Whitney could not accomplish—it officially named the town. There were still a number of residents who insisted on using Chenango Point as the name, partially in opposition to Whitney and his followers' use of the name Binghamton. In this instance, Whitney won over the state, and the name Binghamton officially commemorated William Bingham's vision of the new town.

As work continued on the construction of the Chenango Canal, the future of Binghamton was determined by the state legislature. On May 3, 1834, New York State passed an act of incorporation for the village of Binghamton. It was the formal recognition of the plan of Bingham and Whitney. The increased population of the village had increased its viability as a real force in the southern tier of the state. There had been several attempts at incorporation in the 1820s that had failed. One of these attempts was the first known misspelling of the name of the town as "Binghampton." The state was unable to spell the name of the town and unable to pass the act. Finally, the act passed in 1834, and a new village was created. The act also

There was no official location for the new village government. An election of officials was held in June 1834, and the village was broken into five wards. Each ward would select one trustee and one assessor. The first meeting of the newly elected trustees was held at the tavern of Samuel Peterson, which was located at the corner of Front and Main Streets (now the site of the First Congregational Church). It was a popular stagecoach stop. At the meeting, the trustees selected Daniel S. Dickinson, an attorney from Chenango County who had moved to the village four years prior, as the first president of the village. They also selected a clerk, a treasurer, and five fire wardens. Broome County had its first official village.

Work on the Chenango Canal continued during 1834, 1835, and 1836. Finally, in May 6, 1837, the Chenango Canal opened to great fanfare as the first packet boat made its way along the canal. The project had an original budget of $1 million. But delays, design changes, and cost overruns brought the final construction total to $2.5 million. The over-budget cost overrun was only the beginning of the financial woes of the Chenango Canal.

The opening of the Chenango Canal brought economic changes to the community. It reduced the cost of shipping goods from Binghamton to Utica from $1.25 to 25¢ per ton and shortened the time it took to move the goods from eleven to four days (Bothwell). It created a reliable system that allowed for economic growth in the areas in which it passed. It helped to create entirely new communities based upon canal traffic. Areas such as Port Crane and Port Dickinson were stops along the canal that did not exist prior to the opening of the Chenango Canal.

Several stoneware and pottery manufacturers operated in the Binghamton area by the mid-nineteenth century. Roberts, Whites, and other firms lasted until the closing of the canal in the 1870s. Most of the firms were located in the area called Millville. (Courtesy Broome County Historical Society)

This building was located on the northeast corner of Washington and Henry Street. Used for many purposes including a dyeing and cleaning shop, it was demolished in the late 1800s. The site is now occupied by the Federal Building and Courthouse. (From the *Putnam Collection,* Broome County Public Library)

The canal relied on the transport of goods, with coal being the main product transported. Coal was used for heating homes and factories, and the canal connected Binghamton with the rich coalfields of Pennsylvania. The canal also allowed for finished goods to be brought into the area and for raw materials such as lumber to be shipped and sold in other markets. It allowed for the movement of people, as well. New settlers could move their households and themselves on the packet boats.

Benjamin Sisson and his bride traveled to Binghamton on one of the boats on the canal. A cabinetmaker by trade, Sisson fell in love with Binghamton and the beauty of the Chenango River valley and decided to relocate to the village in 1842. He opened a cabinet shop next to the canal, hoping that the proximity would ensure success of the new business. It did not, and Sisson moved the business to Front Street for a few years. He decided to add several departments and convert the store into a dry goods business. Again, he located to the northwest corner of the canal and Court Street. This time, the new store hosting a line of different goods was successful. Binghamton had its first department store, and Sisson Brothers and Welden would remain open for more than a century at the same location.

New types of businesses opened up along the route of the canal. Near the southern terminus of the canal in Binghamton and located near Evans Basin, a large repair shop and turn-around, there were a number of mill operations. Bartlett and Blanchard ran a planning mill, turning out finished lumber for the manufacture of furniture or for the making of homes and other buildings. Various sawmills and gristmills combined the waterpower of the Susquehanna River and the ability of the canal to transport goods to bring success. This section of Binghamton quickly became known as Millville. Maps of Binghamton just prior to and immediately after the opening of the Chenango Canal show a boom in construction along the man-made waterway.

Despite the appearance of success of the Chenango Canal, it was not the financial boom that its creators had hoped. The canal was both costly to create and costly to maintain. It only operated about nine months of the year. During its closed season, repairs would have to be made along the length of the canal bed where boats had smashed into the sides and gates, causing significant damage. It was also doomed to eventual failure by another type of transportation that was created before the existence of the Chenango Canal.

In 1832, two years before Binghamton became a village and five years before the first packet boat traveled down the Chenango Canal, New York State had authorized the creation of the New York and Erie Railroad Company. Although it would be sixteen years before the first railroad train would traverse Broome County, the death knell for the Chenango Canal had begun to ring. The state already had its first major railroad company, the New York Central, which ran adjacent to the Erie Canal in many areas. Railroad travel had become a reality, and the owners and operators of the various canals across New York State had good reason to be worried.

It was a time for growth and change for Binghamton. The opening of the canal had already resulted in the construction of a number of new buildings in the downtown area. The Iron Bridge was built across the canal on Court Street to allow wagons and carriages to move freely. At first a one-lane bridge, the state ordered that the bridge be made two-lane to avoid creating traffic problems along the village's main road. The 1840s also saw changes in the makeup of the community.

In 1835, James W. White married Rhoda Waterman in Binghamton. She was the daughter of Judge Thomas Waterman. Although marriages were not uncommon,

George Park was the first village clerk for Binghamton as well as an artist. His view of Court Street in 1810 is well known. This view depicted the scene from his bedroom window looking east on Hawley Street. (Courtesy Broome County Historical Society)

CHAPTER 5: CANAL FEVER   73

Religion was an important part of life in early Broome County. In 1791, the Dutch Reformed Church (now Union Presbyterian) was the area's first church and was located in Union.

White was the first Catholic to marry a Protestant in the county. He was the son of Edward White, who was the land agent for the Rose brothers of Susquehanna County, Pennsylvania. The Roses held extensive land holdings and hired Edward White to manage land sales. White was Irish and had offered to bring middle- and upper-class Irish to the community to settle. Hundreds arrived at the county near Friendsville while other settlers helped develop the settlement of Montrose. The year after his son James married Rhoda Waterman, White decided to locate in Binghamton and run the land operations from that village. He built a fine home on Front Street that would later become the home of John Rankin and, subsequently, George Barlow. Two of White's daughters ran Binghamton's first parochial school from that home.

The Whites were the first known Catholic family in Broome County, but they were not the last.

Within a few years, other Catholics moved nearby in the village of Binghamton and in the farmland surrounding the village. Father Wainwright, a priest from Pottsville, Pennsylvania, was allowed to visit and conduct Mass on the lawn of White's home. It became evident that a church was needed. Thomas Waterman offered a site for the church on Oak Street, but it was refused. The members wanted a church setting on higher ground on Leroy Street. The site was obtained, and St. John the Apostle Church was constructed. Various priests held service for the congregation until 1847 when Father James Hourigan was appointed to head the new congregation. It was a post that he would serve for the next forty-five years.

In a smaller but no less important development, two African American churches were begun in the 1830s. The number of African Americans was not large, but the role of religion was essential to their identity as it was with many groups. Small missions were begun in individual homes and eventually in other buildings in the downtown area of the village of Binghamton. In 1838, the Bethel Church was incorporated and operated after 1840 from a building on a lot on Susquehanna Street that was provided by Major Martin Hawley. Its first pastor was

The New (First) Presbyterian Church on Chenango Street as it appeared in 1862. The current church has the only tall spire left in Binghamton.

The First Congregational Church is still on Front Street in Binghamton but without the tall steeple. (Courtesy Broome County Historical Society)

Peter Potter. In that same year, Joshua Whitney provided a lot on Whitney Street (later Sherman Place) to build a church. The First Colored M.E. Zion Church was incorporated in July of that year at the home of Thomas Bell. A structure was built on the Whitney lot in 1840. The church today, Trinity A.M.E. Church, has since relocated but remains a vibrant part of the community. Joshua Whitney also donated land on the southeast corner of Washington and Hawley Streets for a school for African American students. This school would be relocated several times but remain downtown for many decades.

Joshua Whitney was the strength behind and the de facto founder of Binghamton. He had created the model town that William Bingham

The appearance of the White family and other Irish Catholics led to the construction of St. John's Church on Leroy Street in 1838. St. Patrick's Church replaced it in 1872, and the old school was moved to become St. James School. (From *Evert's Atlas of Broome County*, 1876)

had envisioned. It was Whitney who laid out the first street plans, created the first bridge, and laid out the plans for the courthouse and first library. He was the first elected representative to the New York State Assembly from Broome County. Whitney was treasurer of the toll bridge company and was involved in his own mercantile business. He built a distinguished home on the east side of the village in 1810 and had it patterned after another Whitney home in New York City. He was a founder of Christ Church but had stopped going to service after the church had refused to allow him to expand the size of his pew to allow room for his 345-pound body. His personality inspired both the respect of much of the community and provoked many detractors who did not agree with his beliefs. Lawsuits were common in his life but not taken lightly. One incident is illustrative of Whitney's personality:

[Whitney] was sitting in the octagonal drawing room one spring day, with the long windows open, when his Negro manservant announces Mr. Ausburn Birdsell. Mr. Birdsell was a young attorney who had been engaged by some of the plaintiffs in a suit against the General. The General received him courteously in the drawing room and listened attentively to the carefully rehearsed speech of the young man. He had boasted that he would beard the lion in his den, but the General's continued silence finally embarrassed him. Stammering, he requested the General's opinion on his statement of the case. General Whitney only smiled and shook his head as he rose, towering above the guest, who had also risen. Taking the young man by the shoulder, he led him to the open window, bade him good evening, requested him to come again when he had something of interest to discuss, and dropped him to the ground, some distance below. (Seward)

Edward White was the head of first known Roman Catholic family in Broome County. Land agent for Montrose's Rose family, his home on Front Street later became residence for both Mayor John Rankin and industrialist George Barlow before being demolished for a hotel. (From *Art Work of Binghamton*, 1900)

Whitney began to fail in 1844. His son, Virgil, had assumed the day-to-day operations of his father's business. His sons took turns watching over their father, and it took two men to help move him in and out of bed. He had his bed moved to his former office in his home since he found remaining in his bedroom too discouraging. Finally, on April 13, 1845, General Joshua Whitney died. He was buried next to the body of his first wife in the churchyard cemetery of Christ Church. Eventually, his body was removed to Spring Forest Cemetery under a marble monument that cost one thousand dollars. With the passing of the power behind early Binghamton and much of Broome County, the region entered the mid-nineteenth century with new opportunities for change.

As the population spread outward into the rural area, the style of homes grew in size and elegance. This Greek Revival farmhouse from the 1850s is located in the town of Fenton on Route 369; the farm was in operation until recently. (Courtesy Broome County Historical Society)

CHAPTER 5: CANAL FEVER

CHAPTER 6
The Arrival of the Iron Horse
1848–1865

The Starrucca Viaduct in Pennsylvania was the crowning achievement of James Kirkwood, chief engineer for the New York & Erie Railroad. Completed in 1848, it is still in use today and is listed among the engineering marvels of the country. (Courtesy Broome County Historical Society)

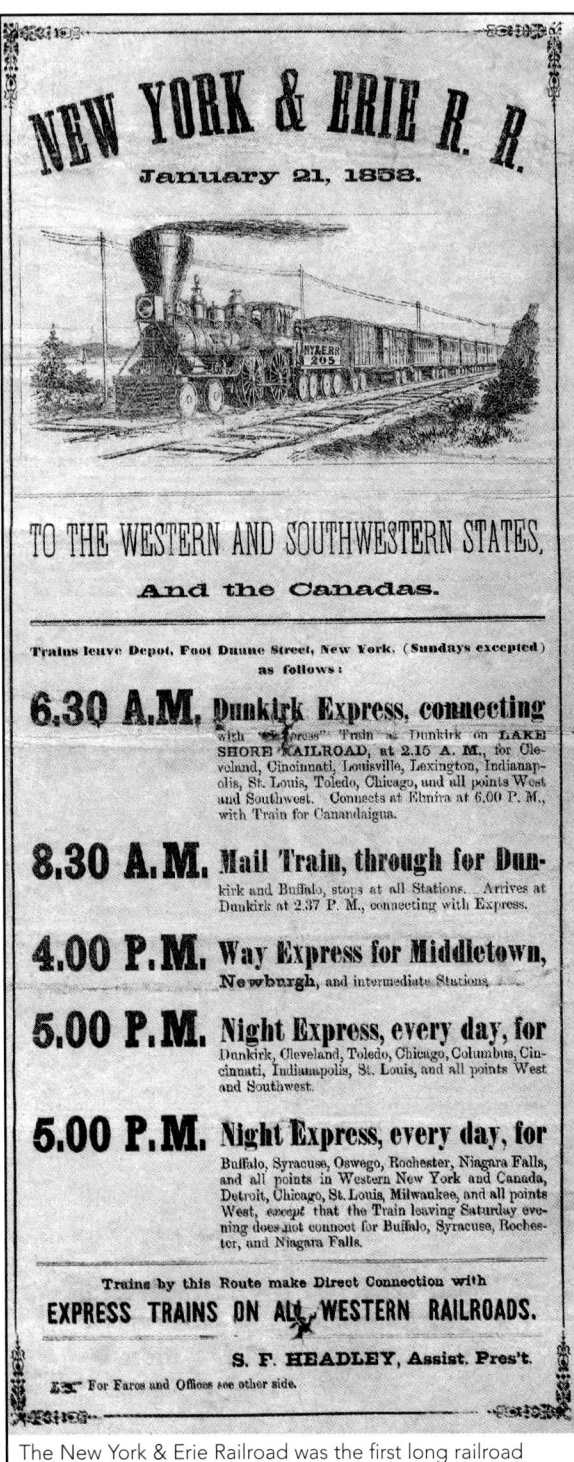

The New York & Erie Railroad was the first long railroad in the country's history. The arrival of the railroad in Binghamton in 1848 effectively ended the viability of the Chenango Canal and forever changed the economy of the area. This brochure dates from 1858. (Courtesy Broome County Historical Society)

IT WOULD TAKE SIXTEEN YEARS and several changes of ownership and direction before the New York and Erie Railroad would become a reality. It was intended to be the first long railroad in the United States. It was originally planned to run from the Hudson River to Lake Erie. The first shovel of dirt in the building of the Erie took place on November 7, 1835, at Deposit, New York. Despite this auspicious beginning, the leadership of the railroad slowed its own progress by infighting. Despite the vision of its original leaders such as Eleazer Lord and John Stevens, who had hoped for the government to underwrite the railroad, the politicians of the canal lobby were stronger and blocked aid. Eventually, however, the New York State government did provide some funds to keep the railroad's development on track.

For the next several years, progress went slowly. The New York and Erie Railroad had chosen a route that would link it to a number of new cities across the northeast, but getting to those cities was another challenge for the fledgling railroad. A major decision to use six-foot gauge instead of the European standard of slightly less than five feet made the railroad unique. The New York and Erie faced other obstacles. Mountains, gorges, and rivers were some of the geographical difficulties. Add to this the constant change in leadership and in its vision, and it is understandable why it took thirteen years for the tracks of the New York and Erie to reach the area of the Susquehanna

This is the Delaware & Hudson Engine Number 501 in front of buildings on North Depot Street in Binghamton about 1890. The expansion of the railroads brought businesses, people, and opportunity to the valley. Today, many of the buildings are being converted to lofts. (Courtesy Broome County Historical Society)

River valley. The progress would have been even slower if the railroad had not done something right in the hiring of James Pugh Kirkwood in 1847.

To lay track near Binghamton, one locomotive, the Orange, was dismantled, floated up the Hudson River and across the Erie Canal, and brought down on the Chenango Canal so that it could be reassembled to lay the track that would eventually destroy the means of transportation that had just brought it to Binghamton. As the route approached Binghamton, it passed over the Cascade Bridge in Susquehanna County, Pennsylvania. This was a beautiful wooden bridge that would last only a few years.

James Kirkwood had previously worked on the Boston railway system. He saw that his major problem was to design a means of moving the railroad across the Starrucca Creek. His design of a viaduct still amazes today's users of the railroad. It was 1,040 feet in length with eighteen arches rising 100 feet above the ground. It was designed so trains could pass each other. The structure cost $320,000 and employed eight hundred men to build it in less than one year. It was originally designed to carry fifteen-ton engines. Today, the Starrucca Viaduct is an engineering marvel; it is still in use 150 years later and carries engines that weigh four hundred tons.

Although it had taken thirteen years to lay the first two hundred miles of track, Kirkwood was able to lay out the final two hundred miles in just three years. The first New York and Erie train made it to this area on December 27, 1848. It had been delayed by a snowstorm, but the weather did not dampen the spirits of the crowds who had waited for hours. Cheers went up as the smoke of the train approached the newly built station on the north side of Binghamton. Two excursion trains reached the station, and a nightlong party ensued at the station and later at a nearby hotel.

Three years later, on May 14, 1851, the entire four-hundred-mile length of the railroad opened. Leaders from the federal and state governments rode the train through the new railroad towns along its route. As the train stopped in Binghamton, President Millard Fillmore announced that the village was now truly connected to the Atlantic and to Lake Erie. Secretary of State Daniel Webster, whose oratory skill was well known throughout country, had ridden the train seated in a rocking chair on a flatbed car because of a back ailment. He rose and addressed the large crowd, saying:

I can hardly more express the pleasure I have in seeing you and the western end of the great work of art. I have crossed the upper branches of the Delaware and Susquehanna, and I know something of these rivers at their mouths, but I have never seen them as they issue from these lofty, sublime and picturesque hills. It is a beautiful and vigorous country. May God bless you and enable you to enjoy all of its healthy blessings.

With those words, Binghamton was connected to the rest of the world by water, land, and railroad.

The New York and Erie provided Binghamton a reliable means of transportation. The railroad could operate through every season, something the Chenango Canal could not. It made travel much faster and reduced the cost of shipping goods. It made Binghamton a viable market for factories, settlers, and other railroads.

In 1851, subscribers began to invest in the Albany and Susquehanna Railroad Company. The route would begin in Binghamton and go through Harpursville, Bainbridge, and Unadilla on its way to Albany. Bonding and investment in the railroad led to the beginning of construction in July 1853, but financial difficulties stopped progress until late in 1858. The route was begun in Albany and made its way to Harpursville in the town of Colesville by Christmas 1867. It would take another two years before a tunnel that was 2,239 feet in length could be cut through a mountain to allow the route to continue to Binghamton. The route that would eventually become the Delaware and Hudson Railroad was finally completed on January 12, 1869 (Seward).

During the time that the Albany and Susquehanna Railroad was under construction, the Syracuse and Binghamton Railroad was busy completing its north-south line to connect to the Erie Railroad. It was built between 1853 and 1854 and opened on October 18, 1854. It quickly ran into financial difficulties and was reorganized as the Syracuse and Southern Railroad in 1856. A year later, the name was changed to the Syracuse, Binghamton and New York Railroad.

In 1850, the Liggetts Gap Railroad Company began operations, hoping to create a route between Scranton, Pennsylvania, and Binghamton. Acquisition of the Cayuga and Susquehanna Railroad gave the new company a line from the Pennsylvania border to the Erie Canal. It soon changed its name to the Delaware, Lackawanna and Western Railroad. It was able to open for operations in 1851 and became the most important railroad transportation line with its large number of branches to many other locations across several states.

The area was evolving from a frontier region to one with all of the amenities of modern life. Education had been an early factor in the history of Broome County but had not developed much since the first school was opened about 1791 in a log building at the foot of Mount Prospect. Colonel Rose was the instructor, but the school did not last long. Another school opened on the east side of the Chenango River near the home of Abraham

In 1869, opposing forces fought for control of the Albany to Syracuse railroad. Two engines filled with men armed with pick handles fought in the railroad tunnel in Colesville. State troops ended the fight. The fight was depicted in Edna Ferber's *Saratoga Trunk*. (Courtesy Broome County Historical Society)

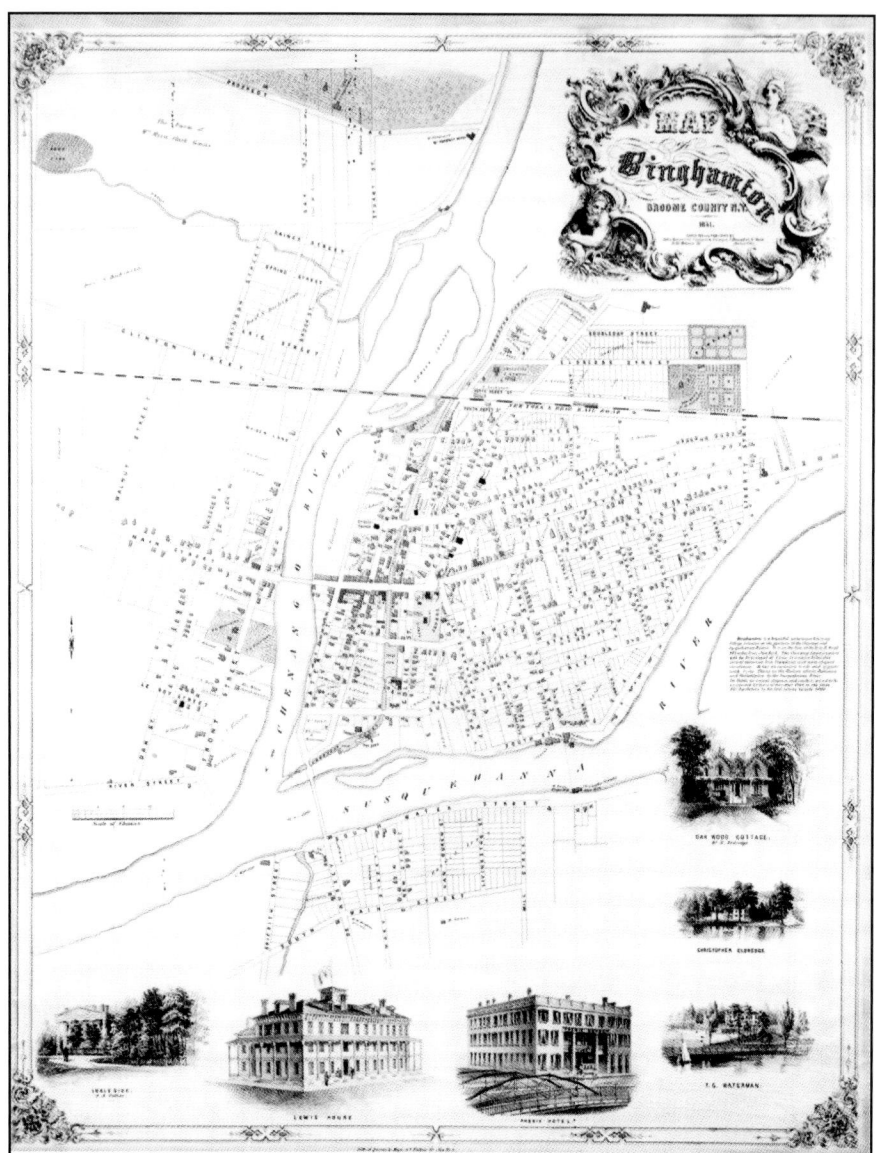

This is the 1851 Bevan map of Binghamton. It shows the rapidly developing village around the railroad tracks and Chenango Canal. The vignettes show the impressive homes of John Collier and others, as well as the hotels of the time. (Courtesy Broome County Historical Society)

created: one on the west side of the Chenango and one on the east side of that river.

Joshua Whitney gave a building lot for a school on the southeast corner of Washington and Hawley Streets. It was eventually occupied by a brick school building that was used for many years. In 1834, William Waterman donated a lot for another school on Main Street on the western edge of the village of Binghamton. Other schools were built in various locations near residential areas, but public schools were not the only avenue for education. Private schools continued to operate during this period. Pamela Wentz and a Miss Waterhouse operated a private school on the northeast corner of Washington and Hawley Streets (across from the Whitney site). It was the first instance of female instructors employed in Broome County.

Bevier. A second school was added across the Chenango River on the west side. These private schools, taught by men, were the first attempts at bringing education to the children of the new settlers. Shortly after 1812, the first organization of a public school system was attempted in Broome County. Two school districts were

Other private schools prospered during the first half of the nineteenth century. As previously mentioned, the White sisters ran the first parochial school. It was originally located at the corner of Lewis and Chenango Streets before relocating to the family home on Front Street. The Reverend Peter Lockwood ran a boys school across Lewis Street from the Whites' school. Harmony Seminary (also called Harmony Retreat) was run by the Marsh family and located on Chenango Street on the north side of Binghamton.

Prior to the outbreak of the Civil War, the largest of the schools was the Binghamton Academy. It opened in 1841 on Courthouse Square. It occupied a three-story brick building and was well financed with the backing of many of the prominent businessmen and political leaders of the time, including Daniel Dickinson. The school had as many as 250 students registered for a well-rounded curriculum including languages, science, mathematics, and writing. As the population grew, it became evident that Binghamton needed a public high school.

In 1861, the Union Free School Act was passed in an attempt to formalize the variety of educational institutions that existed across the state. A Binghamton-wide district was created for the management of the schools. Education commissioners were appointed and allowed to establish schools to meet the needs

Dr. Stephen Hand (1806–1879) was both a major leader of the medical community and a stationmaster on the Underground Railroad. His home on Collier Street and the two Binghamton African American churches were safe stops for escaped slaves in Broome County. (Courtesy Broome County Historical Society)

of the community. With the creation of this commission, seven schools already in existence in Binghamton came under its control. Also included was a school for African American children. This became known as School Number 8 and was located near School Number 4 on the corner of Carroll and Susquehanna Streets. The Union Free School Act also influenced the control of the many one-room and two-room schools that had begun to proliferate in the townships and villages of Broome County.

This building on the corner of Court and Carroll Streets in Binghamton was originally a Methodist-Episcopal church. The church was closed and converted to a livery stable. It was demolished in the 1900s to make way for an automobile dealership (now the site of Matco). (Courtesy Broome County Historical Society)

Opposite page: Christ Church in Binghamton is the city's oldest congregation, dating to 1810. The current church dates from 1854 and was designed by Richard Upjohn, who designed Trinity Church in New York City. Original contractor John Stewart Wells added the steeple in 1903. (Courtesy Broome County Historical Society)

The creation of more schools was a direct result of the increasing population of Broome County and its municipalities. In 1830, the population of the county stood at 17,579. Ten years later, it had increased to 22,338. By 1850, Broome County had 30,600 residents, and just prior to the Civil War in 1860, the population was 35,906 (Seward). Increasingly, the percentage of the population living in Binghamton to that of the rest of the county continued to increase. It increased from 10 percent in 1840 to over 25 percent by 1860.

Some of the new residents were continuing to migrate from New England, Pennsylvania, and New Jersey, but many others were immigrants from Ireland and Germany. Although there were a few Irish in Broome County in the late 1830s, the number did not greatly increase until 1846 after the Potato Famine took its hold on Ireland. An Gorta Mor, or the Great Hunger, began as blight on the potato crop of Ireland. Potatoes were one of the staple foods feeding the millions of tenants living upon land mainly owned by British proprietors. The situation prior to the famine had already begun to deteriorate. Some landowners had already begun to pay for tenants to leave their homes and relocate to the United States. When the famine hit, this situation was exacerbated.

CHAPTER 6: THE ARRIVAL OF THE IRON HORSE   87

Broome County's first Jewish residents arrived in the area in the 1850s. The Sons of Israel constructed the first temple in the county on Water Street. This 1923 building was located on Exchange Street. (From the *Putnam Collection*, courtesy Broome County Public Library)

Prior to the outbreak of the Potato Famine, the population of Ireland stood at eight million residents. By the end of the famine in 1851, the population had dropped by three million people. One million had died from starvation or disease. The other two million had left their native country for other countries. Most of them came to the United States. They settled in all parts of the country, but a large portion settled in the northeastern United States.

In Broome County, the number of Irish also increased. Some worked as transient workers on the Erie Railroad. Other Irish immigrants put down roots in Broome County. There were five main areas of Irish settlement prior to the Civil War. One section was located in Deposit near the railroad lines going through that village. The Irish in that town worked mainly in the smaller factories and in the lumber business that predominated the economic structure of Deposit. To the north of Binghamton, located in the towns of Maine and Chenango, was a large area of Irish farmers that became known as New Ireland. Many were dairy farmers while a few raised crops on the hilly terrain of the area.

In Binghamton, there were two areas of Irish settlement. Many lived near the Susquehanna Street area in the downtown section of the village. The males of the family worked on the Chenango Canal or for one of the railroads servicing the town. Many of the younger Irish females worked as domestics for the wealthier families surrounding this Irish enclave. As they became settled in the community, some of the Irish families moved farther east in the village toward Robinson Street. This area on the "wrong side of the tracks" became known as the Patch (although the Irish settlement in Deposit was also called the Patch). The last area of Irish settlement was located on the south side of the Susquehanna River in the Fifth Ward of Binghamton. It was also known as the Bloody Fifth because of the large number of fights that would break out among the Irish and also among feuding German immigrants in various beer gardens. The Irish in this area settled this region later than the others mentioned. The families began to move in by the late 1860s and 1870s, but today it is still the highest concentration of families of Irish ancestry in the county. Several thousand Irish eventually would call Broome County home.

Beginning as early as 1820, but increasing in the 1850s and 1860s, were waves of German immigrants to the United States. Political unrest in Germany forced many of the native-born of that country to leave their homeland and seek a new life elsewhere. Like the pattern established during the Irish immigration, many first settled in the northeastern United States. Within a few years, large German settlements in the Midwestern states could be found, but many other German families stayed in their first area of settlement, including Broome County. Unlike the Irish, who were mainly farmers or unskilled laborers, a larger percentage of the Germans arriving in Broome County were skilled artisans or of the business class. They, like the Irish, first settled in downtown Binghamton. Some opened businesses while others worked in some of the increasing number of stores in the village. Germans also began to settle on the south side of the Susquehanna River in the area that would later be inhabited by Irish families. As they settled into the community, the more affluent Germans moved to the west side of Binghamton. New streets and housing developments after the Civil War enticed them to relocate to an area known as the German Settlement. Most of the streets in this area are named after German and Austrian writers and composers.

This is also the period of the first Jewish population in Broome County. Many were European Jews, especially German, who migrated with their fellow countrymen. These early immigrants to the area, unlike their Christian German neighbors, did not tend to live for long periods in one area. They would often move to another location within a generation (Sussman, *Beyond the Catskills: Jewish Life in Binghamton, New York, 1850–1975*). By the time of the Civil War, there were only twenty Jewish families living in the county. There would be no synagogue or religious structure until well after the conclusion of the war.

The first known Jews in Broome County were Henry Goodman and Edward Goodkind, who ran the Leading Dry Goods Store. They sold their business in 1857 to Sigmund J. Hirschmann and his brother, Frederick. These men operated Hirschmann Brothers Dry Goods Store until 1902 (Sussman). Sigmund Hirschmann became involved in other businesses, including banks. He also helped start the Hebrew Benevolent Society on July 27, 1862, along with thirteen other Jewish businessmen.

It would be wrong to say that the new immigrants were welcomed to Broome County with open arms. Newspapers of the 1840s and 1850s ran numerous stories in which the Irish were often characterized as "rowdy" or in a drunken state. Non-English-speaking Germans were satirized in national political cartoons, and Jewish residents faced even harsher criticism. This was the one of several periods when racial discrimination would, as in the rest of the nation, rear its ugly head in Broome County.

During this period, the nation was straining with the problem of slavery. Even though the institution of slavery had ended in New York State in the late 1820s, this did not isolate the county from the problem facing the nation. The south's "peculiar institution" did not stop at the borders of those states. The problem invaded every aspect of American society. It is not known when the first slave took the brave step toward freedom and escaped the bonds of involuntary servitude. What is known is that by the first two decades of the nineteenth century, the Society of Friends (the Quakers) began a concentrated effort to assist runaway slaves toward freedom.

Operating mainly in Philadelphia, a network of supporters developed routes and safe houses where slaves could be sheltered en route toward freedom, usually in Canada. Eventually, the network spread beyond the Quakers to other supporters across several states. The network became known as the Underground Railroad, and its supporters were called stationmasters or conductors. The full extent of the network will never be known because of its illegal nature. This is especially true of the period after 1850 when the Fugitive Slave Act made aiding runaway slaves punishable by both prison time and stiff fines.

In Broome County, there were a number of supporters of the Underground Railroad and at least two routes ran through the area. Slaves would leave Philadelphia or the Harrisburg area and travel through Scranton and up to Montrose. There they would pass across the state line and head into Binghamton. In the village, the slaves could be harbored at the home of Dr. Stephen Hand on Collier Street. He was a well-known physician and president of the Broome County Medical Society. In addition, the two African American churches were involved in harboring escaped slaves. The slaves would then go north to Chenango Forks and stay at the home of Nathaniel

Kinyon before following the route of the Chenango River north. This route would end near Peterboro and the home of abolitionist millionaire Gerrit Smith.

The other route went through the town of Union and followed the course toward the hamlet of Maine. There the slave would likely stay at the home of Cyrus Gates before following the route to Whitney Point. The home of George Seymour in that village was used as a stop on the Underground Railroad. The slave would then go through Lisle and continue to Ithaca, New York. The Reverend Jermain Loguen, often called the King of the Underground Railroad, served the Broome County area as a circuit-riding minister for a short time before making Syracuse his home base of operation. His daughter, Amelia Loguen, taught at the African American school in Binghamton before her marriage to Lewis Douglass, son of Frederick Douglass.

The Underground Railroad was not the only answer to the problem of slavery for all residents. Other members of the county's population had other solutions. Dr. Tracy Robinson was the president of the local chapter of the American Colonization Society. The society believed that the only appropriate solution to the issue of slavery was to remove the slaves and ship them back to Africa or other areas. Its leaders could not envision a biracial society. The leading politician of this

Daniel S. Dickinson (1800–1866) was the first village of Binghamton president, a state senator, lieutenant governor, and the United States Senator for New York State from 1844 to 1851. A states' rights Democrat, Dickinson supported the Union during the Civil War. (Courtesy Broome County Historical Society)

period was Daniel S. Dickinson (1800–1866), a states' rights Democrat. Dickinson had risen quickly in state and national politics from his beginnings as village of Binghamton's president. He was a state senator (1836) and lieutenant governor (1842–1844) before being appointed to complete a term in the United States Senate (1844). He was then elected to his own six-year term (1845–1851) during which he was an active participant in ensuring the successful passage of the Compromise of 1850 as an attempt to stave off civil war.

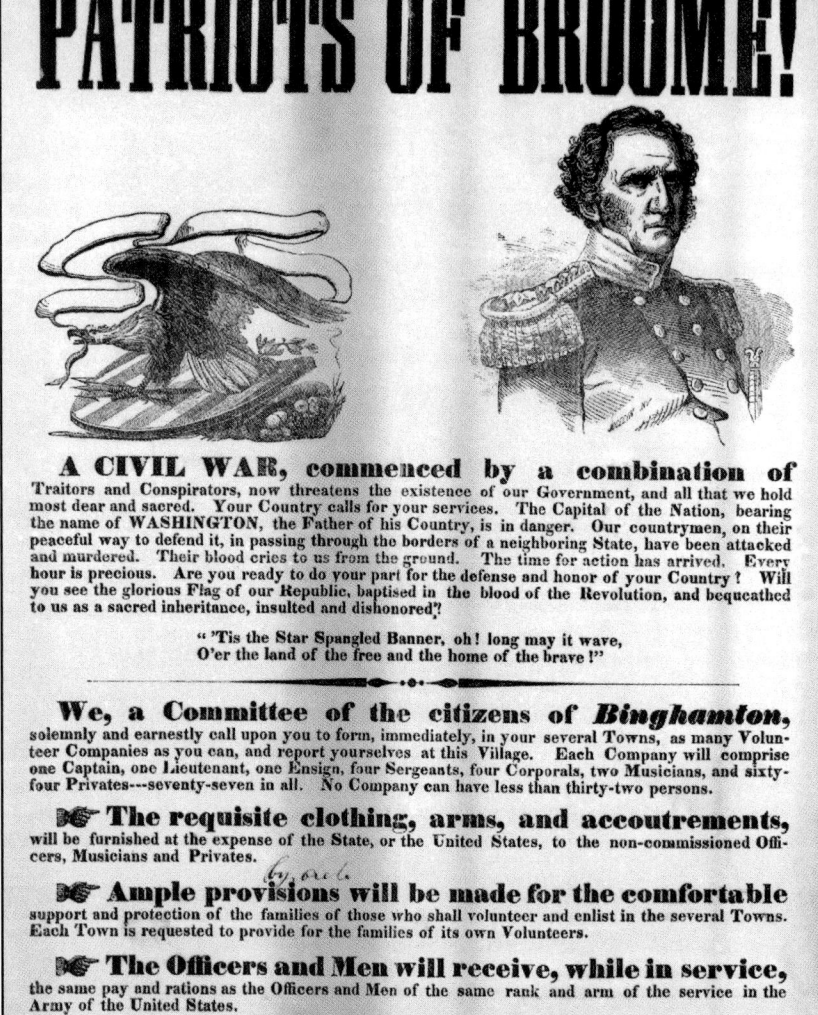

With the firing on Fort Sumter, the citizens of Broome County answered the call for troops. Broadsides such as this one were posted throughout the region. Over four thousand local men served the Union, and nearly five hundred died during the war. (Courtesy Broome County Historical Society)

under the influence of the Whig party of Fillmore. It was staunchly conservative but did not support slavery. It is this element that emerged as the Republican party of John C. Fremont in 1856 and Abraham Lincoln in 1860. For Dickinson to remain so popular a politician in this region shows his personal strengths as an individual.

Dickinson was never fervently anti-slavery, but he was fervently pro-union. He had effectively retired from politics in 1851, but his name was mentioned as a possible presidential candidate during the next two Democratic Presidential Conventions. Each time, Dickinson withdrew from any nomination. The inevitable happened in April 1861 with the firing on Fort Sumter and the secession of the southern states from the country. Civil war had broken out, and Daniel Dickinson was pulled back into the struggle. During the four years of the war, Dickinson spoke over one thousand times in support of the Union and calling for

Dickinson believed that the issue of slavery must be decided by each state rather the federal government. In some ways, Dickinson was an anomaly in Broome County politics. In earlier administrations, much of the county fell

the end of the war. His patriotic efforts did not go unnoticed. In 1864, Abraham Lincoln appointed Dickinson as attorney general for the Southern District of New York. This position required Dickinson to move from his beautiful Italianate home on Front Street in Binghamton to New York City. He died there two years later, and the body was brought back for burial in Spring Forest Cemetery.

Dickinson was not the only local resident to participate in the war. News of the war's beginnings spread quickly. Local newspapers called for men to rush to arms and form regiments to put down the rebellion. Over four thousand men answered the call from Broome County during the four years of the Civil War. Men served in at least twelve different regiments. Those men going to other locations to enlist brought the total regiments that included Broome County residents to nearly twenty. The Dickinson Guard was formed in Conklin and was part of the 89th Infantry Regiment. The Dickinson Light Artillery formed a portion of the 137th Infantry Regiment. In addition, the 27th Infantry Regiment, the 16th Engineers, the 50th Engineers, and the 109th Infantry Regiment were mainly formed in Broome County. There were approximately sixty men who were drafted during the war as a result of the nation's first attempt at military conscription. Although the county avoided the draft riots that had broken out in New York City and other places, some of the men who were drafted were able to avoid service by paying a bounty for someone else to take their place.

There were many valiant and brave men who fought during the war. One of the most notable was General John C. Robinson. Robinson was from Binghamton and had graduated from West Point. He was the commander of Fort McHenry at Baltimore when the Civil War began and held the fort against the Confederates with only six hundred men (Bothwell). Fort McHenry occupied a very strategic position that would help prevent the Southern forces from cutting off communications between the capital and the North. Robinson used a steamer unloading coal as a ruse to make the Confederates think that more troops had arrived at the fort. In addition to saving Fort McHenry, Robinson fought at

Above: The making of rifles and guns during the Civil War helped spur Binghamton's industrial growth. The Joseph Bartlett rifle on top, the Stuart rifle in the center, and the Rufus Howland rifle are three examples of the weapons made in Broome County. (Courtesy Broome County Historical Society)

John Stewart Wells was born in 1822 in Kirkwood. As a contractor, he built Christ Church, the third courthouse, and several schools and banks. He was mayor of Binghamton in 1883. His home on Main Street is now Parson's Funeral Home. (Courtesy Broome County Historical Society)

Captain David Ireland of Binghamton helped to form the 137th Infantry Regiment. This regiment fought bravely at Gettysburg. During the course of the war, the regiment served in campaigns in seven states, and it had more losses than any of the other regiments formed in whole or in part from county residents. The records of military service for local residents for the Civil War are sketchy. However, nearly five hundred men from Broome County did not survive the Civil War. This represents a loss of nearly 13 percent of all those who volunteered to protect the Union. Of those who did die, many died from disease rather than wounds received in battle.

Gettysburg and was wounded at Spotsylvania. He received the Medal of Honor. Upon retirement, he returned to Binghamton. He was later elected lieutenant governor of New York State before his death in 1889.

On the home front, Broome County participated in the war effort in several ways. In Binghamton, the Starr Revolver Company, located in the First Ward, manufactured guns and rifles used during the war. Similarly, Bartlett rifles were made in Binghamton and were also used to protect the troops. In Oakdale in the town of Union, the Bigler Mill received a contract to provide a keel made of oak for a new kind of warship. This mill was selected because of its steam operation, its proximity to the Chenango Canal, and its abundance of oak nearby. The Bigler Mill was able to form the keel but had difficulty moving the massive wooden piece. It took two wagons hooked together to get the keel to the Chenango Canal. From there, it was taken by packet boat to the Erie Canal and then down the Hudson River to New York City. There the keel helped to form the wooden framework of a newly made ship covered in iron plates to be called the *Monitor*.

Prior to the Civil War, the products made at local factories were made by individuals who created the entire piece. During the war, the necessity of making many pieces required speed and efficiency. Companies like Starr Revolver and Bartlett Rifles began using the assembly line to put standardized parts together to form the finished product. This development would propel Broome County into a new period of growth.

The end of the Civil War did not mean an end to its commemoration. Hundreds of veterans joined the G.A.R. posts that sprang up around the county. In 1888, the Soldiers and Sailors Monument was erected at the Courthouse. The mortars were added later. (Courtesy Broome County Historical Society)

CHAPTER 6: THE ARRIVAL OF THE IRON HORSE   95

CHAPTER 7
Immigration and Industry
1865–1880

H. C. Larrabee is seated at the reins of his Sturdevant-Larrabee carriage. The company started in Cincinnatus, New York, before moving to Binghamton. The firm was one of several local companies that manufactured wagons, carriages, and sleighs. The company later became Larrabee-Deyo Truck Company. (Courtesy Broome County Historical Society)

![Advertisement: THE NEW WEIGH / THE OLD WEIGH — EDWARD F. JONES, BINGHAMTON, N.Y. FOUR TON HAY SCALES $75.00. SEND FOR PRICE LIST. THE RECEIVER OF THIS WILL CONFER A GREAT FAVOR IF HE WILL POST IT UP IN A CONSPICUOUS PLACE.]

General Edward F. Jones of Massachusetts (pictured at right) served in the Civil War. After the war, he started the Jones Scale Works in Binghamton. His slogan, "Jones… He Pays the Freight" became one of the first national advertisements. He later served as lieutenant governor of the state. (Courtesy Broome County Historical Society)

THE END OF THE CIVIL WAR not only resulted in peace across a still united nation, but it brought an era of change for Broome County. While the residents of the county recovered from the loss of so many of its citizens, they also moved toward an industrial future that was bright and promising. Broome County was evolving into a transportation hub. It had major railroad lines that ran north to south and east to west. The Chenango Canal was still operating and linked the area to the Erie Canal. The population was continuing to increase, and the number of factories manufacturing products in assembly-line format was expanding. Because of the use of the standardized parts in the new factory system, many of these businesses did not require trained laborers. They could hire anyone and teach the worker how to assemble the pieces.

This brought about a large market for unskilled labor in Broome County. New types of businesses began to evolve. Where once the raw lumbering business had thrived in Broome County, now that lumber was being made into finished furniture. Firms such as Wilkinson & Eastwood and Stone, Crandal & Company began to make parts for wagons and carriages. Sturdevant-Larrabee moved its operations from Cincinnatus in Cortland County to Binghamton in 1884 because of the open land available for the construction of a factory, the number of workers that could be hired from the labor force in the area, and the potential for growth because of the transportation system. The firm prospered for the next forty years and manufactured thousands of beautiful wagons and sleighs that were sold across the entire country.

Many of the new factories were located in the First Ward of Binghamton. In 1866, General Edward F. Jones moved to the area from his native Massachusetts. Prior to the Civil War, Jones had invented a lighting device that had made him some money. He purchased the Starr Revolver Company plant and converted it to the manufacture of scales. Businesses need scales for all types of measurements, and the Jones Scale Works produced

Dr. John Ellis developed a lubricating oil called Binghamton Cylinder Oil, made at the Continuous Oil Company from 1866 to 1869. He moved the company to South Brooklyn and changed the product's name to Valvoline. It is the oldest refining company in the world. (Courtesy Broome County Historical Society)

CHAPTER 7: IMMIGRATION AND INDUSTRY

There were several silk companies operating in Binghamton in the late 1800s. This is the Rossville Silk Mill located on Park Avenue. The buildings were later used by the Gotham Shoe Company. Today, several companies are headquartered in these structures. (Courtesy Broome County Historical Society)

types to meet all needs. In addition, Jones came up with one of the first advertising gimmicks. His company would pay the freight cost of any of their scales. His slogan, "Jones… He Pays the Freight," became famous throughout the nation. The firm prospered and made Jones very wealthy. He built an elaborate twenty-one-room Victorian mansion on the west side of Binghamton, and he dabbled in both writing and publishing. He was also elected twice to the position of lieutenant governor of New York State.

The population of Broome County steadily increased after the Civil War. The rising number of industries and businesses made the area more attractive to new residents.

The transportation system was another factor in bringing both people and business to the community. By 1870, Broome County's population increased by 8,000 to 44,103. Ten years later, in 1880, it had increased to 49,483. An increasingly larger percentage of that population was now living in Binghamton.

Binghamton had started as a small frontier village in 1800 with about 200 residents. Seventy years later, that community had a population of 12,692. It became evident that a village government could no longer meet the needs of the people of the community. Residents demanded better fire and police protection, as well as a full-time government that could keep up with the court and

The railroads ended the viability of the Chenango Canal. A last effort to extend the canal across the Susquehanna River failed, and the empty bed was all that remained. This portion was filled in to become South Side Park, now Veterans Park in Binghamton. (Courtesy Broome County Historical Society)

administrative needs of a community of this size. On April 9, 1867, Binghamton was incorporated as a city.

The new government required a common council and officials of all types, from fire commissioners to a keeper of weights and measures. The first city election was held on May 6, 1867. Abel Bennett, a local hotel owner, businessman, and owner of a major farm on the west side of the city, was elected as mayor over Samuel Hall. The mayor's term was for only one year, and the mayor served without pay. Elected from the five wards of the city as defined in the new city charter, the common council passed laws and resolutions. The newly elected city government met in Firemen's Hall, a three-story brick building located on Collier Street in Binghamton, across from the Broome County Courthouse. Firemen's Hall housed not only the city government but its fire and police forces as well.

With the incorporation of the city, there was also a movement to organize professional fire and police protection. Broome County had created the position of sheriff in 1806, and the village of Binghamton had had constables since 1834, but most firefighters were volunteers working from independent fire companies created around Binghamton. The outlying townships and villages had little in the way of fire or police protection until the end of the nineteenth century. The charter for the new city led to the eventual creation of paid fire and police departments, although some of

CHAPTER 7: IMMIGRATION AND INDUSTRY   101

On April 9, 1867, Binghamton became a city. Abel Bennett, pictured here, was chosen as its first mayor. Bennett was a successful farmer and owner of the Hotel Bennett. His west side lands would become prime residential lots in the early 1900s. (Courtesy Broome County Historical Society)

those organizations were not fully funded until the first two decades of the twentieth century. Chief Hogg of the Fire Department was the first official to have a motorized vehicle—a Cadillac automobile. The other villages and, later, the towns began to create fire departments by the late 1800s and early 1900s. Today, Broome County has more fire equipment than the city of Chicago although most companies are still volunteer-operated.

Police protection followed the same pattern as that of the fire department. The responsibilities for protecting much of the county fell upon the Sheriff's Department. This is still true today, with a large department responsible for protecting the residents of the over twenty-four hundred roads of the county and an academy to train new officers for the many police forces. Binghamton and some of the incorporated towns and villages have their own police forces (Deposit, Endicott, Johnson City, Port Dickinson, Vestal). The costs and issues of running multiple fire and police forces is again an issue being discussed for possible consolidation.

Firemen's Hall on Collier Street was the first government building for Binghamton. Built in 1857 and used until 1896, it housed the city's offices and police. The tower housing the fire department's alarm bell was added in 1874. (From the *Putnam Collection*, courtesy Broome County Public Library)

The newly elected officials of the city of Binghamton faced many new problems as the city continued to grow. An increasing number of people meant more crime, dirtier streets, more housing requirements, and the need for maintenance of the transportation system. The Chenango Canal was one of these problems. Despite the importance of the canal in bringing new residents and allowing raw and finished goods to be moved in and out of the area, the canal was a financial failure. The canal could only operate about nine months of the year, versus the yearlong operation of the railroads. When the canal closed for the season each year, repair and upkeep were needed to restore it to a state that would allow travel the next season. This maintenance became more and more expensive. The number of boats traveling the canal never was sufficient to allow the canal to make a profit.

The third Broome County Courthouse served the community from 1857 until it burned down in 1896. Here, the City Guards Militia is photographed in front of the building. The Victorian bandstand was removed in the early 1900s. (Courtesy Broome County Historical Society)

In addition to these problems, the Erie Canal had widened its canal bed in the 1860s to allow for bigger boats. While this was good for the Erie Canal, the newer boats were too wide to travel down any of the lateral canals. In an effort to make the Chenango Canal more profitable, an extension was planned that would have the canal packets pass over the Susquehanna River and travel along the southern side of that river on the extension, which would connect with the Pennsylvania canal system in Chemung County. The canal extension would bring down the cost of moving goods, especially coal, to make it a viable alternative to the railroads.

Debate over the extension raged for several years. Finally, in 1865, the New York State Legislature passed authorization to create financial backing for the construction. In 1866, work began on the canal extension. The end terminus in Binghamton would be abandoned as the canal moved farther east in the city and passed upstream of the Rockbottom Dam to cross over the Susquehanna. Work continued at a varying pace over the next two years as more

104 PARTNERS ALL: A HISTORY OF BROOME COUNTY, NEW YORK

than thirty miles of the canal bed were dug through Binghamton and Vestal and into Tioga County. Costs mounted as work progressed on the extension until the work ceased in 1871. The next year, 1872, the city of Binghamton closed a section of canal near Prospect Avenue to create a new street. This one act effectively killed the canal, breaking it into two parts. Within a few months, another section was closed to extend the street.

By 1874, the Chenango Canal was closed in Binghamton. The entire length of the canal was closed by 1878. The Chenango Canal extension was never completed and never used. In the history of the canal over $7.4 million had been extended to build the canal and maintain it through its thirty-seven-year history in Broome County. It only took in a total of $744,000 in tolls. The remains of the Chenango Canal extension moldered and lay dormant until the twentieth century. A portion of the extension in Binghamton was filled in to make South Side Park (now Veterans Park). The portion of the extension reaching from the border of Binghamton into Vestal was reclaimed as the bed of a new means of transportation in the late 1950s and early 1960s—the Vestal Parkway. The remaining sections of the canal in Binghamton were filled in with dirt using funds provided by New York State. To thank the government officials for

A separate Broome County Clerk's office building was located on the Courthouse Square. Operating from 1872 until 1916, it helped protect vital documents during the courthouse fire in 1896. It was removed to make way for an addition to the rear of the courthouse. (Courtesy Broome County Historical Society)

allocating the funds needed to create the new byway, it was named State Street.

Despite the failure of the canal, it did not impede the growth of Binghamton and the surrounding area. New types of industries continued to open using railroads and roads

CHAPTER 7: IMMIGRATION AND INDUSTRY   105

Marshall Weed opened this tannery in 1850 near the confluence of the two rivers in Binghamton. In the early 1900s, the building was sold to the Endicott Johnson Shoe Company, who converted it into the BBB Factory. It is now the site of the Arena. (Courtesy Broome County Historical Society)

to transport goods. Marshall Weed came to this area and started his own tannery operation in 1850 in the area near the Chenango Canal known as Millville. Later his sons, James and Frederick Weed, operated the tannery that employed nearly two hundred men turning out leather that could be used to make shoes, belts, and harnesses. The large brick complex of buildings became a significant landmark in Binghamton.

Throughout the city, new types of products of all types were being produced. Glass bottles were made by the Binghamton Glass Works in the First Ward; the Parlor City Box Company made boxes of all sizes to contain products to be shipped all over the world. Beman and Bayless made barrels to hold other types of goods, and Milks and Watson made wagons. Binghamton Soap and Candle Works operated near Spring Forest Cemetery, as did the

In the last half of the nineteenth century, water cures were popular across the state. The Mount Prospect Water Cure began in the 1850s; it was later converted to a brewery. It is now the site of the Ely Park Golf Course. (Courtesy Broome County Historical Society)

Binghamton Lager Beer Brewery on Mount Prospect. Other breweries operated throughout the city including Joseph Laurer on Laurel Avenue. Joseph Noyes came from England to open a comb factory. He found the site he wanted on Lewis Island on the north side of the city of Binghamton. Using a raceway of the Chenango River, he harnessed the waterpower to make combs from animal horns. The island would be renamed Noyes Island, and the factories became a familiar site on that side of the city.

In the 1850s, oil was discovered in western Pennsylvania. The discovery changed the way the industrial world operated. It made some like John D. Rockefeller of Richford, Tioga County, wealthy and famous. It created new types of businesses that operated to bring oil to factories and homes. In Pennsylvania, Dr.

CHAPTER 7: IMMIGRATION AND INDUSTRY

The rise of industry around Binghamton helped bring new firms to the area. E. H. Tichener Wire Goods began in the 1870s. In this photograph, workers are assembling steel wires for shelves and racks. The First Ward firm closed its doors in 2004. (Courtesy Broome County Historical Society)

John Ellis believed that the oil could produce a beneficial medicine. After much investigation, Dr. Ellis abandoned the use of petroleum as medicine. He realized the value of oil was as a lubricant for the many valves and machines used in industry. He moved to Binghamton and founded the Continuous Oil Refining Company in 1866. Located next to the railroad tracks, the company manufactured Binghamton Cylinder Oil. Ellis relied on the patents of Elias Kattell to produce the steam boilers used to produce the oil and on financial backing by several local investors. The company grew for the next three years, but Ellis felt that the business would do better if the company were located in a large market area. He moved the firm to South Brooklyn in 1869 and continued to produce the oil under a new name—Valvoline.

The rise of industry required a rise in the labor force. Increasing numbers of employees were not native residents of Broome County. Many new workers came from the expanding numbers of immigrants who were coming into the community. Unrest in the countries of Eastern Europe in the 1860s and 1870s, the struggle over the unification of Italy, and the beginnings of the economic and governmental failure of czarist Russia all caused citizens of those areas to attempt to find a new life in the United States. Prior to the Civil War, the United States saw an influx of five million immigrants. In the three decades following the war, another ten million immigrants would enter the country. The largest wave of immigrants would occur from 1890 to 1914 when fifteen million aliens would become part of the United States population (Jones, *American Immigration*).

During the period of 1865 to 1880, many immigrants came from the British Isles, Germany, Scandinavia, Switzerland, and Holland. The later and larger wave of immigrants would include new residents from the disintegrating Austrian-Hungarian Empire, Italy, Russia, Greece, Romania, and Turkey. Larger numbers of Jews from many countries began to come to the area. Although the Jewish population would never be larger than 2 percent of the county's residents, many migrants from this later influx of Jews became permanent residents. Many of them entered the mercantile and retail sectors of the local economy. Besides the Hirschmanns, the Rosenthals were among the most prominent Jewish families to enter the market. They opened the first Great Fair Store in 1888 on Washington Street. It later moved to Court Street.

Men, women, and children entered the country through many ports. Immigrants entering our country through New York City came through Castle Gardens until Ellis Island opened in 1892. Those who arrived after 1886 were greeted with the vision of the Statue of Liberty and the words of Emma Lazurus:

Give me your tired, your poor,
Your huddled masses yearning to breathe free.

The expansion of the Binghamton area called for real estate dealers to help with the growing market. Several wagons and workers are located in front of the Hotchkin Real Estate Exchange at 163 Washington Street in Binghamton about 1890. (Courtesy Broome County Historical Society)

This is a member of the Jackson family of Binghamton. He is seen wearing his G.A.R. badge and silk ribbon to show his participation in the Civil War. Although not a large number, several African American citizens from Broome County served in the Colored Troops regiments. (Courtesy Broome County Historical Society)

Isaac Perry is the preeminent architect of Broome County. He arrived here from New York City to design the Inebriate Asylum. Over the next five decades, he designed the Perry Block, churches, and homes and became architect of the New York State Capitol. (Courtesy Broome County Historical Society)

The wretched refuse of your teeming shore;
Send these, the homeless, tempest-tost to me.
I lift my lamp beside the golden door!
   "The New Colossus"

Other immigrants came through Canada, Boston, New Jersey, or Philadelphia. Many of the immigrants went to work in the coalfields of Pennsylvania before moving to work in the industries of Broome County.

Many of the new arrivals settled in the industrial areas of the region—the First Ward of Binghamton and the areas near the railroad tracks downtown. Earlier settlers and immigrants to the area were moving to the "suburbs" of the west side of Binghamton. New homes and streets were quickly being constructed to accommodate the influx of middle- and upper-class families. The homes they had left were quickly being filled with new arrivals from other nations. Many of the new residents would work for one of the several railroad companies servicing Broome County. Others, especially the women, would work as

Dr. Frederick Turner opened the New York State Inebriate Asylum in 1858 to treat alcoholism. Isaac Perry designed the Gothic Revival–style main building to resemble a castle. Now part of the Greater Binghamton Health Center, the building is a National Landmark. (Courtesy Broome County Historical Society)

domestics or, in increasing numbers, in the factories of Binghamton.

If the period of the first two full decades after the Civil War was one of changing population base for Broome County, it was also one of changing social issues and problems for the region. The increasing role of government had brought not only the construction of Firemen's Hall for the village of Binghamton offices, but also the building of the third county courthouse in 1857. A graceful Greek Revival building, it replaced a three-story brick building. By 1890, two larger wings were added to each end of the courthouse to accommodate more offices.

Dr. Frederick Turner came to the area in 1858 with an idea to build a facility that would treat the problems of alcoholism. He hired a young architect from New York City, Isaac Perry, to design a Gothic Revival castle-like building to house patients on a hill overlooking the city of Binghamton. With a number of investors and ample number of patients, the New York State Inebriate Asylum became the first facility in the United States for the treatment of alcoholism. The facility continued to expand with more buildings and more patients. As innovative as Turner was in his beliefs about alcoholism, he was not a good business manager. He ran into managerial and financial difficulties and

Broome County's Poorhouse began in 1830. The main building, the Alms House, was the focus of an institution that assisted elderly, the poor, and children. In later years, it was part of the Broome County Infirmary before it became part of Broome Community College. (Courtesy Broome County Historical Society)

During the 1870s and 1880s, there were an increasing number of children who were not being cared for by family or friends. The death or lack of care by parents left them vulnerable to the ills of society. The Young Men's Christian Association began as an organization to assist this sector of society. The Binghamton chapter opened in 1865. In 1869, Dr. John Orton founded the Susquehanna Valley Home. It began in the former Susquehanna Seminary building on the west side of Binghamton. Within two years, Orton purchased the Griffith Mansion and one hundred acres on the south side of the city.

was, eventually, removed as the head of the institution. In 1879, New York State assumed control of the facility and altered its purpose to the treatment of mental disease. It became the Binghamton Asylum for the Chronic Insane. Today, it still offers treatment for mental health as the Greater Binghamton Health Center.

Opposite page: Isaac Perry designed the Binghamton High School building in 1870. The graceful structure with its tower overlooked the expanding west side of Binghamton. The growth of the population was so great that the building was replaced in 1914 with the current building. (Courtesy Broome County Historical Society)

The Lady Jane Grey School operated from the former Brandywine Hotel from 1861 until 1923. The building was located on Court Street and was built in 1810 by Joshua Whitney. It was removed in 1926 to make way for Binghamton Gas Works. (Courtesy Broome County Historical Society)

The home operated as both an orphanage and as a foster care facility for children. It provided elementary education and craft classes for the children. Boys and girls took classes together at the center, which continued to operate until the early 1980s.

The 1855 Susquehanna Seminary building that had been the first location of the Susquehanna Valley Home later housed another children's home. Father John Hourigan of St. Patrick's Church saw the need for a facility to help children. In 1881, St. Mary's Orphan Home began operations. Thousands of children went through the facility and were well treated for the next century. The old building was closed and demolished in 1963 to make way for Catholic Central High School.

In 1830, the Broome County Poorhouse was created. Poorhouses and poor farms had been established in almost every county in the state.

Walton Dwight (1837–1878, pictured at left) came to Binghamton in 1868 and bought Daniel Dickinson's home on Front Street. Dwight was mayor before he built Dwightsville on the property. The Dwight Block, seen above, was a grand hotel of one hundred rooms. Dwight went bankrupt in three years and died at age forty-one. (Courtesy Broome County Historical Society)

The poorhouse system was an attempt to help those residents who were unable to take care of themselves. Some of the people who lived in the Poorhouse were not poor. Many were elderly or suffered from mental illness or disease. Men, women, and children could be found at the Poorhouse. Additional buildings were constructed including men's and women's dormitories, a hospital, a chapel, dining halls, and numerous barns, garages, and farm buildings. The farm operation helped raise food to feed the numerous inmates of the facility. As the facility entered the twentieth century, other institutions had subsumed many of its operations. Eventually renamed the Broome County Infirmary, it remained in operation until the early 1970s. Today, only the Alms House, originally the Administration building, still remains, part of the campus of Broome Community College.

For women, there were a number of opportunities for advancement. The Young Women's Christian Association opened in 1892. The Lady Jane Grey School opened in 1861 in the former Brandywine Hotel at the corner of Court and Liberty Streets on the east side of Binghamton. The Lady Jane Grey School offered classes for many years to hundreds of young women in the area. The school operated until 1923. The building was demolished in 1926 for the expansion of the city's gas works.

It is during this period of Broome County's history that three of its most interesting personalities make their mark. Walton Dwight (1837–1878) was born in Windsor and served as a colonel during the Civil War. He moved to Binghamton in 1868 with a scheme to make a grand hotel. He purchased the homestead of Daniel Dickinson, the Orchard, which was located on Front Street in the First Ward of Binghamton. Shortly after its purchase, a fire destroyed the home. It was the first of many odd circumstances surrounding Dwight.

Dwight was elected to a one-year term as mayor of Binghamton in 1871. During that period, he hired Isaac Perry to design the Dwight House. Dwight spent over $100,000 on the furnishings of the one hundred rooms of this hotel. It was advertised as a luxury resort that could be a stop for the people using the facilities of the Binghamton Water Cure located nearby on Mount Prospect. The hotel was completed in 1873. The lands of Dickinson's former estate were transformed to create Dwight Park. The park was directly across the hotel and included fountains and a bandstand. Surrounding this hotel, Dwight built Dwightsville, a complex of over thirty homes designed for the "working man" by architect Truman Lacey. However grandiose and ambitious the project, Dwight could not stave off financial failure. Within three years, Dwight was in financial ruin.

The hotel was converted to an apartment complex called the Dwight Block. Dwight's sister and brother-in-law purchased the park at foreclosure, converted it to McDonald Avenue, and developed a small area of Victorian-style

Opposite page: Sherman Phelps, bottom right, was a businessman and banker. Isaac Perry designed his beautiful home (now the Monday Afternoon Club) on Court Street, pictured at top. Phelps ran unopposed for mayor in 1872. A write-in campaign produced more votes for Thomas Crocker, bottom left, an illiterate former slave, but the election was given to Phelps. (Courtesy Broome County Historical Society)

CHAPTER 7: IMMIGRATION AND INDUSTRY 117

homes. Dwight became connected with various schemes including the Cardiff Giant, a hoax based on the "discovery" of a prehistoric giant. In 1878, his health began to fail. Dwight took out a number of insurance policies shortly before he died in his room at the Spaulding House. Numerous stories abounded of poisoning and hanging, forcing the courts to exhume his body and determine the cause of death. Eventually, the courts ruled that Dwight died of natural causes, and his widow received a large sum of money.

In August 1870, three men entered the Halbert Dry Goods Store on Court Street in Binghamton in a robbery attempt. They did not realize that the two store clerks resided in an apartment above the store. The noise awakened the two clerks, who then came down to find the robbers. A fight ensued, and one of the clerks was stabbed. The other, Fred Merrick, was shot to death by the leader of the robbers. All three men ran from the store toward the Chenango River. The next morning, the bodies of two of the robbers were found floating in the river. The corpses were brought to the rear of a nearby funeral home and placed on a wooden board. At that same time, a man was seen crossing the Erie railroad bridge. He matched the description given by witnesses of the third robber.

The man that was captured by the police was Edward Rulloff. Rulloff had been convicted of the abduction of his wife and daughter in the 1840s. Although authorities were sure he had killed both of them and dumped the bodies into Cayuga Lake, they could not convict him of the murders without the bodies. He spent time in Auburn Prison and then spent the next few years burglarizing numerous homes and businesses in New York and Pennsylvania. He traveled with two accomplices, one of them the son of the Tompkins County Sheriff. Rulloff passed himself off as a professor of languages. He nearly convinced police that he was not Rulloff, but he was put on trial for Merrick's death.

Rulloff was convicted of the killing and sentenced to death. It would be the first hanging in the history of Broome County. Rulloff refused to concede to any interviews with newspaper reporters. He was visited by various members of the clergy but, again, refused to see them. A large fence was built around the gallows constructed on the courthouse square. On May 18, 1871, Rulloff was marched out to the gallows. Those in attendance had been given special invitations to the event. Rulloff refused to have a hood placed over his head, and when he was asked if he had any last words, Rulloff was quoted as saying that he wanted the "hangman to hurry so that he could be in hell in time for lunch." Rulloff's body was buried in an unmarked grave in Glenwood Cemetery in Binghamton. His brain was removed and is now in a collection at Cornell University.

The Binghamton mayoral election of 1872 resulted in one of the most interesting episodes in the community's history. Sherman Phelps, a local businessman and banker, was running unopposed for the one-year position. Phelps was extremely successful. His beautiful mansion on Court Street was designed by Isaac Perry and epitomized Phelps' success. Unfortunately, Phelps was not well liked by some of the other voting members of the community. As a joke, some men began an effort to offer a write-in candidate. They chose Thomas Crocker.

Thomas Crocker had been born the slave of the Oliver Crocker family in the town of Union. Crocker claimed to have joined the Union forces during the Civil War but did not like the war and walked home. He held many odd jobs over the next few years, including that of a musician, a wrestler, and a "barker" for a local auction house. Everyone around Binghamton knew Crocker as Old Bay Tom. The effort to put him on the ballots caught on like wildfire. Election day came, and the votes began to come in with Crocker's name written on many of the ballots. When the election commissioners counted the ballots, Old Bay Tom had succeeded in winning the election over Sherman Phelps.

Binghamton had itself a former slave who could neither read nor write as its mayor. This was the first instance of an African American being elected as mayor north of the Mason-Dixon Line. The election commissioners considered this a tremendous embarrassment to the city. To resolve the dilemma, enough votes were thrown out on technicalities to give the election to Sherman Phelps. It is unclear whether Thomas Crocker was aware he had been elected mayor of Binghamton. Although Phelps was declared the winner of the election, the election commissioners refused to sign their names to the certified results, and the official page for that election book was removed. Crocker lived out the remaining years of his life in poverty and died at the Broome County Poorhouse.

CHAPTER 8
A Good Five-Cent Cigar
1880–1910

Newcomers to the area could arrive at the Lackawanna Station and stay at the Arlington Hotel (on the left). It was the premier hotel until it was demolished in the 1960s. The Moon Block on the right was destroyed by fire in 1950. (From *Art Work of Binghamton*)

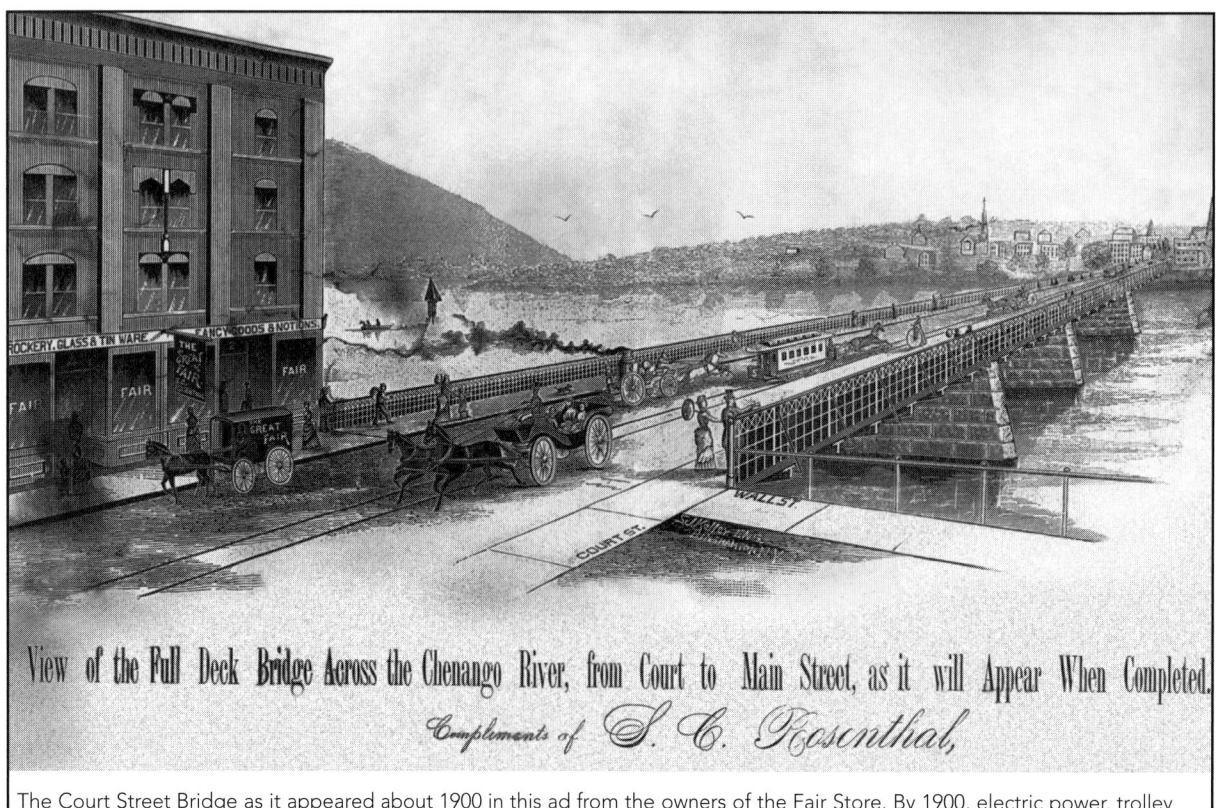

The Court Street Bridge as it appeared about 1900 in this ad from the owners of the Fair Store. By 1900, electric power, trolley cars, and telephones had made their way into the lives of the Binghamton's citizens. (Courtesy Broome County Historical Society)

THE RISING INDUSTRIAL BASE of Broome County in the third quarter of the nineteenth century led to an even larger growth of business and population in the last quarter of that century. If the Civil War was the catalyst that promoted the assembly-line factory system, the beginnings of the Industrial Revolution propelled the valley toward even greater heights. By 1880, Broome County was creating hundreds of different products ranging from heavy industrial equipment to items used daily in households. But the predominant product of this period was the cigar.

The climate of Broome County was not ideal for the production of tobacco. Tobacco could be grown, but the quality would not suffice to produce a good cigar. Tobacco was grown with greater regularity in the area of the Finger Lakes, but it too was not of the quality that smokers of the time demanded. The best quality tobacco was grown in the southern states. But the south did not have the factory or industrial base needed to make large numbers of cigars.

The region that had everything that was needed for the manufacture of cigars was located in the north. The northern states had a substantial labor force, with large numbers of immigrants as its source of cheap labor. The northeast states had well-developed transportation systems. There was ample land for the development of factories, and the tax rates were fairly low. One of the sites that met all those criteria was Binghamton.

The first cigar factory opened in Binghamton in 1858. Cigar factories did not need much heavy industrial equipment. Most of the process of producing cigars required human hands. Tobacco leaves were dried, cut into rough shapes, rolled into the shape of the cigar, and placed into wooden cigar molds. Human hands would trim the ends of the cigar. It was not human hands that formed the round cigar tip, however. It was the human mouth, usually of a female employee, who would form the letter "O" and turn the cigar around inside her mouth, using the saliva to seal the leaves into shape. The finished cigars were packed into boxes and sent to their final destinations in thousands of cigar stores, hotel lobbies, and other establishments across the country.

The industry started small in Binghamton but grew continuously between 1880 and the late 1920s. What started with one factory in 1858 eventually became over fifty factories in the city of Binghamton. There were over seventy factories in the entire county by 1920. Many of these factories operated from single homes or small industrial buildings. The companies

By the early 1900s, over fifty factories produced cigars in Binghamton. The Reynolds, Rogers & Lay Company building was on Wall Street. It employed over three hundred workers. The building was torn down in the 1960s and is the site of the Binghamton Regency hotel. (Courtesy Broome County Historical Society)

CHAPTER 8: A GOOD FIVE-CENT CIGAR

The busy city scene along Wall Street in Binghamton included the Post Office (replaced in 1934), the Binghamton Clothing Company (destroyed by fire in 1913), and Barlow's Cigar Factory (later part of the Fair Store). (From *Binghamton Illustrated*, 1890)

upstate New York. The population of Broome County rose from 49,483 in 1880 to 78,809 in 1910. More significantly, the population of the city of Binghamton exploded during this time. It rose from 17,317 in 1880 to 48,443 in 1910. This represented a 250 percent increase in Binghamton's population in just thirty years.

could employ as few as ten people or as many as five hundred in the production of cigars. At the height of the cigar-making industry in Broome County, there were five thousand people employed as cigar workers in the many factories. Two thousand of those workers were women. It was the first major industry in the county's history where women played a significant role in the workforce.

Many of the workers in this industry were immigrants. What had started as a slow but steady influx of immigrants into Broome County in the 1870s had turned into a flood between 1880 and 1910. Thousands of immigrants from Eastern Europe, Italy, Russia, and other areas escaped their former lives to seek a new life in

Many of these newly arrived residents found work in the many factories of the time. A business survey in 1900 determined that industries were creating over two hundred different items in the city of Binghamton. There was ample work for the new arrivals, especially in the cigar factories. Larger firms such as Barlow, Rogers and Simpson, George A. Kent & Company, Hull, Grummond and Company, and others employed thousands of workers. Many

Opposite page: The millions of cigars produced in Binghamton were sold around the country in businesses like the Acme Pool Hall and Lunch operated by Louis H. Fairchild. This 1903 photograph shows the owner in front of his business at 120 Washington Street in Binghamton. (Courtesy Broome County Historical Society)

120
BILLIARDS
LUNCH
CIGARS & TOBACCO
THE ACME
TEMPERANCE
POOL
&
LUNCH ROOM.
CIGARS.
LUNCH &
TOBACCO.

By 1900, the number of churches grew to handle new immigrants. St. Mary's Catholic Church on Court Street opened in 1897 and was mainly Irish while St. Mary's Assumption of the Blessed Virgin Church on Hawley Street's congregation was predominately Italian. The two churches combined in 1967. (Courtesy Broome County Historical Society)

of the larger companies were located within a two-block radius in downtown Binghamton. Smaller firms were located throughout the city. These companies used the proximity to the railroad tracks to ship the one hundred million cigars. By 1910, Binghamton was the second-largest cigar producing area in the United States. Only New York City, with its large industrial base and huge population base, produced more cigars.

Despite the seeming success of the cigar industry on the surface, it was an industry full of labor unrest. Working conditions were poor. Long working hours and unstable wages dependent on company sales and profits added to labor tensions. Both general and trade unions began to organize many of the workers in the local cigar factories. Efforts at negotiation between the owners and the workers were often at a stalemate. Increasing attempts to provoke responses from owners over poor working conditions, including sit-downs, slowdowns, and absences due to "illness," only served to stiffen the resistance of the owners to any change.

In the summer of 1890, labor unrest reached its highest level. On June 24, two thousand nonunion male and female cigar workers left their workplaces to protest their wages. In the previous two years, owners had lowered wages

In 1887, electric power was introduced to the trolleys of Binghamton. By 1900, the entire line was operating by electricity as seen in this photograph of Washington Street near Court Street. Trolleys moved thousands of workers to and from their homes. (From the *Putnam Collection*, courtesy Broome County Public Library)

during a temporary business depression. When profits rose again for the owners, they did not restore the wages to their former levels. Employees pleaded for the increase to no avail. The rollers left the factories first, followed by the bunch-makers. By the next day, the strike had spread to all types of cigar workers. They held an organizing campaign and set up strike committees. For the next fifteen weeks, the strike rolled on with no real movement. The owners took the matter to the courts. The judicial decision declared the pickets to be illegal and demanded that they end. This decision only exacerbated the situation.

Men, women, and children stayed on the picket lines. They attempted to deter "scabs" who had been hired to take their places at the workbench from getting off the trains in Binghamton (McGuire and Osterud, *Working Lives: Broome County, New York 1800–1930*).

The strike dominated the life of Broome County for the three and a half months of its life. As it continued, tensions rose, until some owners called the police to break up the pickets. The scene became ugly, with police using force against not only the male strikers but also the women and children on the picket lines as well. Newspaper accounts reported scenes of

CHAPTER 8: A GOOD FIVE-CENT CIGAR   127

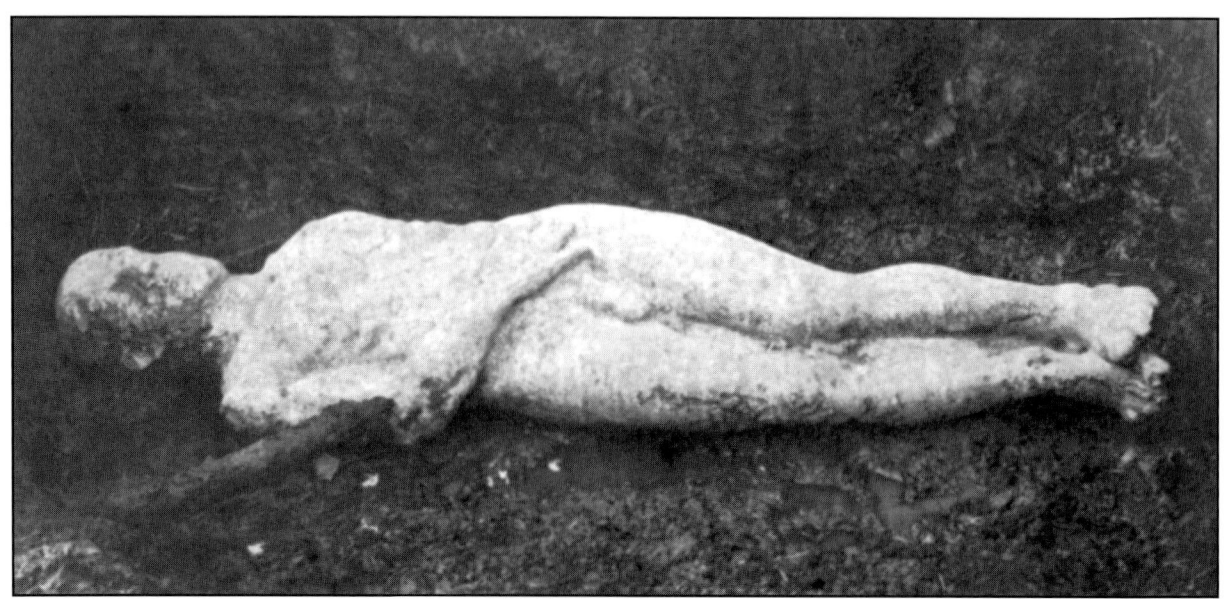

George Hull was both a cigar maker and a scam artist. He created the Cardiff Giant, convincing thousands of the existence of this giant petrified man. The gypsum statue fraud was discovered but not before Hull made thousands. The giant is now in Cooperstown. (Courtesy Broome County Historical Society)

violence, screams, and blood spilled on the streets. This ended what should have ended weeks before. It was the final act that killed both the spirits of the strikers and of the owners to carry on the attempt at change. By the end of October, the strike was called off as workers had been slowly returning to their posts. The lesson of failure and labor unrest was not lost on some of the other business and industry leaders at the time. This was especially true of the owners of the Bundy Time Recording Company and George F. Johnson of the Lester Brothers Boot and Shoe Company. It was also a lesson learned by one particular cigar worker. The apocryphal story is that during this time, Samuel Gompers worked in Binghamton as a cigar worker. He observed the situation of the cigar workers in Broome County and decided there was a need to help them organize and protect themselves against unscrupulous business practices. He left the area to move to New York City and work as cigar worker there before he became famous for his efforts to create what later became the AFL-CIO.

The money that the cigar industry brought into the area made Broome County and Binghamton an attractive location to start a new business. New buildings were being built with great speed and regularity during this time. The area boasted new neighborhoods with new streets and building lots ready for new homes. The city expanded in all four directions. The west side of Binghamton, especially, expanded with Victorian homes for new families. By 1890, the spread of homes into the "suburbs" of Binghamton created a situation where homeowners enjoyed the benefits of city life, such as public sewers and water sources, electricity, and transportation systems, without paying any taxes. The leaders of Binghamton eventually annexed much of this land to the city, but not before one group on the east side of the city tried to start their own village called Fairview. This failed, and the annexations brought the city to its present configuration with thirteen wards.

The spread of population was not just limited to Binghamton. In 1854, George and Horace Lester had started a shoe-making business using the strength of the city's transportation systems and the presence of other businesses such as Weed's Tannery to expand. The company continued to grow during the 1870s

Erastus Ross donated land to Binghamton for a new park in 1875. Within a short time, a zoo was added to the facility. Today, the Binghamton Zoo at Ross Park is the fifth oldest zoo in the country, operated by the Southern Tier Zoological Society. (Courtesy Broome County Historical Society)

This 1905 tornado touched down on the north side of the Susquehanna River and crossed the river, destroying a number of homes in Binghamton. Although not an area prone to such weather, tornadoes again caused damage in 1924, 1998, and 2004. (Courtesy Broome County Historical Society)

and 1880s. They hired George F. Johnson (1857–1948) as one of the factory workers. He later suggested to G. Harry Lester, the son of Horace, that the company could do better if it expanded on open land to the west of Binghamton. Beginning in 1888, the company bought acreage in the town of Union for the construction of a new town. In 1890, the company built a wooden factory that was four hundred feet long by fifty feet wide and four stories in height. The Pioneer factory became the first structure in the planned community of Lestershire that included additional factories, businesses, and homes.

The increasing population was felt throughout the county. The expansion of the railroad lines through much of the area assisted in bringing industries and businesses to many parts of Broome County. In the west, the village of Union was incorporated in 1871. Union thrived after the New York and Erie Railroad line arrived about 1851. On Main Street, the Major House hotel opened under the ownership of Major Mersereau, who housed traveling businessmen. Banks, churches, and homes all were built around the center of the village. In northern Broome County, the villages of Whitney Point and Lisle continued to grow as the homes of area residents and smaller

Charles Stone built the Stone Opera House on Chenango Street in Binghamton in 1892. It housed operettas and vaudeville before being converted into a movie theater in the 1920s. It operated for many years as the Riviera Theater before closing in the 1970s. (Courtesy Broome County Historical Society)

businesses. In eastern Broome County, Deposit and Windsor grew steadily along the banks of the Susquehanna and Delaware Rivers.

But none could compete with the growth of Binghamton. The number and types of companies continued to expand during this period. In 1889, Harlow and Willard Bundy opened the Bundy Time Recording Company in a former gristmill in Binghamton. Willard Bundy had invented a time clock to keep accurate records of the employees of companies. In the era of scientific management, businesses realized the importance of the device. Harlow, who had been postmaster of Oneonta, also realized the potential of the device. He persuaded businessmen such as A. Ward Ford of Deposit and others from Oneonta to invest in the company. Within four years, the firm had built a four-story brick building on Wall Street. It quickly became successful selling its product overseas. It also increased sales in the United States and attracted the interest of other companies making similar products.

132   PARTNERS ALL: A HISTORY OF BROOME COUNTY, NEW YORK

In 1878, S. Andral Kilmer (1840–1924) and his brother, Jonas M. (1884–1912), began operations as Dr. Kilmer and Company. S. Andral Kilmer had invented a patent medicine called Swamp Root. The concoction claimed to cure most ailments and consisted of a variety of herbs, spices, and 12 percent alcohol. The twenty-four-proof "medicine" sold well for a dollar a bottle. In the era of P. T. Barnum, patent medicines, and "suckers born every minute," Swamp Root made fortunes for the Kilmers. Despite the wealth, all was not happy with the brothers. Jonas bought out his brother's interest in the firm in 1893. S. Andral was given enough to focus on his interests at that time—the operation of a "Cancertorium" in Binghamton and a water cure at Sanitaria Springs (formerly called Osborn Hollow) in the town of Colesville. Jonas' son, Willis Sharpe Kilmer (1868–1940) was brought into the firm as the business and promotional expert. It was under his leadership that the firm grew in size and importance.

A devastating fire at the Kilmer building on Chenango Street nearly destroyed the firm about 1900. It was rumored that the suspicious fire may have been the responsibility of S. Andral's son. Although the firm continued to operate from the remains of the building, a new headquarters and laboratory was built in 1902 at the corner of Lewis and Chenango Streets. Soon, other products were added to the company's line of medicines. All of them had greatly exaggerated claims of benefits to mankind. The claims soon came under the investigation of the federal government and the postal service for fraudulent advertising. When Willis Kilmer was once asked what Swamp Root was good for, he allegedly responded, "about two million a year." The result of the investigation was a slight change in the outer packaging of the medicine.

Willis Kilmer used assets of the company to branch into new ventures. A local newspaper ran an unflattering article that alluded to a possible affair between Kilmer and his female ward when they visited a horseracing track out of the area while his wife was alone in Binghamton. The article incensed Kilmer, despite its accuracy (he divorced the wife and married the ward). He swore he would drive the newspaper out of business. He hired the firm of Truman Lacey to design and construct the tallest building in Binghamton. The twelve-story building was the city's first "skyscraper." Kilmer insisted that it be taller than the ten-story Security Mutual building that was being constructed at the same time. He hired away editors and reporters from the rival newspaper. In 1904, the Binghamton Press began

> Opposite page: S. Andral Kilmer (top left) created Dr. Kilmer & Company to produce his "Swamp Root" patent medicine. His brother, Jonas (top middle), and nephew, Willis Sharpe Kilmer (top right), took over operation of the firm that made millions from the "medicine." Jonas' home (later Willis', bottom) eventually became Temple Concord on Riverside Drive in Binghamton. (Courtesy Broome County Historical Society)

Alonzo Roberson Jr. built this Front Street home (1904–1907). Designed by C. Edward Vosbury, the interior of the home was a showcase for Roberson's lumber business. The Robersons left the home to the community, and today it is the Roberson Museum & Science Center. (Courtesy Broome County Historical Society)

operations and the rival newspaper folded a few years later.

On Riverside Drive, Jonas and Willis built adjoining mansions. Designed by C. Edward Vosbury, the mansions reflected the growing affluence of the Parlor City. To the west of the mansions, Willis Kilmer began another venture—breeding thoroughbred racehorses. He built Sun Briar Court, a million-dollar stable complex that included an outdoor track as well as an indoor track inside a circular stable made of stone. Sun Briar was the horse that Kilmer had hoped would bring fame and fortune to the Kilmer operations. While the horse performed well, as did Sun Beau and several other horses in the stable, none lived up to Kilmer's expectations.

In 1918, Kilmer purchased a horse named Exterminator for nine thousand dollars to be the pacer for Sun Briar. The horse had been earmarked for being put down when Kilmer bought him. When the horse was brought to Binghamton, he not only paced the horses in the stable, he outpaced them. Exterminator outraced not only those horses but also every horse that he raced against. Kilmer entered the three-year-old gelding in the 1918 Kentucky Derby, which Exterminator won. In his life, he won fifty races and brought a fortune to Kilmer. He retired a few years later and spent the rest of his thirty-five years at ease at Sun Briar Court where children would come each year for his birthday party and to see his Shetland pony companion, Peanuts.

As the business environment of Broome County began to grow at the turn of the century, so did the transportation system. Horse-drawn trolleys had been in place by the early 1870s. Electricity had been brought into Binghamton in the early 1880s. A new company called the Washington Street and State Asylum Railroad Company petitioned the city to allow it to use electricity to power a new trolley car. On May 24, 1886, the first electric trolley line in New York State began operations. This major innovation toward modern transportation was in operation for only about six months because the company discovered that the car could only reach a top speed of twelve miles per hour. The incline on Robinson Street near the Asylum was so steep that horses had to be brought down to pull

On December 28, 1896, Broome County's third courthouse burned as firefighters tried to stop the flames from spreading. Isaac Perry was hired to design the current courthouse, using the remaining foundation. The Greek Revival–style building opened in 1898. (Courtesy Broome County Historical Society)

the car to the top. The system was abandoned until a new design was accepted as the standard across the country. The trolley system in Broome County finally became fully electric after 1891.

As Broome County's citizens faced the end of the nineteenth century and the beginning of the twentieth century, the residents saw a changing culture approaching. In 1888, the first hospital opened in Binghamton in the former Lowell Harding house near the Tompkins Street Bridge on Court Street. Seven years later, in 1895, the hospital moved to the south side of the city where it continues today as Binghamton General Hospital. Baseball became popular in the last quarter of the nineteenth century. Several minor league teams operated during this period. The Bingos became champions of their league in 1892 and eventually attracted the attention of George F. Johnson. He purchased the team in 1913 and moved the operations to Lestershire.

While the courthouse was being built in 1897, Binghamton built its own city hall. Raymond Almirall designed the building in the École des Beaux-Arts style. It was used until the 1970s when it was converted to what is today the Grand Royale Hotel. (Courtesy Broome County Historical Society)

The incorporation of the city meant the need for regular police and fire forces. Here, members of the Binghamton Police Department appear on their bicycles in front of a store at 104 Court Street about 1900. (Courtesy Broome County Historical Society)

Courthouse Square had been the focal point of Binghamton throughout the nineteenth century. In seven years, the entire look of the square was changed forever. In 1897, the city government decided to construct a new city hall. The new building replaced Firemen's Hall on Collier Street. Designed by Raymond Almirall, the building was in the style of the French École des Beaux-Arts. This impressive structure with its magnificent staircase gave the city government both a new home and a new look, reflecting the growing importance of the city. The five-story structure housed all of the city departments. Many of these departments were new, created to handle the increasing bureaucracy of city government. Clerks filed birth, death, and marriage records, permits for the building of homes, and licenses to operate a business in the city—most of these types of records did not exist prior to 1900.

At the same time, Broome County was busy building a new courthouse to replace one destroyed by fire. On December 28, 1896, a fire broke out in the county's third courthouse. Before the fire department could arrive on the snowy, wintry evening, the fire had spread throughout the building. Flames shot from all parts of the building. Within a few hours, much of the courthouse had been destroyed. The county clerk's office was in a separate building on the courthouse square, saving most of the valuable county records from destruction.

Isaac Perry designed the county's fourth courthouse. He had wanted to create a modern building but was required to reuse the foundation of the previous courthouse and to maintain its design. Perry conceived a graceful Classical Revival courthouse of stone with a soaring copper dome above large tolling clocks

CHAPTER 8: A GOOD FIVE-CENT CIGAR   137

Independent fire companies began in the 1840s but were made part of the regular fire system in the 1870s. The Independent Hose Company was housed in the Number 5 station long before the building was converted to a restaurant in the 1980s. (Courtesy Broome County Historical Society)

around the base of the dome. Steps made from bluestone led up to the large portico. On the pediment was the seal of the county, designed by John Broome. An elegant courtroom on the second floor was used for a variety of trials and functions. Many of the judges' quarters contained their own working fireplaces. A power station, also designed by Perry, was added to generate electricity for several buildings on Courthouse Square.

Across the street from the courthouse, the Security Mutual Life Insurance Company built new headquarters in 1904. The company had offices in the Phelps Bank building on the corner of Chenango and Court Streets but wanted its own identity in the city. The firm purchased the Hagaman Block and the Pope Building on Exchange Street for the location. Both buildings had been constructed thirty years before but were torn down to make way for the new structure. Truman Lacey was hired to design the new building. The ten-story structure was built of yellow brick and included classical appurtenances similar to Lacey's other work at the Press building on Chenango Street. The structure was completed in early 1905.

By that time, another impressive structure had opened on Exchange Street. The city had struggled for years with the problem of creating a library for its residents. The earliest library was a subscription library started in 1800 on the urging of Joshua Whitney and William Bingham. Small subscription library societies existed throughout the nineteenth century, but none lasted more than two decades. In 1865, the Young Men's Christian Association started a national movement to offer books to people to encourage educational growth. Binghamton's YMCA library lasted until the Union Free School opened on Washington Street. In the last quarter of the nineteenth century, the last remaining library society ended, and the Union Free School inherited the books.

It was clear that the school building could not house the material and that a new public library was needed. A committee of five wrote a letter to Andrew Carnegie explaining the virtues of the city and asking for help in the construction

Fire protection expanded beyond Binghamton and into every community by the early 1900s. The J. R. Diment Chemical #1 Company of the Lestershire Fire Department is shown in this 1901 photograph that includes George F. Johnson at far left in the front row. (Courtesy Broome County Historical Society)

Willis Sharpe Kilmer began the Binghamton Press Company in 1904 with the building of the twelve-story skyscraper on Chenango Street. Designed by the Truman Lacey firm, it was the tallest building in Binghamton until the 1970s. (Courtesy Broome County Historical Society)

At the same time as the Press building, the Truman Lacey firm also designed the Security Mutual building for the insurance firm on the corner of Court and Exchange Streets. This ten-story building anchored the courthouse square area with its graceful skyscraper appearance. (Courtesy Broome County Historical Society)

of a library. Carnegie agreed to provide $75,000 for the construction of the library as long as the city provided the land and an annual support of at least $7,500. Isaac Perry was hired as the consulting architect. He chose the Greek Revival design of S. O. and H. A. Lacey. On October 14, 1904, the Binghamton Public Library was opened to the public. It housed a collection of fourteen thousand books and a staff of four. It also housed the Binghamton Museum of Fine Arts in the Art Gallery and the Broome County Historical Society in the History Room.

Nearby on Chenango Street stood the Stone Opera House. Built by Charles Stone, an owner of the trolley car system, the opera house offered operettas as well as traveling troupes of actors and plays. Small moving picture theaters began operations throughout the area by the early 1900s. Families looking for fun could also take the trolley to Ross Park on the south side of Binghamton. In 1875, Erastus Ross had donated ninety acres of land to the city of Binghamton to be used a public park. Soon afterwards, animals began to be housed at the park, and the Ross Park Zoo came into

The Binghamton Public Library opened its doors in 1904. The first public library building in the area, it was a gift of Andrew Carnegie and was designed by S. O. and H. A. Lacey. The $75,000 building was used until 2000, and it is now available for reuse. (Courtesy Broome County Historical Society)

existence. Today, it is considered the fifth oldest zoo in the country.

As culture and society grew in leaps and bounds at this time, so did the expansion of business and the spread of population to new villages to the west of Binghamton. In Lestershire, G. Harry Lester was having difficulties in his efforts to create a company town. The firm had become overextended. Lester had built a factory, a company bank, a company store, and some housing for the workers. He insisted that the shoe workers could only use those institutions. The economy of the country went into a recession in the early 1890s, and the Lester Brothers Company went into a financial tailspin. One of the company's creditors, Henry B. Endicott, agreed to buy the firm and the remaining stock of shoes in 1890.

Endicott also kept on the superintendent of the company, George F. Johnson. Like Endicott, Johnson was from Massachusetts, and Johnson's business knowledge was acute. Endicott saw great potential in the shoemaker. He also realized that he needed someone to run the day-to-day operations of the business. Endicott's main holdings were in the Boston area, and he wanted to remain in that area to manage his own shoe companies. In 1892, the village of Lestershire was incorporated, and the survival of the shoe company was foremost in the thoughts of its residents. Johnson had been the one to persuade the Lester brothers to

CHAPTER 8: A GOOD FIVE-CENT CIGAR   141

move their company to the new village. He had seen the results of the labor unrest of the cigar industry and had wanted the company away from those influences.

Johnson saw that the real success of any business was its ability to cooperate with its workers and with the community in which it existed. In 1899, Endicott saw that Johnson had been able to turn the company around and succeed in making profits. He also saw that Johnson had good rapport with the workers, encouraging their loyalty and their participation in the company. He asked Johnson to become his partner. Johnson did not have the funds to buy the partnership, so Endicott loaned him the money, sure that Johnson would be able to pay him back. The Endicott Johnson Shoe Company was born.

Johnson elaborated on what he called his Square Deal policy. He stated that if the workers were given a decent wage, good benefits, a nice community in which to live, and were made part of the decision-making process, they would give back increased levels of loyalty and productivity. Johnson was not in favor of labor unions and thought it was the responsibility of the company to provide those things that most unions were trying to achieve. The employees of the company instantly accepted the policy. Endicott Johnson thrived and grew. When Henry B. Endicott bought the company in 1890, it had 425 workers. By 1910, the firm employed 4,000 workers (Zahavi, *Workers, Manager and Welfare Capitalism: The Shoeworkers and Tanners of Endicott Johnson, 1890–1950*). New factories began to be built around Lestershire. Each factory specialized in a different line of shoe. The company made shoes for men, women, and children.

In 1899, a group of investors saw a future in farmland about six miles to the west of Lestershire. The leader of this group, G. Tracy Rogers, the president of the Binghamton Railway Company, the trolley car system, led the group. He saw that if Endicott Johnson and other firms built factories there, new residents would build homes, and the trolley system could run lines to move the people back and forth from home to work. Thus, the Endicott Land Company was born. Rogers discussed the possibility with the leaders of Endicott Johnson. George F. Johnson was in favor of the idea and persuaded Endicott to purchase two hundred acres of land on the new site (Fiori, *A History of Endicott*). The other factor in the decision was that the Endicott Land Company promised to name the new village after Endicott.

In 1901, construction began on Washington Avenue, destined to become the commercial

> The care of needy children fell to the community in the nineteenth century. St. Mary's Home operated from the former Susquehanna Seminary in Binghamton from the 1880s until the home was demolished to make way for the current Seton Catholic Central High School. (Courtesy Broome County Historical Society)

Dr. John Orton started the Susquehanna Valley Home in 1869. It operated until the 1970s on a one-hundred-acre plot in Binghamton. Here in this 1906 photograph, the children return to the home from a day at the park via Chenango Street in a twenty-five-car caravan. (Courtesy Broome County Historical Society)

center of the new village. Factories were built on the northern end of the town while residences were built on either side of the commercial center. In 1902, it was estimated that four hundred new homes and buildings would be constructed, including a new home for George F. Johnson. In 1905, the Bundy Time Recording Company decided to build a new factory in the fledging village. It had recently been renamed International Time Recording Company to reflect the merger of several small companies into a more viable business machinery manufacturing firm. New structures like the Hotel Frederick were built to accommodate the increasing number of visitors to the town.

A "splendid little war" was what some called the Spanish-American War of 1898. While many men joined up in Company H as seen in this photograph, few actually saw battle because the war lasted only six months. (Courtesy Broome County Historical Society)

By 1906, the town had a hotel, a bank, factories, and hundreds of workers who lived and shopped in the new town. A complete village had been born in less than six years. The nickname of Magic City seemed appropriate for the planned community. On August 28, 1906, the village of Endicott was incorporated. Harry L. Johnson, the brother of George F., was chosen as the first president of the village.

By 1910, the city of Binghamton and the villages of Lestershire and Endicott were thriving with the growth of business, the influx of immigrants, and the prosperity of the country. Broome County entered the first decade of the twentieth century in a strong condition with the groundwork established for the creation of the Triple Cities.

CHAPTER 9
Which Way EJ?
1910–1936

By the 1930s, Endicott Johnson had over twenty thousand employees and forty factories, tanneries, and other buildings in the area. This is the sales building that was located in Endicott. Only a few of the factory buildings remain today. (Courtesy Broome County Historical Society)

"WHICH WAY EJ?" It was said that this phrase was the only English that immigrants knew as they arrived at Ellis Island. However apocryphal the story, there was a high degree of truth behind it. As Endicott Johnson Shoe Corporation continued to grow in the first three decades of the twentieth century, it had a continual need to find new workers. The company had 4,000 employees in 1910, 13,265 employees in 1920, 14,551 employees in 1930, and 17,858 employees in 1936 (Zahavi).

In order to find enough workers to fill the empty spots, Endicott Johnson advertised in European newspapers, encouraging workers to apply when they arrived in the country. Other workers arrived daily from the coalfields of Pennsylvania as that industry went into decline in the early 1900s. Many were former immigrants from Poland, Czechoslovakia, Hungary, Greece, Ireland, Russia, and many other countries. They had lived in Pennsylvania for a generation, trying to eke out a living in the mines, but found the opportunity of working in the shoe factories more enticing.

This is a rare photograph of Henry B. Endicott (left) and George F. Johnson. Endicott left the operations of Endicott Johnson to Johnson whereas Endicott spent most of his time on his own shoe business in Massachusetts. (Original in the George F. Johnson Memorial Library, courtesy Broome County Historical Society)

This is a typical stitching room of one of the Endicott Johnson factories. Thousands of workers labored for eight hours a day assembling the fifty-two million pairs of shoes the company made each year. (Courtesy Broome County Historical Society)

George F. Johnson and his Square Deal policy transformed not just his company but the community as well. The loyalty between the workers and George F. Johnson was tremendously strong. Although the work was hard, there was a bond between workers and management. It may have helped that Johnson was considered one of them. He had risen from being a poor young worker to head the company. He often would travel through the factories and knew many of the workers on a first-name basis. Johnson's office door was always open, and workers were welcome to come and discuss an idea for the company. It may be that the propaganda used in the company's factories and publications created a sense of well-being and nurtured the feeling that the employees were part of the decision-making process. Throughout the factories were signs like "Live and Let Live" and "For the Benefit of All—Save." In the *E–J Workers Review* magazine that appeared in the 1920s

In four decades, the company constructed over four thousand homes, giving the employees the opportunity to own their own houses. This is one of the streets lined with EJ homes. Although the exteriors might appear different, the floor layouts were nearly identical. (Courtesy Broome County Historical Society)

and 1930s, employees would write letters complaining about gripes in the factories. This was not a guarantee that the situation would be alleviated, but at least the employee was heard.

Above all, the employees and the community enjoyed the benefits that the company offered. In 1916, George F. Johnson realized that employees were tired after working the 9½ hours that was then the industry norm for shoemaking. If workers were less fatigued, he reasoned, they could produce more shoes. He lowered the workday to eight hours, but without any loss of pay. A huge parade was given in honor of the event. Two months later, the name of the village of Lestershire was changed to the village of Johnson City.

Endicott Johnson offered medical care for employees and their families of which the company assumed the total cost. As employees required more extensive care, the company funded the Charles S. Wilson Memorial Hospital in Johnson City in 1912. When the company expanded factory and tannery operations in Endicott, another hospital became necessary. Ideal Hospital opened in 1928. A training facility for nurses was donated by Mrs. George F. Johnson and added to Ideal in 1929.

Babies born to an EJ mother would receive a ten-dollar gold piece and a bank account with another ten dollars as its opening deposit. Each year, children of the Triple Cities would receive a certificate for a free pair of shoes. Recreation played an important part of the EJ benefit package. Johnson realized that if workers had the means to enjoy life outside of the factories, the routine of the assembly line might seem less tedious. Also, Johnson purchased Bennett Park on the west side of Binghamton. It had been a private park where an admission fee was charged. Johnson believed that everyone should benefit from the park, not just those who could afford to pay. The park was donated back to the City of Binghamton with three stipulations: the name would be changed to Recreation Park; there would be no fence around the park to stop anyone from entering; and no admission would be charged.

In Endicott, the company purchased Casino Park located along the Susquehanna River. It had been operated by the owners of the Binghamton Railway Company, which ended its trolley lines at the entrance to the park. Casino Park became Ideal Park (it was renamed En-Joie Park in the 1940s). It offered river walks, lagoons, recreational areas, and the casino building. In Johnson City, George F. Johnson's brother, C. Fred Johnson, was put in charge of reclaiming the former Elijah Brigham brickyard. Located near Main Street in the village, the brick pond was cleaned up and made smaller with boats, swans, and walkways added. Eventually, the playground area was expanded, and the entire pond was filled. In 1927, a gigantic aboveground pool was added to the newly created CFJ Park. The pool was designed by Wesley Binty and could hold two thousand swimmers. The pool was free, but the use of one of the fifteen hundred lockers cost ten cents. The year before, in 1926, the George F. Johnson Pavilion had been added to the landscape. It offered a dance floor that could hold four thousand people. It cost only fifty cents to hear bands such as Benny Goodman, Glenn Miller, or Tommy Dorsey with

Endicott Johnson sponsored public markets in Johnson City and Endicott. It gave farmers a chance to sell directly to consumers. The public markets lasted over thirty years before closing in the 1950s. (Courtesy Broome County Historical Society)

Frank Sinatra. The price dropped to twenty-five cents to hear the local bands that appeared on weeknights.

In 1912, Johnson purchased the Bingos baseball team. He had Johnson Field constructed in 1913 to house the team in Johnson City. The team played for several minor leagues before eventually becoming a farm team for the New York Yankees. Johnson had wanted the team to play Sunday games since it was one of the only days employees had off from work. Blue laws and local ordinances prohibited any admission fees on that day, so Johnson gave away the tickets.

Lights were later added to the field for night games. The team name was changed to the Broomes, but the team was sold in 1919.

In 1928, a new team called the Triple Cities Club began play at Johnson Field. The team name was soon shortened to the Triplets. The team continued to play in the area until 1968 when the baseball field was removed for the expansion of Route 17. Whitey Ford and Thurman Munson were among the many major league players who began their career as part of the Triplets.

Johnson also wanted to offer the residents of the community access to learning and

George F. Johnson believed in the need for recreation for the employees and their families. In 1921, he purchased and then donated what became Recreation Park to the City of Binghamton. The bandstand has been home to thousands of concerts for eighty years. (Courtesy Broome County Historical Society)

The Casino was the main building at Casino Park in Endicott. Endicott Johnson bought the park and reopened it as the free Ideal Park (later En-Joie Park). The casino building burned in a fire and was replaced with the company's West Recreation Building. (Courtesy Broome County Historical Society)

educational opportunities. The Endicott Free Library opened in March 1915 in the Mattoon Building on Washington Avenue. George F. Johnson and his wife later gave use of the former Harlow Bundy House on Park Street for the library. It was called the Ideal Home Library. The Endicott Free Library later added the Hillside Center, which include a branch library, on the north side of the village. Johnson also provided a library for the residents of Johnson City. In March 1917, Your Home Library opened in the former home of Elijah Brigham. This was originally the concept of Harry L. Johnson, brother of George F. Johnson. Like its counterpart in Endicott, the library was meant to also act as community center and included dining rooms and a sunroom. Also, sewing classes were held, and English classes were given for many of the thousands of new Americans now living in Johnson City.

George F. Johnson had a firm belief in the rights of each ethnic group to worship in its own church. He gave money or land to many groups to start their own churches. This includes St. James Catholic Church in

CHAPTER 9: WHICH WAY EJ?   153

Johnson City, as well as many of the "gold-domed" churches of Johnson City, the First Ward of Binghamton, and Endicott. These Eastern Orthodox and other denominations served many of the Eastern European groups who came to the valley in the early twentieth century. The Johnson brothers, George F., C. Fred, and Harry L., gave the funds to start the Sarah Jane Johnson Memorial Methodist Church in Johnson City. The fourth Johnson brother, Oscar, was a Methodist minister, and the church was a tribute to their mother.

The Johnson family also provided the six carousels that still reside in Broome County.

The aboveground pool at CFJ Park in Johnson City was one of the largest in the country. Its slogan "Come On In; The Water's Fine" held true for the two thousand swimmers it could hold at once. It was demolished in the 1970s. (Courtesy Broome County Historical Society)

When George F. Johnson was a small boy in Massachusetts, he did not have the nickel it cost to ride the merry-go-round. He swore that if he were ever rich enough, he would make sure that children of any age would be able to ride for free. Starting in 1919 with a carousel in Ross Park in Binghamton, George F. or his daughter, Lillian Sweet, donated carousels for Recreation Park in Binghamton, CFJ Park in Johnson City, En-Joie Park in Endicott, George W. Johnson Park in Endicott, and West Endicott Park in the town of Union. The Hirschell Spellman Company in North Tonawanda, New York, manufactured all the carousels. Johnson had all of the horses made as jumpers; that is, each horse went up and down. The stipulation was that the carousels be forever free. If not, they are to revert back to the Johnson family.

The greatest of the benefits of the Endicott Johnson Shoe Corporation was the housing program. Harry L. Johnson was concerned that the newly arrived employees should not only have a place to live but also the means to own their own homes. Starting in 1913, a tract of one hundred acres on the north side of the village of Johnson City was purchased for the construction of employee homes. With Harry L. Johnson's untimely death in 1920, C. Fred Johnson assumed control of the housing program. Lumber for the homes came from Roberson Lumber, and Frank Boland was the general contractor of the project. Homes were sold at cost to the employees, and the mortgage costs were deducted from their wages. The program ran from 1913 to 1952. Approximately four thousand homes were built in Johnson City, Endicott, West Endicott, and Binghamton. During the Great Depression, the company wanted to assure workers that their homes would not be foreclosed

The Johnson family donated the six wooden carousels that are still operating in the community. They were given with the stipulation that they would be forever free. As this picture shows, the joys of riding still entertain children of all ages. (Courtesy Broome County Historical Society)

Two industrial giants are pictured together in this photograph from the 1930s. George F. Johnson (1857–1948) and Thomas J. Watson (1874–1956) held tight reins over the economy of the community for the first half the twentieth century. (Courtesy Broome County Historical Society)

CHAPTER 9: WHICH WAY EJ?   155

While thousands of immigrants worked in factories making shoes and business machines, others. such as James Vincent Caciola, ran their own businesses. Caciola's ice cream parlor was at 260 Clinton Street in Binghamton. (Courtesy Broome County Historical Society)

upon. The company defrayed the paying of the principal of the mortgage and only had the employees pay the interest payment of about twenty-five cents per week.

In 1920, in honor of the policies of the Endicott Johnson Company, the workers collected pennies, nickels, and dimes for the erection of two arches: one arch at the eastern entrance into Johnson City and one at the western entrance into Endicott. The twin arches bearing the inscriptions "Gateway to the Square Deal Towns" and "Home of the Square Deal" were adorned with neon shapes of hearts and moons that lit the night. They served as impressive monuments to what many were now calling the Valley of Opportunity. George F. Johnson had risen from a poor man with twelve cents in his pocket and no shirt collar when he arrived in Binghamton to become a multimillionaire. His brand of welfare capitalism was extremely successful. Twice during the history of the company, votes were taken by the employees on whether to join one of the major labor unions in the country. In each instance, the unions lost to the management. The unions could offer nothing the company had not already provided for its workers. It is estimated that George F. Johnson made seven million dollars in his life and gave four million of that back to the community.

While the size and influence of the Endicott Johnson Corporation may have dominated the county, it was only one of many emerging industries in the area. The Bundy Time Recording Company merged with several other business firms to form the International Time Recording Company. Manufacturing time clocks, ITR moved its main factory to the new village of Endicott in 1906. While the company was fairly large by industrial standards at the time with nearly one thousand workers, it did not live up to expectations of its investors. In 1914, the company hired Thomas J. Watson (1874–1956) as the new president of the firm. Watson was born in East Campbell, New York, and had worked previously as sales executive with the National Cash Register Company. That company was under federal investigation for sales fraud because of the practices put in place by its president. Watson needed to get away from that corporation, and the offer to run ITR in Endicott came at the right time.

He quickly took hold and put forth a set of beliefs that was not unlike that of the corporate management system of Endicott Johnson. Watson wanted the firm to make quality business products and enlarged the line from time clocks to include typewriters, scales, and adding machines. He stressed service to the customer at all times. Although it was not written in any employee manuals, all male workers were expected to wear white shirts and ties at all times, even on the assembly line. Watson built a corporate image of a no-

> The expansion of industry also meant the expansion of retail businesses. Fowler, Dick & Walker in Binghamton and other major department stores offered luxuries such as home delivery. This is an 1898 photograph of the store's truck. (Courtesy Broome County Historical Society)

In the early twentieth century, public and private schools abounded. The Parlor City Industrial School was one of two African American–operated schools in the area in the first quarter of the century. It was located on Fayette Street and served people of all colors. (Courtesy Broome County Historical Society)

The third major industrial component during this period started in a piano and organ company in an alley in Binghamton. Edwin A. Link worked in his father's piano company on Spice Alley. His father had returned to the area after a number of years away and after his marriage to Edwin's mother had ended. Edwin was not the best student, but he learned the mechanics of hydraulics and other systems that generated sound in player pianos and organs. An avid aviator, Link had flown planes for several years. He realized that most aviation accidents occurred because of the poor training of the pilots. In 1928, he used hydraulics to design what he called a Flight Trainer to help new pilots learn the mechanics of the airplane before they flew. A year later, in 1929, he began Link Aviation. Initial sales were extremely slow, and Link gave flying lessons to augment his income. The beginning of the company coincided with the onset of the Great Depression.

nonsense firm that was growing. He soon opened up corporate offices in New York City. Watson believed that the firm had to be located there if it was to be truly international.

By 1924, Watson had enlarged the firm, and sales reflected his success in providing the world market with the products needed in an increasing business atmosphere. He changed the name of the firm to International Business Machines, reflecting this change in the focus of the company. IBM plant number 1 was located in Endicott. It and the other white factories were emblazoned with the new logo of the firm, a blue globe with IBM written across the center.

If horseracing was the sport of kings, Exterminator was the king of the sport. Owned by Willis Sharpe Kilmer (second from left), the horse won the 1918 Kentucky Derby, as well as fifty other races in his career. (Courtesy Broome County Historical Society)

By the 1920s, the area was home to a large number of businesses and industries. The economic outlook for the industrial sector of Broome County's economy was strong. Circling the urban corridor of Binghamton, Johnson City, and Endicott was a very active agricultural system. Farming, which had played such an important role in the development of the area during the nineteenth century, continued to be a significant sector of the economy of the region. By the early 1900s, there were hundreds of farms in the county. Many of the farms were dairy operations, producing millions of gallons of milk for residents of the community and for other counties. Larger farms produced a variety of products, including corn, wheat, beans, potatoes, tomatoes, and many other crops. These were sold directly to consumers via roadside markets or through stores in the area. Some farmers participated in the two Endicott Johnson Public Markets located in Johnson City and Endicott. These public markets allowed the

In 1918, a "Jerry Load" of women arrives in Lisle to cast their first ballots. The women's suffrage movement had won, and the American political system was forever changed. (Courtesy Broome County Historical Society)

farmers to sell directly to residents and to keep all of the money received. The markets were popular from the late 1920s through the late 1940s.

In the early 1900s, some farmers had trouble making profits because of the rising cost of transporting goods from their farms to the various markets. In 1911, Byron Gitchell of the Binghamton Chamber of Commerce realized that the loss of area farms and farming would have a direct impact on the business and industrial sectors of the local economy. He invited John Barron, an agricultural expert from Cornell University, to come to the county and demonstrate new ways for farmers to better utilize their lands and produce more crops. He also convinced the leaders of the Lackawanna Railroad to take a number of businessmen, leaders of the community, and representatives from the United States Department of Agriculture on a tour of the farming areas of Broome County. The trip convinced many businesses to become involved in a pilot project to aid local farmers through education and business training.

James Quinn, a farmer in the town of Chenango, was elected as the president of the first Farm Bureau in the United States. Today the Farm Bureau is still a viable agency, aiding and assisting the agricultural sector of the nation.

Despite the relatively isolated location of Broome County, it was not protected from the increasing pressures of international tension in the early 1900s. Ethnic pressures had been mounting since the late 1890s. With the assassination of Archduke Ferdinand in 1914, a Serbian citizen set a series of entangling treaties between the European nations in motion.

This one act of violence plunged the world into war for the next few years. Although the administration of President Woodrow Wilson promised to keep the nation out of war, the sinking of the ship *Lusitania* resulted in Wilson's speech before Congress on April 2, 1917, in which he declared that:

In 1934, the area welcomed its new Federal Building and Courthouse. The building also included the post office and a WPA mural (Johnson City and Endicott also had them). The mural caused a controversy because of a nude in the painting. (Courtesy Broome County Historical Society)

Neutrality is no longer feasible or desirable where the peace of the world is involved and the freedom of its peoples, and the menace to that peace and freedom lies in the existence of autocratic governments backed by organized force, which is controlled wholly by their will, not by the will of the people. We have seen the last of neutrality in such circumstance.

War had broken out, and Broome County responded as it had in all previous wars. Rallies were held in Binghamton encouraging the residents to raise necessary crops, participate in war bond drives, and, of course, enlist in the military service. Karl M. Hyde was the first Binghamton high school student to enlist. The military draft was brought back to fill the ranks of men needed to join in the war efforts. Eventually, over three thousand men were drafted or enlisted from Broome County during the war. Over two hundred of those did not survive.

The rise of industries such as Endicott Johnson and other companies in the area resulted in the influx of thousands of immigrants in the

Medical care expanded greatly during the early twentieth century. Broome County built the Tuberculosis Hospital in the town of Chenango at Chenango Bridge. It aided hundreds over the decades before being converted to the Chenango Bridge Nursing Home. It closed in the early 1980s. (Courtesy Broome County Historical Society)

Opposite page: Although the effects of the Great Depression were buffered in this area by the strength of EJ and IBM, there was a need for an occasional bread-and-soup line. The Broome County Humane Society was feeding this line. (Courtesy Broome County Historical Society)

community. Many of these settled together in certain areas of the county, especially Johnson City, Endicott, and the First Ward of Binghamton. Accents from dozens of languages were heard throughout the area. New churches, new foods, and new customs were introduced to the community. But not all residents of the

Endicott Johnson helped to start both Wilson Hospital in Johnson City and Ideal Hospital in Endicott. In Binghamton, General Hospital (originally City Hospital) and Lourdes Hospital also offered medical care. This is a photograph of a 1920s ambulance. (Courtesy Broome County Historical Society)

CHAPTER 9: WHICH WAY EJ?

The area had other companies beside EJ and IBM. Ansco manufactured a variety of camera and film products. The main complex, seen here, was located in the First Ward of Binghamton. The complex went through several owners before closing in the late 1990s. (Courtesy Broome County Historical Society)

area welcomed the newcomers with open arms. After the end of World War I, there was a rise of nativist sentiment throughout the nation. A pall of isolationism fell across the country, and the sour taste of the First World War left the United States with the tendency toward withdrawal from much that the war had represented. Woodrow Wilson's attempt to have the United States join the League of Nations failed. There was a rise in resentment toward newly arrived immigrants, who were perceived as taking jobs away from "real" Americans.

Into this tension between two groups came an old enemy, the Ku Klux Klan. What had been a bad memory, largely defeated in the post–Civil War period, rose in strength and numbers under a number of names across the country. The organization moved into the North, preying on the fears of its inhabitants. The Ku Klux Klan took up residence in New York State where it targeted two groups—African Americans and new immigrants from Eastern Europe. In cities like Niagara Falls, Ithaca, and Syracuse, the Klan held rallies. But their focus in Binghamton was to target the newly arrived immigrants.

The Klan moved into Binghamton in 1921. Cards announcing the arrival of the Klan were distributed, and rallies were held throughout the area. Cross-burnings were held on both Mount Prospect and South Mountain. The fires were clearly visible in the immigrant sections located nearby. As the strength of the Klan increased, they rented a building on Wall Street as headquarters. By 1925, Binghamton was the statewide capital of the Klan's activities. It even offered a mayoral candidate for the city of Binghamton. Despite the efforts of the Klan to rally the community around its message of fear and intimidation, its efforts backfired.

Local ethnic groups realized that the one way to fight the Ku Klux Klan was to be firm and to protect their own heritage. During the 1920s, groups such as the Polish Community Center, the Czeckslovak Moravian Club, the Jewish Community Center, and others were formed to aid in the perpetuation of their cultures in the community. Another sector that worked against the Klan was made up of local business leaders who realized that Klan's efforts could split the county apart if they were not stopped.

George F. Johnson, head of the Endicott Johnson Shoe Company, worked together with William Hill, his nephew-in-law and editor of the *Morning Sun* newspaper. The newspaper ran a series of scathing editorials profiling the Klan and its intimidation techniques in the community. Johnson stated that he

The Drybak Corporation was located along the Brandywine Highway in Binghamton. It made men's sporting wear and work pants before the firm closed. The building later became home to both Link and Stow Manufacturing. (Courtesy Broome County Historical Society)

After a tumultuous period of milk strikes, farmers grouped together to form organizations like the Dairymen's League Cooperative Association. The cooperative helped stabilize prices for milk and other dairy products. Here, farmers gather in front of the Kalurah Temple during a 1927 state convention. (Courtesy Broome County Historical Society)

would fire any employee of the company who was a member of the Ku Klux Klan, and several employees were fired for this reason. These efforts worked, and the strength and importance of the Klan diminished quickly. By 1928, the Klan had abandoned its offices and moved on, but not before leaving an indelible mark on the history of the community.

By the late 1920s, the community had survived the threat of the Klan, but it could not escape the failure of the nation's economy. During the 1920s, there had been a meteoric rise in the stock market. Millionaires were being made every day as the price of stocks rose steadily. The regulation of the stock market was weak, and much of the rise was not supported by actual funds. The world came apart in a matter of days. In late October 1929, the stock market began to tumble. A short rise in stock prices was met with an even more sickening fall. On Black Tuesday, October 29, the market fell at a dangerous pace that did not stabilize until November 13 when the prices finally hit bottom. By that time, most stocks were worth less than half of what they had been worth only a few weeks before.

The stock market crash set off a series of failures throughout the economy. There were runs on banks with many creditors losing everything. In Broome County, however, only one bank was forced to close, and only for a short time. Nationwide, the failure of the economy resulted in massive layoffs from businesses, a loss of orders for new products, calls by banks for immediate payment of outstanding debts such as mortgages, and thousands of foreclosures of farms and other institutions. By 1933, at the depth of the Great Depression, many urban areas had unemployment rates between 10 percent and 25 percent.

Despite the statistics in many areas, Broome County was able to buffer the worst of the Great Depression. Watching the failing economy made the leaders of the two major employers of the time, Endicott Johnson and IBM, work to protect their workers and the area. George F. Johnson and the leadership of his company vowed to minimize the worst of the effects of the downturn in the economy. The company did not lay off any employees, but it did lessen the hours each employee worked. In this way, everyone had some income to provide for families to survive the depression. The company also refused to foreclose on any EJ employee homes. Instead, Endicott Johnson only required each employee to pay the interest payment on the home and not the mortgage. This usually equaled about twenty-five cents per week. Many employees took wooden shoe lasts that were no longer used and burned them for fuel to save money.

Thousands of immigrants flooded the valley to work in the factories. This 1920 cover of the EJ magazine demonstrates the diversity of the community. Unfortunately, the ethnic groups faced a decade of turmoil at the hands of the Ku Klux Klan. (Courtesy Broome County Historical Society)

The Ku Klux Klan used Binghamton as its base as it waged its campaign of hatred and terror. The group even ran a mayoral candidate before people like George F. Johnson and many ethnic groups worked together to remove the KKK from Broome County. (Courtesy Broome County Historical Society)

Thomas J. Watson saw the downturn as an opportunity rather than a disaster. He believed that the businesses and industries would need a large amount of business equipment once the economy came out of the depression. He increased the number of workers employed by the company and, in some instances, raised wages. The theory held true, and after the end of the Great Depression, IBM stock rose significantly.

These two companies did help to lessen the impact of the Great Depression on Broome County. Their actions did not, however, prevent all from losing their jobs or prevent some farms from being foreclosed during the depression. At least one soup kitchen was kept open in Binghamton during the Great Depression, feeding hundreds during the late 1920s and early 1930s. The election of Franklin D. Roosevelt signaled a move toward greater federal government responsibility. By the end of the 1930s, many stores and businesses showed evidence of the New Deal programs. Posters in store windows displayed the blue eagle of the National Recovery Act, and workers employed by the Civilian Conservation Corps were busy putting in water and sewer lines or building the Chenango Valley State Park in the town of Fenton. Artists under the Works Progress Administration painted the murals that adorned the post offices of Binghamton, Johnson City, and Endicott, although the mural in Binghamton raised questions of the use of public funds for art because it depicted a nude as part of the artwork. It is interesting to note that, despite the popularity of Franklin Roosevelt as president, he only carried Broome County in one of his four presidential elections.

During the period of the 1910s, 1920s, and 1930s, Broome County endured three tremendous disasters—one of fire and two of water. The Binghamton Clothing Company was located on Wall Street and employed about one hundred workers making men's overalls and pants. Many of the workers of the four-story brick building were women, some of whom were immigrants who spoke little or no English. Reed Freeman was the owner and had followed all contemporary safety regulations. In 1911, the Triangle Shirt Waist fire had claimed over one hundred lives because of

The Beautiful Plan Baptist Church on Pine Street (shown left) and the Berean Baptist Church (later Mt. Nebo Church, shown right) were two of the African American churches located in the community. Both churches continue to serve the community today. (Courtesy Broome County Historical Society)

doors locked to keep out union organizers. The Binghamton Clothing Company did not operate in this manner. There was a fire escape that went up to the second floor. Periodically, the company held fire drills when the building had to be evacuated. The structure contained one single wooden staircase near the middle of the building and an elevator nearby.

On July 22, 1913, the calm world of this company came to an end. A fire broke out in the basement or first floor of the building near the stairway and spread onto stored clothing material. How the fire started has been the focus of much investigation. The history of the fire written by the granddaughter of the owner points much suspicion of arson by one employee who later was convicted of a similar crime in another city (Stevens, *Fire! The Story of the Binghamton Clothing Company Fire of July 22, 1913*). The fire quickly spread up the staircase that acted as a catalyst, pulling the flames up all four floors within a few minutes. A fire alarm was sounded in the building. Alice (Mrs. Reed) Freeman, the company secretary, made at least two calls to the Central Fire Station located one block away from the fire.

Workers were told to evacuate, but some thought this was just another fire drill. Many of the women employees tended to remove their long woolen skirts when they were working because of the heat, and when they went outside, male employees from nearby companies often jeered at them. They held back to be sure of the alarm. Other women left the building only to return to retrieve their purses and personal items. They found themselves trapped by the quickly spreading fire. Some attempted to jump out of the third- and fourth-story windows, only to fall through flames or be killed or horribly injured from the fall. Others were trapped inside and had no way to escape once the staircase collapsed in the flames.

170 PARTNERS ALL: A HISTORY OF BROOME COUNTY, NEW YORK

In less than fifteen minutes, the fire had engulfed the building and much of structure fell into a smoldering ruin. Of the one hundred employees known to be in the building at the time of the fire, thirty-one died at the scene or within hours of the fire. Nineteen of the bodies could not be identified and were buried in a mass grave at Spring Forest Cemetery in Binghamton. An investigation cleared the owners of any wrongdoing but resulted in regulations that required fire escapes on all floors and the installation of sprinkler systems in factories. Reed Freeman was a broken man and spent his remaining years trying to raise funds to repay the families of the victims.

On July 8, 1935, a series of torrential thunderstorms headed into the Ithaca region. The Chenango River valley had been experiencing a drought, and the river measured less than two feet deep that morning. The storms dumped a tremendous amount of water on the Central New York region in a matter of hours. The water caused streams and brooks to become torrents, pushing the rivers up at an alarming rate. Little or no warning was sent out to the residents of the area as the floodwaters pushed southward toward Broome County. One

This area is blessed with a number of "gold dome" churches representing the variety of ethnic groups in the community. Churches like the Holy Spirit Byzantine Church on Clinton Street (top left), St. Stanislaus Kostka (now Church of the Holy Trinity) on Prospect Street (bottom), and St. John the Baptist Ukrainian Orthodox Church in Johnson City (top right) help to keep their heritages alive. (Courtesy Broome County Historical Society)

by one, communities were hit by the onslaught of the flood. Lisle, Whitney Point, Chenango Forks, Chenango Bridge, Binghamton, Johnson City, Endicott, and Vestal were all struck. Barns and houses were ripped off their foundations. Cars were swept away. In Binghamton, travelers were stopped from going across the Ferry Street Bridge only fifteen minutes before the raging water undermined the bridge abutments. It collapsed into the Chenango River now fourteen feet deep. Downstream, the O'Day house on Front Street toppled into the river and was smashed against the Court Street Bridge.

As the flood subsided a few days later, the community began to recover from a disaster that caused $1.6 million in damage to Broome County. Worse than the monetary damage was the loss of human life. Eighteen people died during the flood, including many who were swept away from their homes or cars. Entire families had been killed. Over fifty people died in the entire flood-hit region. Within a few days, pleas went out for better flood control. By 1936, there was a call to build a dam for protection from future floods. A new steel bridge was soon under construction over the Chenango River to replace the Ferry Street Bridge. Work on this bridge had been stopped because of the winter when another disaster hit the region.

Only eight months after the worst flood in Broome County history, another deluge brought

The First World War was not popular with many citizens, but everyone celebrated when the war ended. This 1918 photograph shows a parade down Clinton Street and includes such diverse groups as the Workmen of the World United and the Socialist Party marching together. (Courtesy Broome County Historical Society)

destruction to the area. On March 17, 1936, a steady rain had been falling on the thawing ice of the winter. As the ice broke up and formed ice jams in many places, the waters from the

Opposite page: The call for troops during World War I was answered as can be seen in this photograph of men headed toward the trains that would take them to boot camp. (Courtesy Broome County Historical Society)

rain caused the rivers to rise above the ice jams significantly. This time, the worst flooding was on the path of the Susquehanna River. Again, major sections of Binghamton, Johnson City, and Endicott were flooded. Most of the bridges in Binghamton were closed, and the city's waterworks plant was threatened. Gas tanks

CHAPTER 9: WHICH WAY EJ?   173

The area's worst human disaster occurred in 1913 when the Binghamton Clothing Company was destroyed by fire. The Wall Street building was consumed in fifteen minutes, and thirty-one people lost their lives. The unidentified are buried in a mass grave in Spring Forest Cemetery. (Courtesy Broome County Historical Society)

located on the east side of Binghamton began to tip over as the ground softened and gave way. Sandbags prevented the possible explosion from the gas tanks. In the First Ward of Binghamton, many families had to be evacuated from their second floor windows by boat.

When the floodwaters finally receded, the community had suffered $1.35 million in damage. The new bridge under construction in Binghamton had been destroyed, and work had to begin again to build the new East Clinton Street Bridge. There was no loss of life in this flood because better warning had been given.

Yet, it did give credence to the need for better flood protection. Concrete floodwalls were placed along the Chenango and Susquehanna Rivers throughout the city of Binghamton. Plans were finally developed for the construction of an earthen dam on the Otselic River at Whitney Point. Both Governor Lehman of New York State and President Franklin D. Roosevelt visited the area to assess the damage and to ensure that adequate floor protection would be provided. The United States Army Corps of Engineers designed the dam, and the Whitney Point Reservoir was completed in 1947.

Torrential downpours that flooded the Chenango River area caused the July 1935 flood. Eighteen people lost their lives while bridges like the Ferry Street Bridge in Binghamton and many homes and businesses were destroyed. In March 1936, storms and ice jams caused major damage along the Susquehanna River area, but no lives were lost. (Courtesy Broome County Historical Society)

CHAPTER 10
The Rise of IBM
1936–1950

This is an aerial view of the IBM plants in Endicott. By the 1940s, IBM was quickly rising as a leading employer in the area. It was involved in the manufacture of typewriters, time clocks, and other business machines. (Courtesy Broome County Historical Society)

Thousands were working for IBM during World War II as seen in this photograph of employees of the firm on North Street in Endicott. (Courtesy Broome County Historical Society)

IF THE 1920s AND EARLY 1930s was the era of the growth of Endicott Johnson into a mega-industry, the period of the late 1930s and 1940s saw to the rise of IBM as the next predominant industry in the community. As the region began to emerge from the Great Depression in the late 1930s, the theory of Thomas J. Watson held true. Watson had speculated that once the country came out of the depression, companies would need new business equipment at a faster pace than previously.

New orders for typewriters, clocks, adding machines, and scales added to the sales volume of IBM. Thomas Watson was a firm leader. He, like George F. Johnson, disliked labor unions. He thought of them as disruptive to the efficient running of the business. He openly borrowed concepts of employee benefits from Endicott Johnson. IBM offered good wages and benefit packages to its employees. Each employee was encouraged to "THINK," which became the company motto. Watson had taken the Computing-Tabulating-Recording Company of 1914 and turned it into a very profitable and growing company in only a few years.

The world of International Business Machines was a male-dominated society until the outbreak of World War II. There were a few women working as typists and nurses and a few held factory positions, but nearly everyone else was a male dressed in white shirt and dark tie. It was also evident that the employees were overwhelmingly white, Anglo-Saxon,

One of the famous events of IBM was the 100 Percent Club Convention where hundreds of salesmen stayed in a "Tent City." It was located on the grounds of the IBM Homestead. (Courtesy Broome County Historical Society)

and Protestant. There was no written policy that Catholics, Jews, African Americans, and women were not to be hired, but it was an informal practice that was followed until the labor shortages brought on by World War II (Rodgers, *THINK: A Biography of the Watsons and IBM*). IBM was not alone in this practice, as William Rodgers writes:

Nor was the company distinguished by its exclusionary policy, which was practiced in much of the country, by both intention and oversights. IBM did not create this aspect of the American character; rather, it exemplified it and subscribed to it.

Indeed, similar practices could be found at Endicott Johnson during this same period.

The IBM Homestead was a private home before a fraternal organization bought it. In the 1930s, IBM purchased the home and used it for an educational center and apartment for Thomas J. Watson Sr. Today, it is part of the Traditions at the Glen golf course. (Courtesy Broome County Society)

Even in the original Endicott Johnson homes, the houses were technically leased and then sold back to the company to ensure that the homes were not sold to certain types of ethnic groups. This policy ended by the late 1920s, as the company faced the huge influx of many ethnic groups and their growing strength in the community.

While the Johnson family was interested in bringing merry-go-rounds, parks, and baseball to the community, the Watsons were interested in collecting art and cultivating culture. Thomas J. Watson never had a permanent home in the community. He rented a local apartment in his early years at IBM but quickly worked to establish the New York City area as the home base of the corporation. He built a large home in New Jersey for his family. When he did visit the area, he would stay at an apartment in the IBM Homestead. He worked diligently to move IBM away from the blue-collar image of EJ and toward the image of the quintessential white-collar company. The symbol of the company, the globe emblazoned with the letters IBM, epitomized the move of the company into international markets and away from area of the Triple Cities.

As technology changed, IBM was there as the company leading the change. The company's promotion of the electric typewriter beginning in 1933 helped make it an essential tool in the modern office. Watson promoted the constant evolution and adaptation of business equipment to meet the needs of the customers. IBM was able to continually transform itself while Endicott Johnson was not. EJ did not have the capability to move away from the staid technology of making shoes. Although the styles changed, the technology did not alter significantly during this period. It would be a problem that would seriously injure the company in future decades.

IBM was not the only company to grow during this period. The photographic history of the community began shortly after the invention of the photograph by Louis Daguerre in 1837. By the 1850s, a number of itinerant photographers were working in the area. Many would stay for only a few months or years before moving on to another location. In 1842, Edward Anthony had begun a photographic supply business in New York City. It merged with the Scovill Manufacturing Company in 1901, moved to Binghamton, and formed Ansco in 1907. By the second decade of the twentieth century, the company employed several hundred employees in the manufacture of cameras and film. In 1928, the company was sold to Agfa of Germany, and Agfa-Ansco was created. The First Ward company was the main competitor of the expanding Eastman Kodak Company of Rochester.

The benefits of working for IBM included the recreational opportunities, such as bowling, found at the IBM Country Club. (Courtesy Broome County Historical Society)

Link Aviation also grew steadily during the 1930s. Edwin Link continued to provide flying lessons to beginning pilots at Bennett Field in Binghamton, but his real love was for the manufacture of his "blue box." The pilot trainer was the first simulator that effectively trained pilots to fly before they flew actual

Thomas J. Watson Jr. took over the reins of IBM from his father and chaired its board from 1956 until 1971. He pushed the company toward the development of the computer. (Courtesy Broome County Historical Society)

airplanes. The United States Postal Service ordered ten of the trainers in the late 1930s to train airmail pilots.

In 1936, the Tri-Cities Airport was built in the town of Union near the village of Endicott. Broome County now had two airports to service the increasing air traffic of the Northeast. Link Aviation was ready for growth, but needed a catalyst that would propel the company to greatness.

In 1939, Adolf Hitler provided that catalyst. The German Army invaded Poland on September 1. Great Britain and France declared war on Germany two days later—the Second World War had begun. Although Franklin D. Roosevelt pledged to keep the United States neutral in the war, many of the country's residents realized that would be impossible. There were too many ties and alliances to Great Britain and France. Orders for war materials began to increase dramatically in 1939 and 1940. Roosevelt's Lend-Lease Act of 1941 only brought more alliances between the Allied Powers and the United States. Local companies were already contributing to the war effort. IBM was making and selling business equipment to both the Allied forces and Germany during the first few years of the war.

On Sunday, December 7, 1941, a wave of Japanese airplanes moved toward their target on the United States Naval Base at Pearl Harbor in Hawaii. The attack began shortly before eight o'clock in the morning and caught the base entirely off-guard. Within ninety minutes, the strike was over, leaving over twenty-four hundred dead and much of the naval fleet of the United States destroyed. Word of the attack reached the White House in the early afternoon (Eastern time), and then radio news agencies began the long series of bulletins to

> The development of air flight also led to the creation of airports in Broome County. In Binghamton, Bennett Field served the area while the Tri-Cities Airport in Endicott offered smaller planes a safe harbor from any storm. The airport also offered flight instruction. It still operates today. (Courtesy Broome County Historical Society)

alert the country of the attack. In Broome County, the word reached residents in many ways. In a movie theater, the film was stopped and an announcement was made. Everyone walked out dazed and went home. Radios blared announcements, but many people did not have their radios on in the afternoon. Neighbors called each other on their party-line telephones and spread the word. Before long, the county's population realized that their warm and protected world was forever changed.

Edwin A. Link (1904–1981) was the leading pioneer in the simulation industry. His invention of the flight trainer assisted thousands of pilots during World War II in learning how to fly. The company made ten thousand "blue boxes" during the war. (Courtesy Broome County Historical Society)

Departing soldiers would see this sign erected by Endicott Johnson at the Lackawanna railroad station to remind them that Binghamton would always be in their hearts and minds during World War II. Radio host Ralph Carroll is at the far right. (Courtesy Broome County Historical Society)

The next day, December 8, Franklin Roosevelt appeared before Congress. He declared that December 7 would be a "date which will live in infamy." Congress granted a declaration of war against Japan. Shortly thereafter, it voted to include Germany and Italy. The United States had entered the war. Local men quickly went to recruiting stations and enlisted in the military. Others were drafted in the largest military inscription in history. Thousands marched down to the Lackawanna train station in Binghamton to begin their service to protect their country.

At home, residents took up the charge of the government's challenge to start Victory gardens and become more self-reliant, freeing up food supplies for the troops. Others became trained in recognizing aircraft to ensure that another enemy attack would be detected. Thousands bought war bonds to help support the nation's fight to protect our country. In almost every community, there were scrap metal drives to collect valuable metal to make ships, airplanes, and bombs. A strange sight to many as they drove by was to see old fire engines, garbage cans, and other items piled high on the main streets in the towns and villages around Broome County. Shortages of gas, sugar, and other substances were handled with the War Ration Books that everyone carried.

Certain residents were exempt from military service because of their occupations. Many farmers were not called because of the food they grew. Nurses and doctors provided essential medical service to the thousands of

Laurella Barnum (Christensen), standing, and Marjory Barnum (Hinman), seated, were members of the local 4-H. They were trained to watch for enemy aircraft at a Civil Defense building on Oakdale Road in Johnson City. (Courtesy Broome County Historical Society)

wounded from the war. If it seemed that the country had been divided and disillusioned by the First World War, the nation's entrance to World War II was a rallying point for its citizens. Women signed up for service as nurses, WACs, WAVES, and as training and ferry pilots. They also entered the industrial workforce by the thousands. The image of Rosie the Riveter was certainly true in Broome County. Women took over many of the jobs vacated by the men at Endicott Johnson and IBM who had entered the armed forces.

Link Aviation suddenly became very important to the war effort. Link's flight simulator was crucial in the training of the pilots as they flew missions over Europe, Africa, and the Pacific. During the four years of the United States' war participation, Link Aviation manufactured ten thousand flight simulators. The company and its creator were credited with saving hundreds of lives of pilots and crewmembers that had trained with the Link invention. The war catapulted the company and its device into national prominence.

The Endicott Johnson Shoe Corporation made millions of pairs of combat boots for the armed services. The company continued to increase the number of employees during this period. At the height of the war, Endicott Johnson had nearly nineteen thousand workers. Every aspect of shoe manufacture was handled locally, from the tanning of the leather to the creation of cardboard boxes to ship the boots overseas. At nearby IBM, the company was involved in the design and construction of guidance systems and data systems for many of the armament systems used by the Army Air Corps and the Navy. This was the first time that IBM began to employ large numbers of women in the assembly line of the company.

Other companies produced a myriad of war products. Twenty-millimeter aircraft cannon, the M-1 carbine, three-inch gun parts, Browning guns, firelocks, hand grenade parts, and bomb-tail fuses were produced at various companies. The Drybak Corporation of Binghamton converted from manufacturing hunting clothes to making Navy pants and Army combat suits. In Westover, a suburb of Johnson City in the town of Union, the Defense Department purchased a large tract of land for the construction of a military plant. The Remington Rand Company leased the facility. Although the company had produced typewriters before the war, at the plant in Westover they created airplane propellers. The federal government also built the Army Medical Depot in the Hillcrest area of the town of Fenton.

Ansco made a number of products during the war, including a sextant, Driftmeter, Collinator, aerial photographic films, papers, printers, and a color film that could detect camouflage and be developed in the field (Hartzell, *The Empire State at War*). There was a serious problem at Ansco, however. In 1928, the company had become a part of the German I. G. Farben conglomerate as Agfa-Ansco. In 1939, it was combined with another Farben subsidiary, the General Aniline & Film Corporation (GAF).

Five days after the attack on Pearl Harbor, the United States government felt threatened by the German-based ownership of the camera

This is a photograph of the 730th M.P. Battalion marching in Albany in 1942. The battalion was stationed in Broome County to guard local bridges against sabotage. (From the *Claude Fawcett Collection*, courtesy Broome County Historical Society)

V-J Day in Broome County is celebrated with dancing in the street, as the community gives thanks for the end of hostilities during World War II. (Courtesy Broome County Historical Society)

company. The Alien Properties Commission seized the plant. Many of the German-born administrative officers of the company were taken out of the plant and not allowed to return. These included Leopold Eckler, the Austrian-born vice president of the company. The workers were upset at the removal of the popular leader of the firm and refused to come to work until he was allowed back. He was reinstated at a lower position within a week. Although the federal government seized other companies in the country because of the possible foreign threat to national security, it was the length of the seizure of Ansco that raised eyebrows. The government did not relinquish control of the company into private hands until 1965, over twenty years after it had been seized. The company was sold and again became part of General Aniline and Film.

From the beginning of the United States' war effort in 1941 until the conclusion of the war in 1945, over eighteen thousand residents of Broome County served in the armed services.

the "Greatest Generation." After horrific battles in Normandy, North Africa, Italy, and at the Battle of the Bulge, the fall of the Nazi empire occurred with the surrender of Germany on May 8, 1945. Three months later, on August 6, the *Enola Gay* B-29 bomber delivered a payload unlike no other in history. The first atomic bomb was dropped on the city of Hiroshima, Japan. In an instant, the city lay in ruins, and thousands lay dead. Three days later, a second bomb was dropped on Nagasaki. The Japanese empire surrendered on August 14, 1945.

The Second World War had ended. When all casualties were reported, the estimate of war dead was thirty-five million across the world. Another ten million Jews and others had perished in the concentration camps of

As the population increased in Broome County, so did the need for more schools. These are some of the students of the Benjamin Franklin Elementary School in Binghamton during 1933. (Courtesy Broome County Historical Society)

The centralization of most of the area's school districts in the 1930s and 1940s led to the creation of junior high schools. In Binghamton, the West Junior High School was built on former farmland. (Courtesy Broome County Historical Society)

They participated in every branch: Army, Army Air Corps, Navy, Marines, Coast Guard, and Merchant Marine. The men and women who fought for their country were truly members of

Nazi Germany. In Broome County, 642 residents died in military service to their country, including 2 women. Honor Roll boards had been erected in Binghamton, Johnson City, Endicott, Windsor,

The returning veteran came back to a world where college quickly became a necessity. The Triple Cities College opened in 1946 in Endicott as part of Syracuse University. The former Bowes home on Park Street became Colonial Hall. It is now the Endicott Visitor Center. (Courtesy Broome County Historical Society)

America traveled by bus, automobile, train, and airplane as mobility became easier after the end of World War II. The Greyhound Bus Station with its Art Deco exterior has been a landmark on Chenango Street in Binghamton for many decades. (Courtesy Broome County Historical Society)

and other locations to list those in military service. At the conclusion of the war, these temporary walls of names were taken down and mostly forgotten.

There was a concerted effort to move away from the war and to attempt to get society "back to normal." It was reported that there were five thousand jobs available in the shoe industry in Broome County. Housing was desperately needed for the returning veterans. On Macarthur Park on the south side of Binghamton, temporary housing was built using prefabricated corrugated steel Quonset huts from military surplus property. Dozens of veterans and their families now had a place to live. The housing would remain for the next decade.

The returning veterans not only needed housing but also training and education to allow them to re-enter the job market. The call for higher education continued until 1946 when Syracuse University decided to locate an associated facility in Endicott. Endicott Johnson provided

Life seemed to return to normal in the late 1940s, as people could enjoy a good movie at one of the many theaters in the area. Chenango Street, seen here, was blessed with the Strand, Riviera, Star, and Symphony Theaters. (Courtesy Broome County Historical Society)

land for the construction of Quonset huts to be used for classrooms, and IBM provided money for the transformation of the area around the former home of Alphonsus and Julia Bowes. The house was built in 1904 for Julia, the secretary of George F. Johnson. The home was renamed Colonial Hall and became the administration building of Triple Cities College.

In 1948, the school became a four-year institution. Classes were held in the Quonset huts as well as at nearby Union-Endicott High School. The library was housed in the former Harlow Bundy House. In March 1948, the college became part of the newly created State University of New York system. It soon became apparent that the college needed more space than was available at Endicott, but it would be several years before a new location could be determined.

In 1947, another facility for higher education was created. The New York State Institute for Applied Arts and Sciences opened in

Even the youngest farmers could help feed the residents of the area, especially if they were riding a BMC Tractor Junior. Owned by the Botnick family, the BMC Company made a number of products, including these peddle cars. (Courtesy Broome County Historical Society)

The need for larger government offices resulted in the construction of the George R. Harvey Justice Building. The Art Deco–style building offered more courtrooms and office space for the growing bureaucracy. At present, the building is unused. (Courtesy Broome County Historical Society)

the armory building on Washington Street in Binghamton. While Triple Cities College emphasized a liberal arts education, the new school provided essential college-level education aimed at the skills needed for many of the industrial jobs in the area. Shortly after opening, the school changed its name to Broome Technical Community College.

In 1948, George F. Johnson died at the age of ninety-one. Johnson had risen from a poor shoe worker with a sixth-grade education into a leader of a giant industry. He had become an advisor to presidents and corporate leaders and had developed a system of welfare capitalism that was unrivaled across the country. Endicott Johnson had effectively thwarted the development of labor unions because of its generous benefits programs. Johnson had created a corporate culture of paternalism that permeated the entire county.

Even if the work at Endicott Johnson was hard, the loyalty and love for George F. was ingrained in every worker and in his or her family. While Thomas J. Watson was the quintessential corporate leader of white-collar workers, Johnson represented the "everyman" image of the blue-collar worker. His funeral was held at Union-Endicott's Ty Cobb Stadium with ten thousand attendees. His death marked the ending of one chapter of the area's history and the beginning of another.

While George F. Johnson was gone, his former baseball team was not. The Triplets had become an integral part of the farm team system of the New York Yankees. Each year, the Yankees would play an exhibition game against the Triplets at Johnson Field. The baseball field was located next to the first Endicott Johnson housing project. It had a short right field, which made hitting home runs a bit easier than at some other fields. When Babe Ruth came up at bat on his first visit to Johnson Field, he delivered a home run that went out of the park. Many baseball players destined for long careers in the sport played with the Triplets. In 1949, Ed "Whitey" Ford played for the Triplets, helping them to win the championship that year. Mickey Mantle was scheduled to play for the Triplets but was moved directly into the major league team before he could play a single game in Johnson City.

Regular radio broadcasting had started in 1929 with WNBF in Binghamton. Radio played an important role in providing daily entertainment and news to the area residents. In 1946, Endicott welcomed its first radio station. But at the conclusion of the Second World War, the country was moving toward a new technology—television. Television had been around for a number of years, but regular operations did not begin until the conclusion of

Edwin Arthur Hall represented Broome County in the House of Representatives during the 1940s and 1950s. The maverick Republican from Binghamton became a popular favorite with the people but not with his party. He quit politics and led a secluded life after leaving Washington. (Courtesy Broome County Historical Society)

A familiar face to broadcasting, Ralph Carroll entertained thousands with his daily radio show on WNBF radio starting in the 1930s. He later also hosted his own television show, Carroll's Caravan, in the 1960s. (Courtesy Broome County Historical Society)

the war. As the decade of the 1940s came to a close, the area joined in the modern world of broadcast media.

In 1949, WNBF began regular television broadcasts. The shows often lasted for only fifteen minutes, and the station was on the air only a few hours a day. But the popularity of the new medium took off. People clustered around neighbors' television sets to watch early programs such as *Milton Berle* or *Kukla, Fran and Ollie*. Local broadcasts focused on the issues of the day such as interviews with Binghamton mayor Donald Kramer. Television brought the world into the homes of Broome County. Television may have been a "vast wasteland," but it connected all parts of the globe to one another. No longer isolated by the hills and valleys of the area, Broome County was a direct participant in the affairs of the country.

While the end of the Second World War brought peace back to the country, it did not bring the sense of calm for which many had hoped. The dropping of the atomic bombs had dashed that hope. If the Americans could develop the technology to split the atom and release almost immeasurable energy and destruction, how long before another country such as the Soviet Union could do the same?

In 1950, fire claimed the Moon Block on the corner of Chenango and Lewis Streets in Binghamton. The elegant structure was demolished, and a diner car took its place for a short time. It is now the site of the U-Haul Rental Company. (Courtesy Broome County Historical Society)

Diners did not have to wear wooden shoes, but they would have fit in at the Dutch Mill Restaurant located in the town of Chenango. Joseph Hauptfuehaer owned the unique eatery. It burned down twice before being replaced with what became Morey's Restaurant. (Courtesy Broome County Historical Society)

While the United States had allied with the Soviet Union to defeat Germany, it was, at best, an uneasy alliance. The Soviets, under the control of the brutal Joseph Stalin, were not considered trustworthy. The spread of Communism appeared to be a real threat to democratic societies in Europe. Foreign policy in the Truman administration was under the control of Secretary of State John Foster Dulles. His belief in the threat of the Communist bloc and the "domino theory" would influence the direction of the country for the next twenty-five years. However well intentioned, it prevented many companies from reverting to peacetime activities and moved others toward a continuous wartime level.

CHAPTER 11
The Valley That Came In from the Cold
1950–1968

The Broome County Airport began operations from Mount Ettrick in the 1950s. The new facility greatly eased the growing air traffic coming into the region. Today, the facility is called the Greater Binghamton Regional Airport. (Courtesy Broome County Historical Society)

In 1962, demolition began in Binghamton to make way for the construction of North Shore Drive. In this photograph, homes were torn down at Carroll and South Streets. The highway took out several streets and disrupted many lives. (Courtesy Broome County Historical Society)

ON JUNE 25, 1950, COMMUNIST North Korea invaded South Korea, capturing the capital city of Seoul. General Douglas MacArthur was placed in charge of the United Nations forces that began to battle with both the North Korean and later the Chinese Communist forces to regain the sovereignty of the South Korean nation. The Korean War had begun, ending less than five years of peace for the United States. The invasion by Communist forces added to the "domino theory" as defined by John Foster Dulles.

In Broome County, the Cold War was reflected in efforts to thwart Communism wherever it reared its head. Link Aviation was sold to become part of General Aviation. Edwin A. Link had made a decision to step away from aviation and devote more time to deep-sea oceanography. The direction of General Aviation followed the trend of many area industries that tried to obtain government contracts to provide goods and services essential to the Cold War efforts.

Increasingly during this period, companies such as IBM, Universal Instruments, and General Aviation relied on government contracts to sustain the growth of the firms. Thousands of workers were employed in top-secret projects. Remington Rand vacated its plant in Westover, but the facility was soon taken over by General Electric. The firm was busily engaged in the development of guidance systems for military aircraft and missiles.

198   PARTNERS ALL: A HISTORY OF BROOME COUNTY, NEW YORK

The spread of Communism meant the spread of government contracts as the federal system sought new military weapons, better airplanes, and clothing and boots for the military. For the first time in the nation's history, a wartime draft did not end at the conclusion of the Second World War. Young men were still receiving letters that started "Greetings from Uncle Sam," and Endicott Johnson continued to manufacture military boots into the mid-1950s. EJ reached its height of employment in the area in 1951 with 20,909 workers (Zahavi). Endicott Johnson made shoes in not only Broome County but also in former shoe facilities in Pennsylvania and distributing facilities across the country, making the shoe manufacturing firm one of the largest in the nation.

Returning veterans began to marry, and these new families added to the baby boom that had begun in the late 1940s. In turn, these new families and new arrivals that came to work in the burgeoning industries of the Cold War added to Broome County's population. The Census Bureau estimated that by 1953 Broome County had a population of nearly 200,000 and the city of Binghamton residents numbered 83,000. It appeared that the Valley

The General Electric plant at Westover in the town of Union was instrumental in the development of many guidance systems and engine systems such as the A-R System in this photograph. The plant is now operated by BAE Systems. (Courtesy Broome County Historical Society)

of Opportunity was growing at a rapid pace. Many of the new residents were no longer required to live next to the factories and businesses. Better transportation and highway systems allowed workers to live farther from their workplace.

In March 1951, the Vestal Avenue arterial highway bypass opened. The new Vestal Parkway had been built partially atop a section of the former Chenango Canal extension. It allowed for more and faster automobile travel between Binghamton and the rural bedroom community of Vestal. In that same year, the Broome County Airport opened atop Mount Ettrick. Larger aircraft and increased air traffic

required long runways that could not be accommodated at the out-of-date Bennett Field. The new airport offered a modern terminal building with a restaurant and game room.

Residents moved to new ranch-style homes in recently created housing developments such as the Stair Tract in Vestal, or onto new streets in Kirkwood, Conklin, Chenango, Union, and other locations near the urban area. These suburbs offered more land and the attractiveness of lower taxes. There was also less traffic for the families driving one of the thousands of new automobiles coming out of Detroit. Prosperity was no longer just around the corner—it seemed to have arrived.

The election of Dwight D. Eisenhower in 1952 added to this feeling. The respected leader of the former Allied forces brought a sense of calm to the White House. Eisenhower promoted the development of the Interstate Highway System. These highways would connect all of the urban areas of the country to allow for faster and more efficient movement of freight and goods using the newly developed tractor-trailers. The new superhighways promised to be a boon to the areas where they went through. It was thought that travelers would stop at these cities and towns on the way to their final destinations.

The prosperity of the 1950s was a welcome change from the struggles of the Great Depression and the rations and war bonds of the Second World War. The freshness of television added to the image of the family-oriented America. With wholesome shows like *Ozzie and Harriet, Donna Reed, I Love Lucy*, and *Your Show of Shows*, the country was entertained and amused with little threat to the nation's morals. Unfortunately, below the seemingly serene surface simmered the seeds of unrest and dissent.

In Washington, DC, Senator Joseph McCarthy saw the threat of Communism as pervasive throughout every corner of American society. McCarthy was a complex man who sought to do what he deemed best to save the country while feeding his own need to further his power and notoriety. Using the forum of the Permanent Investigations Subcommittee of the Senate Committee on Government Operations in 1954, the "McCarthy Committee" attacked the alleged spy ring on one army base. For the next four weeks, McCarthy used the televised hearings to attack much of the army system. He implied that Communists had infiltrated much of the military, as well as other parts of the American system. What started with a small flame of reality degenerated into smoke with no substance in fact. Finally, McCarthy went too far

> Opposite page: Link Aviation underwent many ownership changes in the last forty years, but it has continued to develop simulation systems used by the military and NASA. Today, its Kirkwood plant is part of L-3 Communications. (Courtesy Broome County Historical Society)

Ozalid was a subsidiary of General Aniline and Film. The firm was located in Vestal and continued until the 1980s when, like many of the other firms involved in Cold War contracts, it closed. Today, the site is the location of Parkway Plaza. (Courtesy Broome County Historical Society)

and tried to impugn the reputation of a young attorney, a member of the army's counsel. McCarthy showed himself for the inhumane bully he had become. Edward R. Murrow of CBS News used the strength of television to destroy the vestiges of power to which McCarthy clung. Although "McCarthyism" may have ended at that moment, the fear of Communism lingered in the American mind.

The Civil Defense program became a serious part of American society and its education system. Plans for the construction of bomb shelters were widely distributed to American homeowners. These personal concrete fortresses against the "A-bomb" were dug into backyards or built in countless basements across the nation. Many of these were built in Broome County where employees were actively involved in Cold War industries and felt the threat of total annihilation. It was widely reported that Binghamton was high on the list of sites that would be hit by an atomic bomb if the Soviet Union took the first step toward nuclear war.

In Broome County schools, students were trained in the "duck and cover" method of protection. Drills were a regular part of student life. Radio stations played air raid drills using realistic sounds of bombs dropping and cities being destroyed to encourage residents to protect themselves. The government practiced a mass evacuation of portions of eastern Broome County to demonstrate that entire areas could be moved in the event of war.

In Endicott, Triple Cities College underwent a name change in 1950 as it emerged as a growing liberal arts school. It was dedicated as Harpur College at a ceremony presided by Governor Thomas Dewey. The name was chosen for Robert Harpur, professor at King's College (Columbia University), and the secretary of the New York State Land Board in the 1700s, whose home was in Harpursville in the town of Colesville.

The area's other institution of higher learning survived near destruction. On Labor Day 1951, a large fire broke out at the Washington Street Armory in Binghamton. The building was destroyed, and one fireman lost his life trying to save the home of Broome Technical

Community College. The school moved up Washington Street to "Fraternity Row" and occupied the former Kalurah Temple building for several years. But it was evident that both colleges needed space in which to expand.

In 1954, land in the town of Vestal was selected as the future home of Harpur College. The tract included the Vestal Hills Country Club, requiring the golf course to be relocated to town of Binghamton. Plans for the development of the campus began with a series of buildings built in a quad pattern. In that same year, Broome Technical Community College purchased land in the town of Dickinson, adjacent to the Broome County Poor Farm. This campus was also laid out in the quad pattern. It opened for classes in 1957.

In 1954, Roberson Memorial opened in Binghamton. The new museum occupied the former home of lumber merchant Alonzo Roberson and his wife, Margaret. The couple had left the home to the community to be a center for the promotion of art, history, and science. Keith Martin was hired as the first director of this new institution. The Binghamton Museum of Fine Arts vacated its quarters at the Binghamton Public Library,

Triple Cities College outgrew its Endicott campus by the 1950s and moved to the town of Vestal by the 1960s. It also changed its name to the State University of New York at Binghamton. Today, Binghamton University hosts over fifteen thousand students each year. (Courtesy Broome County Historical Society)

CHAPTER 11: THE VALLEY THAT CAME IN FROM THE COLD

and the Broome County Historical Society left their history rooms in the Broome County Courthouse to become two of the first five constituent groups to form the core of the Roberson Memorial Museum. Martin and his wife, Laura, promoted a wide array of displays and educational programs, including television, to promote the new museum. Martin appeared on Saturday morning television with a fifteen-minute program called *Treasure House* to interest young children in the collections of the museum.

The area's second television station, WINR, went on the air in 1955. Area broadcasts became longer, with news programming as well as children's shows becoming a staple of Broome County family life during this time. Television shows originally used radio broadcasters to supplement their staff. Ralph Carroll, who had been broadcasting on the radio since the early 1930s, easily moved into the new medium with *Carroll's Caravan*. Another area broadcaster, Bill Parker, launched a fifty-year career on radio but did double duty with children's programming in the 1950s and 1960s with shows like *TV Ranch Club* and the *Officer Bill Show*.

In the early 1950s, the leaders of IBM were seeking new technologies in data retrieval to market. Thomas J. Watson Jr. had sought his father's permission to develop an electronic computer. The new technology sought to develop a device to hold large amounts of data that could be used to create answers to myriads of problems. Although IBM was not the first to develop the computer, it was the first to successfully market its potential. The company was in competition with other firms, such as Remington Rand, owner of the UNIVAC (Universal Automatic Computer). The new mainframe computers

A 1951 Labor Day fire destroyed the Washington Street Armory, killed a fireman, and left Broome Community College without a home. The school later moved to a new campus in the town of Dickinson where it continues to operate more than a half-century later. (Courtesy Broome County Historical Society)

occupied an entire room and sorted data using punch cards at first, before developing magnetic tapes and disks to hold the data. By 1960, IBM had established itself as the leader in the industry.

In 1957, the Soviet Union launched the Sputnik satellite. The reaction of the United States government was immediate. It created the National Aeronautics and Space Administration to develop a rival space program. Contracts to develop guidance systems, computer programs, and weapon systems went to a number of area firms. IBM became integrally involved in NASA's Mercury, Gemini, and Apollo missions. Link simulators were used to train the astronauts to operate complex space vehicles. General Electric developed guidance systems used in the space program.

Ansco, which had languished under the control of the federal government since World War II, was released to private control in 1965. It was split into two companies. Ozalid was located in Vestal and Johnson City and made photographic papers. General Aniline and Film (GAF) purchased the other portion of the company. The Ansco name was kept on many cameras and on film products. The company also received a number of government contracts during this period. The firm produced much of the film and technology used in

Many local merchants began to worry when chain stores moved into the valley. Stores such as Acme Markets, Neisner's, and Montgomery Ward, seen here in 1951 on Main Street in Binghamton, moved the retail market away from traditional family-owned ventures. (Courtesy Broome County Historical Society)

NASA's Gemini and Apollo programs. Many of the best-known lunar photographs were produced on Ansco film.

In 1957, a not-so-innocent barbeque altered America's perception of crime. Joseph Barbara was the owner of the local Canada Dry distribution and a beer distributorship in Endicott. His home was located in Apalachin in Tioga County. Barbara was also alleged to be a high-ranking official in the Mafia. Barbara was asked to host a barbeque with representatives of various Mafia families to settle territories and to quell some rising tensions between the factions. Although the gathering was supposed to have been a secret, the word was out to many families in western Broome County to stay away from that area.

A state trooper investigating a fraudulent check charge at the Vestal Motel saw several suspicious cars parked there and found one

Beccye Fawcett was the first African American employee in any of the Broome County area libraries. She remained an employee of the Binghamton Public Library for several decades and was an influential proponent of civil rights. (Courtesy Broome County Historical Society)

of them belonged to Barbara's son. Calling in local police officials and, eventually, the FBI, the trooper trailed the cars to the barbeque. Surrounding the home, the police raided the outing. Men were seen fleeing through windows and across fields. Within a few hours, sixty-four leaders of the Mafia had been taken into custody. The problem with the raid was that none of the men detained were doing anything illegal. The men were released, but not before FBI leader J. Edgar Hoover had to admit for the first time that an organized crime syndicate was at work in the United States. Some of the leaders like Anthony "Guv" Guarnieri lived in the Endicott area before moving up in the Mafia's structure.

If the population of Broome County seemed to flourish during the 1950s, there were clear signs of change by the beginning of the next decade. The number of African Americans in Broome County was on the rise. In 1950, there were only 855 African Americans in the county. By 1960, the number had increased over 50 percent to 1,290. The movement of African Americans to the urban areas of the northeastern United States was in direct response to the increasing industrial base of the cities. Meanwhile, although many of the area's residents continued to work in Binghamton, Johnson City, and Endicott, they were choosing in greater numbers not to live there. Binghamton's population fell for the first time. The suburbs were on the rise.

Another major change was in the leadership of its largest employers. Endicott Johnson began to suffer a series of losses in the late 1950s. Much of this loss was due to the influx of foreign-made shoes into the country. Many of the American shoe manufacturers asked the federal government to establish tariffs against imported shoes to protect the shoemakers' interests. Both the Eisenhower and Kennedy administrations refused to agree to any tariff terms. In 1957, Charles A. "Mr. Charlie" Johnson suffered a stroke. Frank Johnson, George F.'s grandson, replaced him. Three years later, in 1960, the company suffered a $1.5 million loss. The board decided to replace Johnson with Pasquale J. Casella, a former executive with RCA (Zahavi). In 1961, the company suffered a $12 million loss; Eli White replaced Casella in 1963. The era of the Johnsons was over.

Thomas J. Watson Sr. passed away in 1956. His son, Thomas J. Watson Jr., assumed control of the firm. It had rapidly moved away from building time clocks and had entered the computer age. As Endicott Johnson began to fail and decrease its number of employees in the late 1950s and early 1960s, IBM increased its workforce. While the electric typewriter was still a staple of the company, it moved further into the world of transistors and computer circuit boards. New IBM factories were being constructed along the North Street area in Endicott, at a new site at Glendale on the western edge of the town of Union, and at a major new complex at Owego in Tioga County.

In 1960, General Aviation sold the Link division to the Singer Corporation. The change in ownership was the beginning of a decades-long trend, moving area industries away from local control and toward national ownership of local firms. The company continued to make flight simulators, expanding from airplanes to include helicopter simulators. Its operations were diversified into sectors for military operations

Television came to the area in 1949 with WNBF-TV. In this photograph, a cooking show is being aired from the Arlington Hotel. Today, the county supports four television stations, as well as a cable system that airs over one hundred channels. (Courtesy Broome County Historical Society)

and commercial operations. This was another indication of the area's reliance on the Cold War.

The period from the late 1950s and through the 1960s was an era of new school buildings in Broome County. The Binghamton City School District erected the Macarthur, Calvin Coolidge, Horace Mann, and Theodore Roosevelt elementary schools during this time. Many other school buildings were constructed in the outlying districts to match the increase in suburban population. Chenango Forks, Chenango Valley, Harpursville, Maine-Endwell, Susquehanna Valley, Vestal, Union-Endicott, Whitney Point, and Windsor all built new schools.

On March 6, 1962, a can of salt was mistakenly labeled as sugar in the maternity ward of

CHAPTER 11: THE VALLEY THAT CAME IN FROM THE COLD   207

In 1963, the first national fast-food restaurant, McDonald's, opened its first eatery on State Street in Binghamton. It was an indication of the area's increasing reliance on national chains of stores and businesses. F. W. Woolworth had been a part of the national chain of five-and-ten-cent stores since the late 1800s, but in 1950 they built a larger facility on the corner of State and Court Streets in Binghamton. The store demolished the older Exchange Hotel that had been constructed during the era of the Chenango Canal. Kresge's built a new store in 1947 directly across from the Woolworth store. The era of the chain department store had begun in Broome County. By 1965, the Kresge store had changed to the Jupiter Department Store before closing. Kresge's did not disappear altogether. It reappeared under a new name, Kmart, opening in strip plazas across the area.

Tom Cawley was a reporter and columnist for the *Binghamton Press* for four decades. His daily stories of life in the community brought pleasure and humor into everyone's lives. (Courtesy Broome County Historical Society)

Binghamton General Hospital. The substance was used to mix the formula fed to newborn infants. The babies quickly became ill and dehydrated. Doctors were at a loss as to the cause. By the time the discovery was made, six of the infants had died. The case of the "Salt Babies" made the national newscasts, including a broadcast by a new reporter for CBS News, Dan Rather. An investigation revealed that it was simple error that had caused the calamity, and new measures were put in place to prevent a future tragedy.

As the population of the Binghamton area began to decrease, local officials looked to find answers to revitalize the city. Many saw a city filled with older Victorian-era architecture and tired-looking houses. Binghamton, especially downtown Binghamton, was no longer able to attract new businesses and residents. Many urban centers in the northeastern United States experienced the same problems. Many of these cities sought to remedy their dilemma by looking to the federal government for assistance. That assistance came in the form of urban renewal. The concept was simple: tear

The problem of an aging population base was met with the development of retirement and nursing home facilities. Elizabeth Church Manor on Front Street in the town of Dickinson was one such facility. Today, Broome County plans to replace its aging Willow Point Manor. (Courtesy Broome County Historical Society)

down the older, dilapidated structures and clear the way for the construction of new buildings that would be more attractive to business development.

In 1964, Binghamton became part of this program, which the Urban Renewal Agency was created to oversee. Planners, leading businessmen, and others were tasked to develop a master plan for the downtown area. Groups such as the Valley Development Corporation were created to use federal funds to identify areas of urban blight and develop new uses for those sites. While the plan seemed sound, there were two major problems with the program. The existing businesses in buildings targeted for demolition were forced to relocate or to close, and although there were federal funds to demolish buildings, there was very little money available to rebuild on those sites.

The other problem with what many have now termed "urban removal" was that it disrupted a number of residential neighborhoods and destroyed many reusable structures. One of the large areas affected included the former

Robert F. Kennedy ran for United States senator from New York with the help of his campaign manager, former Binghamton mayor John Burns, seen here. Kennedy would later seek the presidency, but an assassin's bullet killed him in 1968. (Courtesy Broome County Historical Society)

On Labor Day in 1952, students and educators took a relaxing moment from their studies at Union-Endicott High School to enjoy water-skiing on the Susquehanna. (Courtesy Broome County Historical Society)

Millville area of Binghamton, along the north side of the Susquehanna River. North Shore Drive was planned to connect the Brandywine Highway with the Memorial Bridge and Riverside Drive. The development of the drive took out a number of streets populated by mainly Italian and African American families. An entire block was removed nearby for the construction of a central location for city, county, and state office buildings. Over one hundred homes and businesses were removed for the Government Plaza. Adjacent to this property was the former Weed's Tannery, later used as the Endicott Johnson BBB Factory (Binghamton Busy Boys), the George F. Johnson Factory, and the Binghamton Police Station (the former Union Free

In 1963, Timba the lion killed an attendant at the Ross Park Zoo. Both Timba and its mate, Tina, were later destroyed. It was four decades before lions once again made an appearance at the zoo. (Courtesy Broome County Historical Society)

School). These and several other buildings were demolished to make way for an arena. The arena had been planned since the late 1940s as a memorial to the veterans of World War II, but plans had sat unused for two decades.

Along the Chenango River, the buildings that had held a number of cigar factories were taken down, leaving a large empty pit. Nearby, plans called for the demolition of both the Arlington Hotel and the Carlton Hotel on Chenango Street. The Arlington Hotel was considered to be the premier hotel in the area. It had been built in 1887 and contained the beautiful Spanish Ballroom. Conventions, railroad passengers, newcomers to the city, and permanent residents used both hotels. The Arlington Hotel had been home to WNBF radio and television stations. Despite the protests of many residents, the Carlton was demolished in 1966 and the Arlington in 1969. The site of the Carlton is now a postal building with a parking lot on the site of the Arlington. These demolitions alerted residents that the program was not fulfilling its promise to revitalize the city. It merely made Binghamton look a bit like London after the blitzkrieg.

On November 22, 1963, while riding in a motorcade in Dallas aimed at increasing support for his 1964 presidential reelection bid, President John F. Kennedy was assassinated. His death shocked the nation and seemed to end its naiveté about the issues of society. There were storm clouds on the horizon, and the deluge was just beginning. The issue of civil rights had been stirring since the 1950s and the Supreme Court decision in *Brown vs. the Board of Education* (1954) that promulgated the desegregation of schools. Rosa Parks refused to sit in the rear of the bus in 1955 and triggered the Montgomery bus boycott in Alabama. In 1963, 250,000 attended the march on Washington, DC, led by the Reverend Martin Luther King Jr. The next year, the Civil Rights Act was signed into law, but not before a number of violent acts had been committed, including the murders of Medgar Evers and other civil rights workers.

A busy day in downtown Binghamton can be seen in this photograph of Court Street near the Kresge store. Today, the building is the home of a branch office of HSBC Bank. (Courtesy Broome County Historical Society)

The civil rights movement reached Broome County in the person of William Moore. Moore had been a postman in Binghamton who had spent time in the State Hospital for schizophrenia. After his release, he wrote a book entitled *The Mind in Chains*. Moore felt deeply for the plight of African Americans in the Southern states. He went on a one-man civil rights march to meet the governor of Mississippi and plead for the end to segregation. On his way through Alabama, a gunman took his life. Moore's name is listed among the civil rights martyrs on the memorial in Selma, Alabama.

The conflict in Vietnam escalated quickly in the early 1960s. What had been originally perceived as an effort for the Vietnamese to shake off the shackles of their colonial period became another conflict of Communism versus the rest of the world. By the time of the death of John F. Kennedy, the conflict had risen from a few military advisors to armed servicemen fighting to protect the interests of the South Vietnam government. The Gulf of Tonkin resolution in 1964 gave the administration of Lyndon Johnson almost a free hand to confront North Vietnam. But what had been predicted to be a quick war to reduce the Communist threat and establish a strong South Vietnam soon became a quagmire in which the United States government could not find solid ground. While various attempts were made to bring some type of conclusion to the war, United States soldiers were dying, and resentment toward the war was rising at home.

Protests against the war increased as the conflict continued. The demonstrations had started in major urban areas and were often linked to college campuses such as Berkeley. But as public opinion polls showed growing uneasiness about the war, protests spread to smaller areas. In Broome County, many of the demonstrations were staged on the campus of the newly built State University Center at Binghamton (Harpur College) in Vestal. As the college protests continued, it increased local opinion of the campus as a hotbed of "liberal thinkers." Marches were also held in Binghamton, and demonstrations were held in front of the Federal Building on Henry Street.

This was not the only change that Broome County experienced during this period. Great changes in transportation and business were also taking place during the last half of the 1960s. The Penn-Can Highway was under construction. It was planned as an interstate highway that would go across Pennsylvania and through New York to end in Canada. It reached the New York State border in the town of Kirkwood in 1961. Construction of the highway through Binghamton forced the removal of two streets and adjoining homes as it made its way toward the north.

At the same time, a new Route 17 Expressway was being built with an eventual plan to convert that roadway to an interstate highway. The route chosen for the highway forced the removal of Johnson Field in 1968. It also ended the Triplets baseball team and its long association with the New York Yankees.

The two highways converged on the edge of Mount Prospect, creating an intersection that quickly became known as "Kamikaze Curve" because of the large number of accidents in that section of the highway. The new highways succeeded in speeding up the flow of traffic, but they failed to live up to the expectations that some of that traffic would funnel into the

Henry's Hamburgers was located on Main Street in the city of Binghamton. It was the first fast-food restaurant in the area and opened a second facility in 1963 (seen here) on the George F. Highway next to Endwell Rugs. (Courtesy Broome County Historical Society)

A nearly deserted Lackawanna Station marks the passing of an era in Broome County. The end to passenger railroad service came in 1966 with the last trip of the Phoebe Snow train. (Photograph by Ira Current, courtesy Broome County Historical Society)

A sign of the passage of time can be seen in loss of the drive-in movie theater. The Endwell Drive-In on the George F. Highway in the town of Union has been removed, as have all of the Broome County drive-ins. (Courtesy Broome County Historical Society)

cake was wheeled out for the hundreds in attendance. While local officials touted the proud history of Binghamton and the surrounding area, signs of change were all around the audience. Urban renewal had destroyed much of the intrinsic architecture of the community. Sisson Brothers and Welden department store had closed in 1963 after ninety years of operation. Nearby, the Hill, McLean and Haskins store was beginning to show signs of wear. At the end of Collier Street, the new government plaza was under construction.

In business, change was also altering the established structure of the area. The Endicott Johnson Shoe Corporation continued to lose funds. It suffered from the competition of low-priced foreign shoes as well as from its own management. The company was also hurt by its inability to alter its product line. Endicott Johnson had staved off a takeover attempt in 1961, in which current and former employees purchased thousands of shares of stock to prevent the sale. By 1968, interest in keeping the company in local hands was

urban area. Instead, travelers tended to bypass local hamlets, villages, and cities on their way to their final destinations.

In 1967, the city of Binghamton celebrated it centennial with an elaborate ceremony in front of City Hall on Collier Street. A large birthday

not as strong, and EJ was sold to an outside firm. The community had lost financial control of its leading employer of the previous seventy years.

In April 1968, while standing on a hotel balcony waiting to participate in a march in

Memphis, the Reverend Martin Luther King Jr. was assassinated. As the horrible shock of the loss of the civil rights leader was absorbed by the nation, it experienced another shock in June when Robert F. Kennedy, the brother of slain president John F. Kennedy and senator from New York State, was struck down in a hotel kitchen after winning the California primary in his bid for the presidency.

The Binghamton Press left its home in the Press Building in 1965 to move to a new structure built across from the State University on the Vestal Parkway. In 1968, the Montgomery Ward department store, which had already moved from downtown Binghamton to Main Street, announced that it would be moving to a new store in a planned mall in the Oakdale section of Johnson City. Binghamton Plaza, the first shopping plaza in the area, had opened on State Street in 1964. It was built as a strip plaza, with all the stores in a line, requiring shoppers to step outdoors between stores. The Vestal Plaza opened on the Vestal Parkway a few years later, followed by Campus Plaza a bit farther west. The news of the Oakdale Mall construction across from the newly built Route 17 Expressway further shook the retail and business sectors of Broome County. The decade of the 1960s had come in with the hopes of stabilizing the population base, revitalizing the urban corridor, and helping traditional businesses. By the end of 1968, it was clear that the winds of change had become a tornado.

Governor Nelson Rockefeller (center) receives advice from Mayor Joseph Esworthy of Binghamton (at right). Rockefeller would later serve as vice president to Gerald Ford. (Courtesy Broome County Historical Society)

CHAPTER 11: THE VALLEY THAT CAME IN FROM THE COLD

CHAPTER 12
The Decline of Industry
1968–1995

Urban renewal changed the look of Binghamton forever. One of the completed projects was the construction of the Treadway Inn (now Holiday Inn-Arena) on Hawley Street. (Courtesy Broome County Historical Society)

RESIDENTS AND POLITICIANS could not quell the spiral of change. The change was too great, and it came too quickly. Also, it was not contained within the borders of Broome County. Many of the developments in this area were mirrored in other communities of the Northeast. Change came in many areas. The agricultural sector of the economy had been an important part of the life in Broome County since its creation. But since the end of World War II, this sector had been undergoing change.

At the conclusion of the Second World War, there were thousands of farms located within Broome County. Most of these were family farms where the children helped to keep the farms operating. Many were dairy operations with hundreds of head of Holstein, Hereford, and other breeds. Farmers also raised beef cattle, pigs, sheep, and chickens. Some farms' operations focused on crop cultivation. Wheat, oats, corn, squash, tomatoes, and potatoes were among the more common crops raised in Broome County.

But the rewards of working the land seven days a week lost some of its luster for younger farmers. In the 1970s and 1980s, farmers saw milk prices freeze while costs for livestock, feed, electricity, insurance, and equipment continued to rise. It was not unusual to read about farmers selling off their farms. Much of the farmland was sold to adjoining farms. While the number of farms dropped dramatically during this period to under a thousand farms operating in the county, the average acreage of the remaining farms increased. By 2000, the number of farms of any size had dipped below six hundred and was declining at the rate of 6 percent to 10 percent every five years.

The First City National Bank building was built next to the Treadway Inn. The building is now occupied by M&T Bank. (Courtesy Broome County Historical Society)

The "Black Box" is what some have called One Marine Midland Plaza on Hawley Street in Binghamton. It opened in the early 1970s and is now the home of a branch of NBT Bank. (Courtesy Broome County Historical Society)

The land that was not sold to other farmers became an attractive purchase for those wanting to move into the expanding suburban areas of Broome County. Expansion outward from the urban corridor continued during this period. Residents built new homes within planned developments in places like Whitney Point, Endwell, Chenango Bridge, Fenton, Colesville, Windsor, and Barker. Many homes were located where barns and outbuildings once stood. It was not unusual to see a large modern house juxtaposed near an old

CHAPTER 12: THE DECLINE OF INDUSTRY 219

stonewall of the farm that once operated on that site.

But agriculture was not the only sector of Broome County's economy to undergo significant change. When Endicott Johnson was sold to the McGowan Corporation in 1968, there was no large-scale effort to stop the sale. Frank Johnson had been removed as the last family member involved in the firm, and the sales and employment numbers had been declining for more than fifteen years. Within a few months of the sale, the company began to divest itself of many of the properties that made Endicott Johnson unique. The tanneries had been shut down by the mid-1960s. The company sold CFJ Park in Johnson City and En-Joie Park in Endicott to the respective villages. The interests in Your Home Library and the George F. Johnson Library were also turned over to the villages. The company medical programs were ended, and health insurance was converted to a Blue Cross/Blue Shield program.

Ownership of the company changed several times during this period. Eventually, the firm was sold to Hanson Trust of Great Britain. Hanson Trust, using the Endicott Johnson name, operated U.S. Shoe, but the value of the firm continued to drop. The remaining buildings in Endicott were sold off to IBM and torn down. The remaining operating plants were at Glendale and adjoining CFJ Park in Johnson City. There, the Paracord factory manufactured boots until it was closed in 1994. The retail portion of the company, both the Endicott Johnson Shoe Stores and the Father and Son Shoe Stores were closed in 1995. The remaining manufacturing arm of the firm was at Glendale. It finally closed in 1998. Although some office portions of the parent company remained until 2005, the company came to end

The construction of Government Plaza on Hawley Street created new offices for the City of Binghamton, Broome County, and the State of New York. Edwin Crawford, the first Broome County executive, shows off the new legislature chambers in this photograph. (Courtesy Broome County Historical Society)

Opposite page: Public art was purchased for the new Government Plaza, causing some citizens to complain about the misuse of tax money. Louise Nevelson, world-famous sculptor, created this work that stands outside City Hall. (Courtesy Broome County Historical Society)

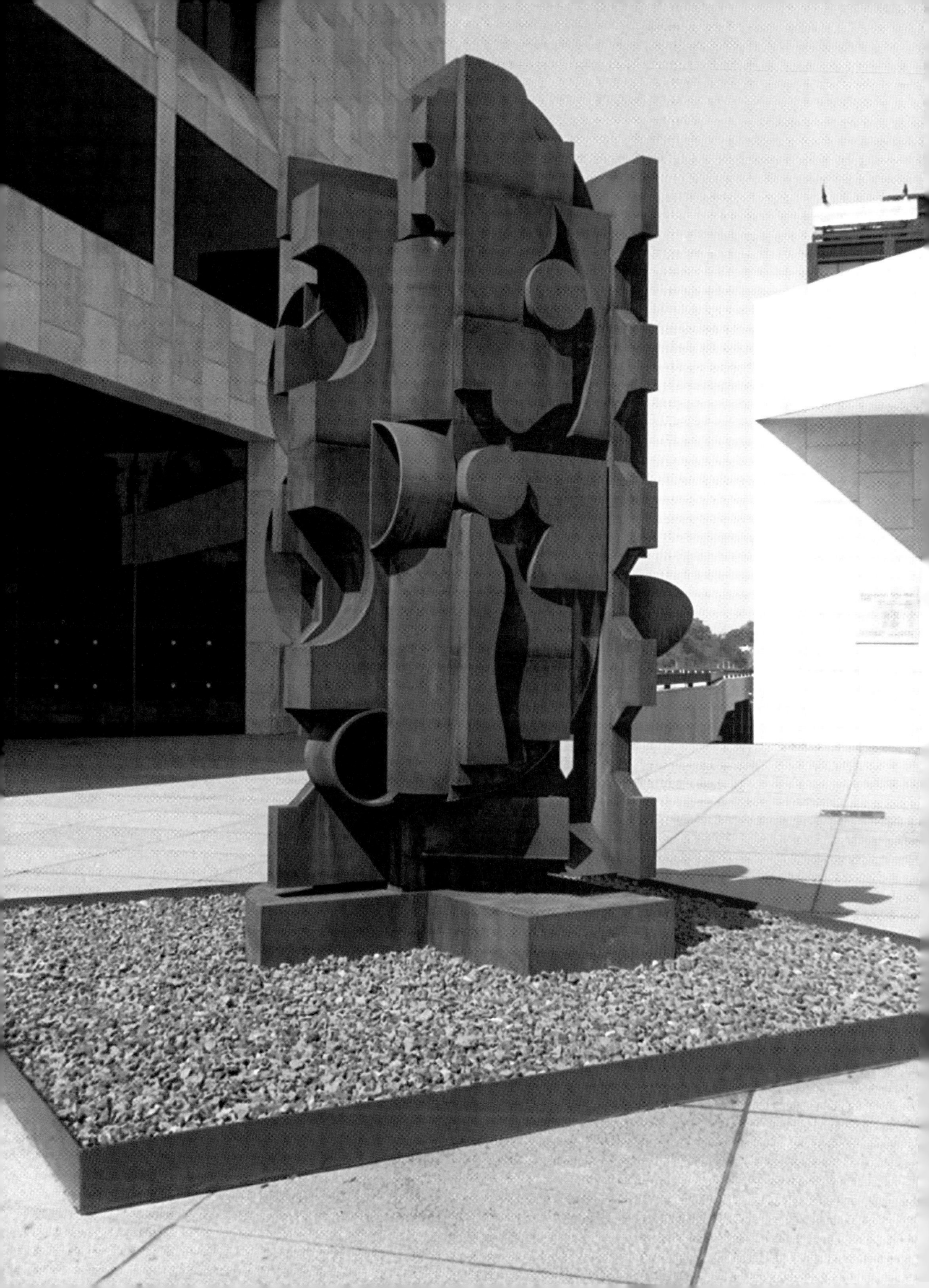

Strip plazas expanded from the 1960s to the 1990s. The Vestal Plaza opened with Britts as its anchor store. That plaza has now been transformed into Vestal Park with the addition of University Plaza, which houses over seven hundred students. (Courtesy Broome County Historical Society)

106 years after it had evolved from the Lester Brothers Company.

The demise of Endicott Johnson shook the region. It had been the leading employer of the county for several decades, but like the cigar industry before it, it disappeared after failing to transform to changing tastes, technologies, and management systems. Other industrial firms also felt the changes. When Edwin A. Link sold Link Aviation to General Aviation in 1950, he could not have known that the firm would change ownership several times in the next three decades. In 1968, the firm was Singer-Link. The Singer Company was sold to Wall Street financier Paul Bilzerian, who had a reputation for buying firms, raping them of any profits, and selling them off or closing them. His reputation was well deserved; the firm was sold to his leverage company in 1988. By the end of that year, Bilzerian split the company into two portions, commercial enterprises and military enterprises. Both portions were sold: the commercial to Singer Link-Miles Simulation (now GSE Systems), which moved all operations out of the area, and the military portion to CAE. While some operations continued at the firm's facilities in the town of Kirkwood, the number of employees decreased from a high of three thousand to only a few hundred.

In 1995, Hughes Training subsumed the company in an effort to expand its involvement in the simulation industry. The company originally said that the facility in Kirkwood would be closed, and employees were given the opportunity to move to its facilities in Texas. While some employees chose to relocate, a number of them decided to leave the firm and stay in Broome County. Hughes Training reconsidered closing the plant and left a small workforce in place. Three years later, in 1998, Raytheon purchased the Kirkwood facility but kept it only for two years. In 2000, the firm was sold to L-3 Communications, a Canadian firm with United States offices. That firm decided to bring back the Link name to help with recognition of its role in the simulator industry.

Similarly, Ansco went through a period of being sold, divided, and resold to other firms. It had been operated by GAF since 1942, and that firm had purchased the business in 1963. Ozalid was involved in a process that eventually replaced traditional blueprint. The Ansco division continued to manufacture cameras and film papers in their complex of buildings in the First Ward of Binghamton. In 1981, GAF decided to divest itself of the firm. The Ansco portion became Anitec and Ozalid remained as an independent corporation. In 1985, Ozalid closed its doors and laid off over three hundred employees. Anitec operated until 1987 when it was sold to International Paper. That company continued operations in Binghamton until 1998 when Kodak Polychrome, a subsidiary of Ansco rival Eastman Kodak, approached it. The firm was sold to Kodak who promised to keep the employees working. The promise lasted only six months, and the firm was closed, forcing over one thousand workers to seek new employment.

The skyline was also undergoing change during this period. The huge gas tank located on the east side of Binghamton that had served as a landmark for traveling motorists was removed in 1969. In the downtown area, new buildings were finally being constructed as a part of the urban renewal program. Government Plaza was built over a one-block area near the Susquehanna River between 1968 and 1972. The State Office Building rose seventeen floors above the ground. The Press Building, which had long stood as Binghamton's tallest structure, was now demoted in rank to number two. The Broome County Office Building and the Binghamton City Hall completed the tripartite government complex. The modern

The Kopernik Observatory opened in 1974 in Vestal as a gift from the Kopernik Society. Here, Frederic Savage directs a group of Polish Americans being filmed. The observatory, which has expanded to include an education center, is now operated by Roberson Museum & Science Center. (Courtesy Broome County Historical Society)

architecture included a second-floor deck with large steps leading up to that level. Only a few months after opening, the floor of the deck began to heave, and large uneven paving stones made the deck unusable. The steps leading to the deck deteriorated and were closed to the public.

Nearby, the Broome County Veterans Memorial Arena opened on August 29, 1973. The facility was the culmination of three decades of discussion. The new facility was home to major concerts, including Elvis Presley in 1977 and Frank Sinatra in 1979. It was also home to professional ice hockey with the Broome Dusters. In the intervening years, several others including the Whalers, the B.C. Icemen, and the Senators replaced that team.

The Treadway Inn built a new facility next to the Arena. The hotel later became part of the Holiday Inn chain. Across Washington Street was the new One Marine Midland block. A large black glass monolith, the bank building also featured a courtyard and public art. This block was interconnected with a series of overhead walkways that allowed pedestrians to move easily over the automobile traffic on the street below.

The Binghamton Plaza had opened several years before, but the move toward new retail venues was just beginning. In 1969, Montgomery Ward moved its Binghamton store to the Oakdale Mall in Johnson City. The first enclosed mall structure in the area, the Oakdale Mall, was completed in 1975. It held several anchor stores, including Montgomery Ward, Sears & Roebuck, and J.C. Penney. As the new stores opened in the Oakdale Mall, their counterparts in Binghamton closed. The suburban landscape was also home to new strip plazas. The Chenango Plaza in the town of Chenango; the Campus Plaza, the Vestal Plaza, and Westins in the town of Vestal; Grant City in the town of Union; and Grandway in Endicott opened between 1965 and 1975.

The unpopularity of urban renewal led to a reaction in favor of historic preservation. Stephens Square Marketplace in Binghamton opened as a result of the work of James Mowry, who renovated several older buildings into new space. (Courtesy Broome County Historical Society)

Ethnic heritage is still strong in Broome County with groups such as these Ukrainian dancers who are performing "Negabutky" at Highland Park in Endwell in 1977. (Courtesy Broome County Historical Society)

Across much of the United States, locally owned department stores were having a difficult time competing against major chains like Sears, Wards, Macy's, and others. The Broome County region was one of those areas. Some of the stores closed without putting up much of a struggle against the new type of competition. Sisson Brothers and Weldon store closed its doors in 1963 shortly after it had been sold to another chain of stores in a last-ditch effort to remain open. Most of the newer chains did not own the buildings in which they were located. This allowed the flexibility to open and close stores without the fear of entangling real estate. The newer chains were less committed to the regions where their stores operated. Older local stores often participated in local events, helping out in times of disaster or when families were in need. This was less true of national chains where the profit line was the decisive factor determining whether a store would stay open or close.

To compete in the changing retail market, locally owned stores attempted to open secondary stores in the new malls and plazas. Fowler, Dick & Walker opened a major store in 1975 at the Oakdale Mall while keeping their downtown Binghamton store open. In 1972–1973, the company had completely renovated the exterior and interior of the Binghamton store to remove the vestiges of its Victorian

CHAPTER 12: THE DECLINE OF INDUSTRY

For twenty-five years, the Otsiningo PowWow brought Native American heritage to the people of Broome County. The Iroquois Studies Association ran the festival, usually at Otsiningo Park in Dickinson. (Courtesy Broome County Historical Society)

architecture and give it a more modern appearance. Fowler's had been sold to L. S. Good & Co., which was bankrupt when they closed the downtown store. Other stores in Binghamton, such as Compton Dunn, Resnick's, and Lowry Music, closed downtown stores while continuing to operate in suburban plazas and malls.

Hill, McLean and Haskins fought to stay independent for many decades. They operated the Binghamton store and then expanded to Endicott, Owego, and Ithaca. As national chains became stronger and invaded their market areas, McLean's followed the lead of other locally owned stores by retrenching to a smaller size. The Endicott, Owego, and Ithaca stores were closed initially. Eventually, the firm was sold to the Rothschild Brothers of Ithaca who operated a chain of stores. They closed half of the Binghamton store in 1972 and then closed the entire facility in 1979. Within a few years, Binghamton had lost all three of its anchor department stores, as well as chain stores like W. T. Grant. The last remaining locally owned department store was Burt's of Endicott. It closed in 1995.

Binghamton planners fell into the common trap that there was the single answer to revitalize the urban corridor. As northeast cities had believed that urban renewal was going to be the single answer to solve urban blight, the cure-all solution to answer the spread of retail markets to the suburbs in the 1970s and 1980s was the urban mall. Binghamton attempted two failed schemes that followed this theory. During the administration of Mayor Al Libous, the city became embroiled with the Mondev development. A Canadian firm, Mondev proposed a plan that would have made much of Court Street a closed pedestrian walkway. Modern retail and office towers would have replaced much of the remaining downtown buildings. This was promised as the means to bring back retail and business growth to Binghamton. The city spent several millions of dollars to plan and implement the development. The City Council and the Binghamton Urban Renewal Agency finally became tired of delays and cost overruns and ended the relationship in 1980.

In the mid-1980s, the administration of Mayor Juanita Crabb attempted a number of redevelopment concepts. Boscov's department store chain from Pennsylvania was persuaded to open up a store in 1984 in the closed Fowler's building. Nearby, a small remnant of the Mondev scheme called the MetroCenter opened the same year. In 1988, the city once again promoted a plan to develop an urban mall using the Wilmorite firm of Rochester. This plan called for using Boscov's store as one anchor store and creating another anchor farther south along the Susquehanna River. The mall would be developed along the riverbank and would be called the Town Square Mall. Again, time and money killed the plan with no real progress.

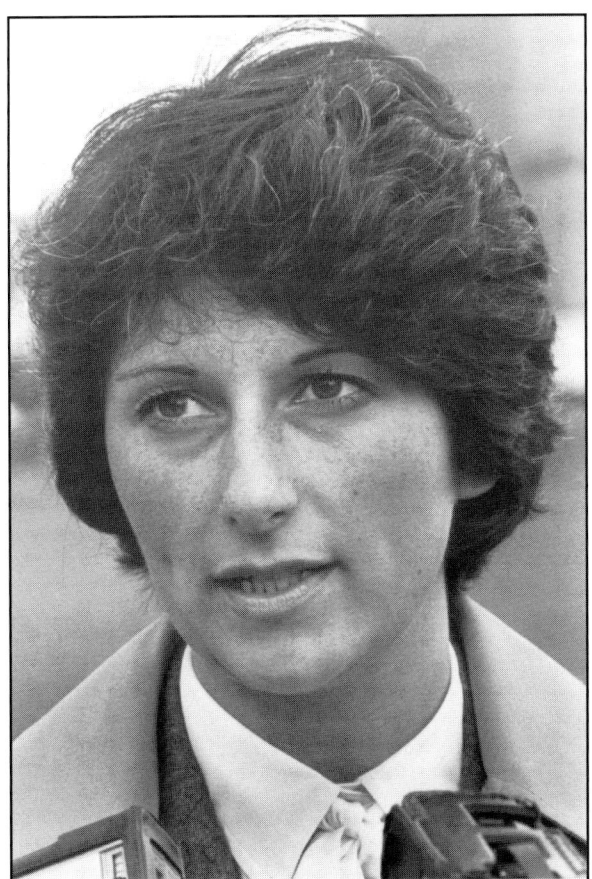

Juanita Crabb was the first female mayor of the city of Binghamton and held that office from 1982 through 1990. She and Marion Corino, the first female mayor of Endicott, helped to change the way the political system worked in Broome County. (Courtesy Broome County Historical Society)

John Gardner was a best-selling author before he came to Binghamton University to teach creative writing. His novel *Mickelsson's Ghosts* is based on this area. He died in a motorcycle accident in 1982. (Courtesy Broome County Historical Society)

In 1984, Boscov's of Pennsylvania took over the space formerly used by Fowler's in Binghamton. Boscov's continues to operate from this and several other locations in the Northeast. (Courtesy Broome County Historical Society)

While the city looked to redevelop its image, another movement was gaining momentum. Historic preservation had been relegated to the back burner in the days of urban renewal. A new look at the surviving buildings gave some local residents hope that they could salvage much of the remaining architecture. They saw an old building not as something to be demolished, but as something that could be refurbished into new purposes and reused.

The earliest large project was the redevelopment of the former City Hall building on Collier Street. Local architect James Mowry saw a new use for the building. The structure was reconfigured with a new entrance and had a new life as a luxury hotel. He also refurbished the Stephens Square building on State Street. The building had been used as a paper factory and cigar plant before closing. The structure reopened in the 1980s as a mixture of retail and office space. Mowry connected this to the Stephens Square Marketplace, the former Home Dairy on Court Street, as new restaurant space. Nearby, the former Hull, Grummond & Company cigar factory found a life as Cahill Office Supplies, later the Lost Café coffee house. On the south side of the city, a former fire station was refurbished into the Number 5 Restaurant. The old Landmark Society that had floundered in the 1960s was revamped into the Preservation Association of the Southern Tier (PAST).

While some looked toward the past to help improve the image of Binghamton, others looked toward the future to help answer some of the pressing needs of society at the moment. The problem of garbage became an important issue during the 1980s and 1990s. Broome County had developed a landfill in the town of Barker, but the increasing amount of garbage threatened the lifespan of the facility. A major effort began to recycle many everyday used household items. The plan was successfully promoted, and Broome County became a good example of using recycling to extend the life of a landfill for many years.

Another issue during the period was the handling and treatment of hazardous materials. During an era when places like Love Canal and Three-Mile Island made national news for the lack of control of toxic materials, Binghamton became the focus of the issue. On February 5, 1981, a fire broke out in the transformer located in the basement of the State Office Building in the Government Plaza. The fire in the oil-based transformer poured smoke and soot through the ventilation system of the building. It also spread deadly PCBs and dioxins through the entire building. The building suddenly became, quite literally, the "Toxic Tower." The incident forced experts to determine safe levels of these substances and to create new technology to clean up the building. Eventually, over $40 million was spent to remove much of the interior of the building, including walls and floors. Finally, the structure was reopened after fourteen years of disuse.

There were changes in the medical field as well. The smaller population and increasing medical costs created the need for consolidation. The loss of Endicott Johnson company funds for medical care was one factor in this change. The increasing age of Broome County's population was another factor. In 1980, Wilson Hospital in Johnson City merged with Ideal Hospital in Endicott. Within a short while, United Health Services was formed, also incorporating Binghamton General Hospital. Only Our Lady of Lourdes Hospital remained as an independent facility. Ideal Hospital was closed and converted into a long-term nursing facility in 1984. But along with the smaller number of hospital and maternity beds available came new types of medical care: coronary surgery and oncology care are

The urban renewal program left several block-wide lots devoid of buildings. The lot at the corner of Water Street and East Clinton Street was finally developed in the 1980s. The Binghamton Regency hotel was constructed on the site. (Courtesy Broome County Historical Society)

Sports played an important role in the resurgence of the area. The B.C. Open is held each year at En-Joie Golf Course in Endicott. The PGA event draws thousands of people and has helped raise millions for charity. (Courtesy Broome County Historical Society)

some of the new procedures and treatments developed for the problems of the aging population.

The period that had opened with the shrinking of Endicott Johnson ended with the near demise of IBM in the valley. With the decline of Endicott Johnson, IBM had become the largest employer in Broome County by 1970. At its height, IBM had employed fourteen thousand residents in its area facilities. But IBM had become reliant on the inflated government spending prevalent during the Cold War. Like many other industries that thrived at least in part on defense contracts, it seemed to be impressed with its own size. IBM avoided risky, experimental ventures. It had become complacent. The time for a change reached the firm, but that change would mean large changes for Broome County.

Growing dissension and problems within the Soviet Union had created an environment for change. The movement of its leader, Mikhail Gorbachev, toward *perestroika* led the Soviet Union to further democratic changes. It also gave the outlying satellites of the Soviets the opportunity to pull away and become independent. By the end of the 1980s, the Berlin Wall had come down and Germany had been reunited without violence. Poland and other Eastern European nations had become free of the dominance of the Soviet Union. Indeed, the Soviet Union ceased to be. The domino theory that had been proposed decades before by John Foster Dulles as a justification for the Cold War did work, but in the reverse. Communism fell rapidly under its own weaknesses.

The fall of the Soviet Union and the end of the Cold War also reduced the need for large government contracts for equipment and weaponry. Many firms in Broome County felt the loss of this huge source of revenue. IBM began to lower the number of workers in the area, first through retirement and attrition, and, finally, through layoffs. The firm had been proud that it had never "laid off" any employees in this area, but beginning in 1994, this could no longer be said. The firm sold its Owego plant in 1994 to Loral Corporation. It would be the first of many drastic changes in the computer and aerospace industries.

Broome County suffered the worst job loss in its history during this period. Soon many businesses and homes stood empty. The value of real estate also fell dramatically as the valley entered the middle of the last decade of the twentieth century. Broome County had faced

Despite an increased awareness of the value of older buildings, some structures were lost. The Rose Mansion, seen here, was torn down in a failed effort to develop the property. The lot remains empty two decades later. (Courtesy Broome County Historical Society)

Ice hockey is a popular sport in Broome County. The Broome County Arena has played host to the Broome Dusters, the Whalers (seen in this 1982 photograph), and now the Senators. (Courtesy Broome County Historical Society)

the winds of change of the previous quarter century. As the county approached the coming of the new millennium, it faced many problems and had few solutions.

CHAPTER 12: THE DECLINE OF INDUSTRY   231

CHAPTER 13

The New Millennium

1995–2006

Although the Triplets ended in 1968, the area once again has minor league baseball with the Binghamton Mets, who play at NYSEG Stadium in Binghamton. Thousands of children of all ages can still enjoy watching America's pastime. (Courtesy Broome County Historical Society)

DECLINING POPULATION, rising costs of services, an eroding industrial base, and an influx of new immigrants were only a few of the problems faced by the residents of Broome County as the twentieth century came to a close. By 1995, it was apparent to many residents and officials that the old parochial attitude that the problems of Binghamton were only those of Binghamton and did not affect the rest of the county no longer was true. The loss of employment opportunities meant the loss of residents and families throughout the area. Binghamton's population fell below the 50,000 mark in 2000. It was approximately the same as the population shortly after the end of the First World War. The decline in population hit Broome County as well. Total population fell in 1990 and 2000. By the time of the county's bicentennial in 2006, the Census Bureau estimates its population will be approximately 198,000 residents.

Corporate merges and selloffs continued until the end of the century. Loral sold off the

Mike Dellapenta trims the edge of a shoe at the Endicott Johnson factory. In 1995, the last manufacturing plant at Glendale had closed its doors while the last remaining office of EJ's successor, the Lehigh Safety Shoe Company, ceased operations in 2005. (Courtesy Broome County Historical Society)

Owego facility to Martin Marietta in 1996, only two years after purchasing it from IBM. Martin Marietta also purchased the former GE facility in Westover. In a short time Martin Marietta became Lockheed Martin. The firm operated both facilities briefly before selling off the Westover plant to BAE Systems. By the early years of the twenty-first century, this trend of constant sale and mergers of local plants seemed to have ended.

In the last few years, the number of contracts and orders to the former Cold War companies have stabilized. The bleeding away of local residents has slowed, if not stopped. Lockheed Martin Federal Systems in Owego recently acquired the contract to build a fleet of new presidential helicopters. It is hoped that the rising number of employees will bring new residents helping to fill the homes of Broome County. Meanwhile, the incidence of layoffs and departures of firms has lessened, and slow growth has been noted.

There were also new residents who entered the area during the last decade of the 1900s. New immigrants from Southeast Asian, Russian,

State Senator Thomas Libous was elected to the seat formerly held by Majority Leader Warren Anderson. His uncle, Alfred Libous, was mayor of Binghamton, and Senator Libous holds several high positions on state senate committees. (Courtesy Broome County Historical Society)

and Hispanic countries again changed the ethnic makeup of the community. Newcomers to the area faced many of the same issues that confronted the immigrants of the early 1900s. Questions of discrimination and ethnic hatred were heard in places like the halls of Johnson City schools where a large number of Vietnamese students attended. But unlike the period of the 1920s when the KKK had reared

its ugly head, school and area leaders worked together to bring about a dialogue between area immigrants, residents, and officials. Acclimation and accommodation were seen as better prospects for keeping peace and calm in the area.

The fall of value in real estate during the late 1980s and early 1990s was found to have a beneficial effect for the community. It made the county more attractive to new residents and businesses. In the suburbs, the empty fields of former farms became attractive for the building of new homes. At the same time, the costs of mortgages fell in the country, and new home sales soared dramatically. The cost of vacant land actually rose as new buyers from the downstate area began to see Broome County as a good place to build and live.

In Binghamton, a new attitude began to take hold. Owners and developers began to salvage and enhance older buildings and to promote older architecture as a common theme in the city. Urban planners and city officials realized that the answer to growth was not to be found in one answer but in many. The turn-of-the-century look of many of the older buildings in Binghamton was used to bring a cohesive look to downtown.

Opposite page: In 2001, work began to restore the mansard roof of the Phelps Mansion on Court Street in Binghamton. The Monday Afternoon Club raised $750,000 to bring the building back to its former glory. (Courtesy Broome County Historical Society)

Period lighting and street treatment began on one street and was continued on several others. The Washington Street Bridge, which had remained closed to traffic since the late 1960s, was rehabilitated for pedestrian and bicycle traffic. Across the Susquehanna River, the city stressed the development of a section called South Bridge on the south side of the city. Memorial Bridge, which had been built in 1925, was restored to its original look in 2005, as its counterpart, the 1936 East Clinton Street Bridge, had been ten years before. The Court Street Bridge is slated for restoration to its 1900 appearance in 2006.

The development of river walks was nothing new in the Broome County area. The Chugnut River Walk was developed in the village of Endicott. The town of Vestal rehabilitated a former railroad line for a walking and biking trail. Otsiningo Park enlarged its operations and extended the river walk area almost one mile into the town of Chenango. The calls to stress the beauty and importance of the rivers did not fall on deaf ears in the city of Binghamton. Plans finally emerged to develop a river walk along the Chenango River. With the creation of Confluence Park at the meeting of the Susquehanna and Chenango Rivers, the walk became a viable plan. It connects the area along the riverbank for more than a mile. It is interesting to note that the original plan to develop this river walk was proposed in 1911.

Historic preservation continues to play an important role in the look of the community. The 1876–77 Perry Block is a fine example of cast-iron architecture that now houses a dental clinic and several shops. (Courtesy Broome County Historical Society)

New housing projects have been or are being developed throughout the urban area. The increasing size of the student population of Binghamton University (State University of New York at Binghamton) has resulted in new dormitories being constructed, the creation of the Binghamton University Events Center, and the creation of private housing for area students. In Binghamton, the redevelopment of the area surrounding the railroad yards is bringing a new type of loft-living into former factories and warehouses. There is an increased awareness of the importance of neighborhoods as west side residents work to protect the historic importance of their Victorian homes.

The arts have risen in importance in the community. Nationally known area artists have propelled an increased interest in developing our arts scene. Arts walks, new galleries, and the development of loft space for incoming artists have helped bring back some of the glory of Broome County. Local schools have also placed a higher importance on developing new programs to keep the interests of its students. The importance of education has raised the numbers of local high school graduates who continue on to college. The student enrollment at both Binghamton University and Broome Community College are at all-time highs.

An awareness of the problems of health hazards to our community has been made all the more important by the discovery of more "brownfields" and toxic sites in the urban area. New efforts are underway to monitor and clean up spills from decades of industrial activity in Broome County. Major efforts have recently been undertaken to clean up one toxic spill in the ground in the village of Endicott. IBM has assumed much of the cost of this operation. But this is only one example of this problem of modern life in Broome County. It is a struggle that will continue for many years to come.

The area also continues to struggle with the weather. In 1996 and again in 2005, major floods hit the region, causing millions of dollars of damage to the rivers and to properties on the floodplains of the valley. In 1998, tornadoes hit the area causing three deaths and millions of dollars of damage. The consolidation of Emergency Services under the control of the Broome County government has aided in the time and efficiency of the use of the fire, police, and emergency medical services of the area.

The retail sector continues to move away from the traditional bases of Binghamton, Johnson City, and Endicott and move toward the malls and plazas that are scattered along the Vestal Parkway. But like the days when Binghamton was developing as a center of retail stores, the costs of increasing traffic flow, police protection, and better water and sewer construction are now affecting the town of Vestal. Retail shifts will be common for a number of years, as the sales via the Internet will again affect the way residents purchase the luxuries and necessities of life.

When the millennium approached in 2000, there was great fear over the possibility of failure of major computer systems that could not handle the change of year. Y2K fear swept across the country, and Broome County was also affected. Computer experts claimed a major disaster was looming. Several municipalities purchased extra stop signs in case of the failure of traffic signals. In the end, nothing happened, with the possible exception that Broome County moved from one century into another and approached its own anniversary.

Residents have lived in Broome County for the last two hundred years. Sometimes it appears that the issues and problems associated with government, businesses, and industries will overwhelm the day-to-day lives of the thousands who have called this county home. On September 11, 2001, terrorists commandeered airplanes and flew them into the World Trade Center, the Pentagon, and a field in Pennsylvania. But much more importantly, they used them as weapons against the American people. Perhaps on that day we, as a society, were altered in the way we think about each other. People realized that we must protect each other, or we are all at peril.

That is the way Broome County has operated for much of its history. It is the story not only of those businesses and industries that formed our buildings or provided jobs. It is the story of every resident who came here to find a better life. That was as true in 1806 as it is in 2006. Broome County has been called the Valley of Opportunity. In looking historically at our past, and in looking at the prospects for growth and resurgence at its bicentennial, it remains the Valley of Opportunity.

It remains so because of its residents. Despite the many ethnic heritages that make up this county, despite the different occupations, lifestyles, ways we worship, and languages we speak, we realize that we are all part of the success of this county. Many years ago, Endicott Johnson published a book of photographs demonstrating the family of workers and how they were *Partners All*. Broome County has been through a tough battle in recent decades because of the changes in industry and business. It has evolved from farm to factory, and again, from smokestacks to high-tech. These changes have not been easy. Some have resulted in major job losses and instability in traditional businesses. But the residents of Broome County are also tough. Today, we work together to find the answers that will help Broome County thrive and grow. We now realize that truly we are *Partners All*.

The dome of the Broome County Courthouse presents a constant reminder of the area's past and a connection to its future. It was restored in the 1990s, and the clock mechanisms were replaced to again allow citizens to hear its mellow chimes. (Courtesy Broome County Historical Society)

CHAPTER 14
The City of Binghamton

The entrance of Fowler's Department Store was always decorated for Christmas. Victorian-dressed carolers would appear on the deck to entertain customers as they entered the building. (Courtesy Broome County Historical Society)

This panoramic view of Binghamton shows the downtown area as it appeared about 1909. The Chenango River winds its way through the picture, as traffic flows down Court Street. (Courtesy Broome County Historical Society)

WHAT BEGAN AS A VISION for a model town at the confluence of the Chenango and Susquehanna Rivers in the minds of William Bingham and Joshua Whitney gradually evolved into a small country town by the early 1800s. In 1834, Binghamton became an incorporated village. Thirty-three years later, in 1867, Binghamton became a city. In the next one hundred and forty years, the city of Binghamton evolved from a village of 1 square mile to a city comprising 10.4 square miles of land within Broome County.

Binghamton was selected as the county seat of the newly formed Broome County in 1806 when the country crossroads was still called Chenango Point. During its history, twenty-six men have served as village president and forty-six men and one woman have served as its mayor. Countless hundreds have served as village trustees, city council members, clerks, department heads, police, firefighters, and other employees of a city that at its height had a population of nearly 85,000 residents. Today, there are 47,380 people living in Binghamton, the city that helped launch major corporations such as IBM (Bundy Time Recording Company), Endicott Johnson, Link Aviation, Valvoline, and Whirlpool.

There are 654 streets in the city comprising hundreds of miles of roadway. Court Street and Chenango Street both follow Native American trails; State Street was once the Chenango Canal, while two-block-long Lisle Avenue has had four different names during its existence. There are nine bridges in the city for vehicles and pedestrians (not including railroad bridges and many overpasses). These bridges connect the residents of the north side, south side, west side, and east side of the city to the downtown section of Binghamton. There are thirteen wards that were originally used to elect city council members but today help define the various neighborhoods that ring the city. Some are well known by name, such as the First Ward or the Bloody Fifth, while the boundaries of others are best found on a map.

Until the mid-twentieth century, the downtown section of the city was laden with a mixture of stores and factories. Adjoining the former Chenango Canal and surrounding the railroad tracks that transect the city were numerous buildings where workers assembled and built over two hundred different types of products. These products ranged from cigars to furniture, to silk, to cameras, to bottles—almost every type of home product was made in Binghamton

The flying truck of DiRienzo Brothers Bakery is a familiar site to many of the citizens of Binghamton. The bakery is located on Henry Street and celebrated its centennial in 1984. (Courtesy Broome County Historical Society)

at one time or another. Many other factories were located in the First and Second Wards of the city.

As the city developed into both a transportation and an industrial hub by the late nineteenth century, the residential neighborhoods surrounding these factories expanded outward. Thousands of immigrants arriving to work in the area populated a large percentage of these neighborhoods.

An explosion of the construction of homes in the city met the population explosion of Binghamton in the last quarter of the 1800s. New streets were being laid out yearly during that period, with developers constructing both small and large Victorian period homes throughout the area.

Binghamton has long been called the "Parlor City." Many of the residents believe that this was due to the large number of Victorian

An addition to Binghamton High School in the 1980s included this glass-lined walkway that connects the old to the new. The school continues to educate thousands of students each year. (Courtesy Broome County Historical Society)

homes scattered in almost every ward of the city. Like many sobriquets, this one was not penned with great love for Binghamton but with a note of sarcasm. A firemen's convention in Binghamton in the 1870s prompted a reporter from the rival industrial city of Scranton to describe his stay in the city as having been pleasant in the sleepy little Parlor City. What was meant as an insult to the residents became a quickly spreading moniker for the growing city. City fathers and business leaders even took out an ad in the local newspaper asking citizens to stop using this nickname because the residents were not sitting in their parlors, they were busy working in the factories. Nevertheless, the name stuck and is still used today.

Binghamton has often been perceived as staunchly Republican and conservative in its politics. This perception is somewhat misleading. In the early 1800s, many of the leaders of the community were followers of the Whig Party (many of whom joined the Republican Party when the Whig Party collapsed). The leading politician of the nineteenth century, however, was Democrat Daniel S. Dickinson. Republican Party leaders such as Harvey Hinman, George Hinman, William Hill, and the former New York State Majority Leader, Senator Warren Anderson of Binghamton, have influenced local and statewide politics in the twentieth century. At the same time, the number of registered voters is almost evenly divided between the two major political parties and nearly half of the elected mayors of the city have been Democrats. Franklin D. Roosevelt carried the area when he was running for governor yet only carried it once during his four elections for the presidency. George W. Bush failed to carry Binghamton against John Kerry in his 2004 bid for reelection, and Edwin Arthur Hall, the maverick Republican representative of this area in the 1950s, was from the south side of Binghamton.

There have been many firsts in the city of Binghamton. Aside from the aforementioned first electric trolley car in the state, the city also played host to the Continuous Oil Refining Company that created Valvoline. The first Kinney Shoe Store began in Binghamton in 1889 when George Kinney, a clerk in the Stone, Goff & Company shoe firm, bought the remaining stock of the Lester Brothers Shoe Company and sold it to the public at a greatly reduced price. The first modern matchbook was made in Binghamton; Cornelius Webster operated the Binghamton Match Company. The company was located next to the railroad tracks and made long parlor matches for fireplaces. Webster came up with the idea of making short matches in a protective cover so men could carry them to light their cigars. The idea may have seemed a sure moneymaker until another firm came up with the flexible match. Henry Bradley, another store clerk, came up with a patent for a product he called an improved culinary compound, later called oleomargarine. Although Bradley had the first patent, he never made any money on the invention. Other companies improved on what Bradley had invented and made it more palatable to the tongue.

In 1868, the area's first trolley car system, the Binghamton and Port Dickinson Railroad Company, was incorporated (although operations did not begin until 1873). During the next six decades, trolleys provided thousands with the means to live farther away from workplaces and establish residential neighborhoods. Hundreds of miles of track were laid on all of the major streets in the city by at least six independent trolley companies. Eventually, the various firms merged to become Binghamton Railway Company, later reorganized as the Triple Cities Traction Company. In 1932, a massive parade was held with several trolley cars followed by a fleet of new buses that replaced the once popular means of transportation. Today, BC Transit, operated by the Broome County government, maintains an extensive bus service through much of the Triple Cities area.

Binghamton has also been the hometown of several celebrities. The most famous of these was Rod Serling (1924–1975). It is interesting to note that although Serling was born in Syracuse and moved to Binghamton when he was two, he always considered this area his home. His father, Samuel Serling, ran a delicatessen store and lived on the west side of the city. Serling spent much of his youth in and around Recreation Park. He graduated from Binghamton Central High School in 1943 and served as an Army paratrooper in the Pacific Theater during World War II. He graduated from Antioch College in Ohio in 1950. It was here that he met his future wife, Carol. Although he is best known for his two television series, *The Twilight Zone* and *Night Gallery*, he received many of his six Emmy awards and a Peabody award for other writing, including *Patterns, Requiem for a Heavyweight, The Comedian*, and *Planet of the Apes*. Several Binghamton locales were used in his scripts, including Recreation Park as the backdrop for a *Twilight Zone* episode called "Walking Distance." Among other well-known Binghamtonians are Richard Deacon (Mel Cooley on *The Dick Van Dyke Show*), comic movie actor Hugh Herbert, and actor William Prince.

The meeting place for Binghamton's government has moved several times in the last two hundred years. The first meeting of the Village of Binghamton was held in 1834 at Peterson's Tavern. The tavern was located on the corner of Front Street and Main Street on the west side of the Chenango River. It was a stagecoach stop and popular meeting place for the upper class of the town. The first official building constructed for use by the government was Firemen's Hall, also called Village Hall, built in 1857 on Collier Street. Located across from the Courthouse Square, a bell tower was added several years later. The building served as village hall, fire station, and police headquarters for many years. In 1897, the structure was removed for the first City Hall. The new City Hall building was home to all city departments with the exception of the fire and police departments who used other buildings to house their personnel and equipment. In 1972, the current City Hall building was opened in the Government Plaza on Hawley Street. Returning to the usage of the earlier building, the structure also serves as the central location for both the fire and police departments.

As well as serving as the county seat for Broome County, Binghamton has served as the home to the industrial, retail, and service sectors. While the various neighborhoods have changed in terms of their ethnicity, size, and appearance, they still remain the vital link to

Art has become an important part of life in Binghamton. The First Friday Art Walk, the opening of new galleries, and the relocation of artists to the community have helped Binghamton resurge in the new millennium. (Courtesy Broome County Historical Society)

the success of the city. In recent years, there has been an important stress on the resurgence of these neighborhoods. Grant programs, historic districts, and groups such as the West Side Association have helped to promote the neighborhoods and the development of programs to ensure their success. Despite the passage of time, Binghamton remains the central focus of government and business. As it works to restore the downtown to an earlier appearance, it remains the Parlor City.

CHAPTER 15
The Town of Barker

Azaiah Westover purchased this property in 1839. The 1880s Victorian house was used as the Town of Barker offices for several decades. In the early 1990s, it was sold and is again being used as a residence. (Courtesy Broome County Historical Society)

THE TOWN OF BARKER was created on April 18, 1831, when it was broken off from the town of Lisle. Barker is located in the northwestern quarter of Broome County and has a population of 2,738 (2000 census figure). There are 35.22 square miles of land within the town. It was named for John Barker, an early resident of Chenango Forks who had come to this area from Connecticut. His daughter Mary married Simeon Rogers, another early resident from Connecticut, who opened the first store, kept a tavern, and established the first school at his home. Mary Barker Rogers survived two different encounters with drunken Native Americans who were very upset over her refusal to sell them more whiskey.

The Tioughnioga River that flows southeasterly until it meets the Chenango River at Chenango Forks transects much of the township. It was at this site in 1787 that a treaty conference was held for the relinquishment of Indian claims to the Boston Purchase area. The hilly geography of Barker provided little area for the growth of large-scale industry. Agriculture was the largest occupation of the residents of the town. At one time, over a hundred farms were located within the boundaries of Barker. By 1860, 58 percent of the town had been improved for cultivation. In the early years, sheep farming was more extensive than dairy operations. But, as in the rest of the county, the total number of people who farm has declined significantly. Today, there are only three operating dairy farms remaining in the town.

There are six distinct settlements within the town. Adams Settlement is located on Route 11 (originally called Adams Street). It was named for Joseph Adams who came from Dutchess County to Broome County in 1800 (Thomas, *Naming the Hills and Hollows of Broome County*). Anoka is located on Dunham Hill Road and is sometimes called Dunham Hill. The word Anoka is derived from a Native American term meaning "on both sides of the river." The area was renamed either for John Dunham, who came to the area from Dutchess County in the 1820s, or for Albert Dunham, who arrived in 1830.

Simeon Rogers built a gristmill in Chenango Forks in 1795. This building replaced the earlier mill. Lee Peters (seated) and his son Harry (standing) operated the mill. The 1935 flood destroyed it. (Courtesy Broome County Historical Society)

The Central Hotel was the main structure in the hamlet of Chenango Forks. It housed travelers on both the railroad and the nearby Chenango Canal. Torn down in the 1970s, it was replaced by a gas station. (Courtesy Broome County Historical Society)

point. Chenango Forks also prospered because of the opening of the Syracuse & Binghamton Railroad through the area in 1854. The railroad later became the Syracuse, Binghamton & New York Railroad. In 1876, the Utica, Chenango & Susquehanna Valley Railroad opened a spur on the eastern side of Barker. Eventually, the lines were merged under the Delaware, Lackawanna & Western line.

Chenango Forks is a unique hamlet that encompasses portions of the towns of Barker, Chenango, and Fenton in Broome County, and crosses into Chenango County and the town of Greene. Much of the business section of Chenango Forks is located in the town of Barker. At one time, the hamlet included two hotels, two grocery stores, a jeweler, several blacksmiths, three bars, a sawmill and gristmill, a doctor, a soda fountain, and a combined undertaking parlor and furniture store.

Much of this development of Chenango Forks was dependent on the creation of the Chenango Canal, which followed the route of the Chenango River through this area. Although the actual canal was located across the river in the town of Fenton, there was a guard lock that allowed boats to enter the canal at this

Hyde Settlement was named after Major Chauncey Hyde, a Revolutionary soldier who came here from Lenox, Massachusetts, in 1793 (Thomas). Hyde paid $4.00 an acre for his property. The small settlement grew and soon included a post office. It was a stagecoach stop between Binghamton and Cortland until the railroad opened. One of the more interesting characters of the town was LeGrand Lawrence. He was a farmer who lived on Hyde Street in the home of Lillian Hyde until his death in 1988. Lawrence took great pride in the stories he told to whomever would listen. His reputation was so great that on the door of his woodshed was a sign that said "World's Greatest Talker lives here" (Christine Gillette, Town of Barker Historian).

CHAPTER 15: THE TOWN OF BARKER

Ed Bowe (seen standing on the left along with his wife) built this grocery and general store on Main Street in Chenango Forks about 1850. The porch collapsed and was removed. William Dutcher later owned the structure. (Courtesy Broome County Historical Society)

Itaska is located on the north side of the Tioughnioga River. It was originally called Fuller's Settlement after Benjamin Fuller, who came to Broome County from Dutchess County in 1796. The settlement once included a post office, grocery store, and railroad depot. Parsons' Corners was named after Captain Jacob Parsons who came here in 1792 from Berkshire County, Massachusetts. He was one of the sixty proprietors of the Boston Purchase (Thomas).

Early settlers to the area included John Hurlburt who settled at Halfway Brook in 1794. He built a log home that was succeeded by a frame house. In 1850, Chauncey Hurlburt constructed a Greek Revival brick home that still stands today. The bricks were produced on the farm, and the large stones were brought in from Oxford. Aaron Gaylord arrived with his wife, Elizabeth Shevalier, in 1812 from Connecticut. The Gaylords lived on the Joiner Road area with eight of their eleven children. Nathaniel Kenyon was one of the first settlers on Sap Bush Road. He would later operate the Gothic House, a tavern on the edge of Chenango Forks located in the town of Chenango and said to be a stop on the Underground Railroad. The children of these last two families married into many other early families of the town, including Lyon, Stoughton, Gray, Brown, Thurston, and English. Zenas Eldredge also came with a large family that married into many of the town's older families.

The first school in Barker was located at Chenango Forks, but by 1858, there were fourteen one-room schoolhouses located throughout the town. Students today attend either the Whitney Point or the Chenango Forks School District. The Charlotte Kenyon Elementary School, located in Chenango Forks, was the original central high school for Chenango Forks. The school was closed in 2002, and students now attend an enlarged elementary school in the town of Chenango adjacent to the new high school.

These are the students of the Adams Street (Number 10) School, taken about 1905 with Emma Carley (seated). The school was part of the Barker School District. The building was closed in 1936, and the students later attended Whitney Point School. (Courtesy Broome County Historical Society)

Lumbering was an important early industry in Barker, but it declined after 1830. Beginning about 1825, there was a salt mine operation on Halfway Brook in the town. Native Americans living and hunting in the area used the salt. The salt mine operated intermittently throughout the nineteenth century. In recent years, the area has been explored for natural gas. Adelaide Gaylord Wooster (1846–1936), a granddaughter of early settler Aaron Gaylord, recalled seeing Native Americans heading north on Hyde Street to go to Onondaga Lake to obtain salt. Today, the largest industrial operation is the Broome County Landfill. It is located off of Dunham Hill Road on land that was sold to the county by Reginald Haist in the 1970s. The land also includes a section of the town of Maine. There has been a recent expansion site added on the north side of Dunham Hill Road that will allow the landfill to operate for many more years.

In the early development of the town of Barker, churches played an important role in the growth of the various hamlets of the town. There was a Methodist Episcopal Church at Hydeville, while in Chenango Forks the Congregational Church opened in 1822 and St. John's Episcopal Church began in 1877. The Itaska Methodist Episcopal Church began in 1825, and the Adams Street Methodist Church opened in 1871. All of these churches have since closed. Today, Countryside Christian Chapel in Itaska services the town and the Wat Lao Samakhtham Buddhist Temple was established in 1995 on Route 11.

CHAPTER 16
The Town of Binghamton

This "wood-bee" in the town of Binghamton includes the shed, ladder, and chair. Francis Buchanan stands with the axe over his shoulder in the back row. (Courtesy Broome County Historical Society)

Until the twentieth century, at House's Hill on Mill Street in the town of Binghamton stood the Morey log cabin, constructed in the early 1800s. Will Harris stands in front of the remains of this early residence. (Courtesy Broome County Historical Society)

THE TOWN OF BINGHAMTON was created on December 3, 1855, from the town of Chenango. Located south of the city of Binghamton, the population of the town is 4,949 (2000 census figure). The town is named after William Bingham, the major landowner of the area. (It should be noted that throughout this book the words *township* and *town* are interchangeable. Common vernacular and colloquial use of the word *town* is often inappropriately applied to hamlets such as Hawleyton or Chenango Forks, and *township patents* was a phrase used for military tracts created at the end of the American Revolution.) This township was one portion of the original land patent that Bingham purchased in 1786 at the cost of 12¼ cents per acre. When the township was originally created, it included the village of Binghamton and a northern portion that is now the town of Dickinson. The creation of the city of Binghamton in 1867 divided the township into two halves without any connection. In 1890, the northern portion was split off to form the town of Dickinson. Today, there are 23.48 square miles of land in the town.

The original inhabitants of the town were squatters living on the lands of William Bingham. Ezra and Ira Keeler were the original settlers on these lands. Ezra and his brother Ira arrived sometime before 1798. Ira Keeler traveled to the area on a raft floating down the Chenango River from Cooperstown to

Chenango Point (Keeler, *Keeler Family*). He brought his mother, Mary, wife, Rosabella, and two children along with him on the raft. Ezra and Ira were two of the residents who signed the 1798 petition to William Bingham asking him to allow them to pay rent and eventually purchase the land on which they lived. Ezra Keeler shortly moved to Schuyler County where he died in 1818. Ira Keeler lived in the town long enough for his son, Revillo, to be born there in 1797. He later moved to Union Center where he died in 1837.

In 1818, Major Martin Hawley arrived in Broome County and settled in the part of the town of Chenango that later became the town of Binghamton. He purchased land there in 1829, including the original 250 acres of the Keeler family. He eventually owned 2,500 acres of land in the town but not without a legal suit against him by several squatters. The courts sided with Hawley in 1833, and he and his son, James, operated a sizable farm. Martin Hawley later moved into the village of Binghamton to operate a general store. Hawley Street in the city of Binghamton is named for him. His son James operated the farm for only a few years before dividing portions for his five children. James left the area and moved to Pennsylvania where he became a judge.

The only settlement in the town is Hawleyton, named after the Hawley family. Some of the original residents called the area The Hemlocks (Thomas). The hamlet grew out of the improved lands of James Hawley near the intersection of the current Park Avenue and the Hawleyton Turnpike. The turnpike was constructed between 1845 and 1846. It was the first road specifically created to connect this area with Pennsylvania and was an extension of the Montrose Turnpike. A section of the road became Park Avenue, and another section that had been surfaced with logs would later become Pennsylvania Avenue.

One of the few industries of the town was the cheese factory that was located in Hawleyton. James Hawley began the company in the mid-nineteenth century. The Hawleyton Creamery Company operated for many years in the hamlet. Hawleyton also supported several stores, blacksmith shops, and wagon and buggy factories. From 1850 through 1902,

This is the Hawleyton School with its pupils in a photograph taken about 1920. Students of this one-room school later attended the Susquehanna Valley School System. (From the *Putnam Collection*, courtesy Broome County Public Library)

The Hawleyton Methodist Church was built in 1855 on lands donated by the Hawley family. A newer church stands near this building that is now the home of the Town of Binghamton Historical Society. (Courtesy Town of Binghamton Historian)

the hamlet also had its own post office. The town hall was located in Hawleyton from 1855 until 1970. At that time, the town hall was relocated to the former Common School District Building Number 7, near Park Terrace, where it remains today.

The first church in the town was the Methodist Episcopal Church in Hawleyton. It was constructed in 1855 through the gift of James Hawley. It was used until 1969 when a new church was constructed. The Town of Binghamton Historical Society now uses the old church structure. Today, there are two more churches in the township: the Park Terrace Gospel Chapel located on Park Avenue in the Park Terrace section of the town and the Faith Baptist Church that was founded on the corner of Ingraham Hill Road and Pennsylvania Avenue in 1975.

The one-room and two-room school buildings that populated the town in the nineteenth and early twentieth centuries were replaced by the 1950s. Today, the Brookside Elementary School located on Saddlemire Road educates hundreds of students as part of the Susquehanna Valley Central School District. A small portion of the town of Binghamton is part of the South Mountain-Hickory Common School District. Approximately 175 families participate in one of the few common school districts left in the state. The students in that district attend the City of Binghamton School District.

The history of the town of Binghamton has been one of a rural existence. Several farms still operate within the township, but most have given way to contribute more to a bedroom community atmosphere. Residential developments have sprung up around the town.

They include Park Terrace Heights, Sherwood Heights, Ridgeview, and Orchard Park. Hawthorne Heights (which includes the South Mountain-Hickory Common School District) includes an area of more expensive homes on land that was once part of the Stone farm.

During the nineteenth and early twentieth centuries, there was some industry in the town of Binghamton. Stone quarrying was found at several locations in the town. Granite and other materials were quarried from operations that ceased prior to World War II. In addition, some work was done to construct a state line railroad that would have connected the city of Binghamton to the village of Montrose in Pennsylvania. The railroad would have allowed trolley and/or rail traffic to flow between the two areas. This intermodal system was not as unusual as it may sound. Some major urban area trolley systems used interconnected railroads to advertise that you can travel long distances via trolleys. While some tracks were laid and paths cleared for the development, the system was never completed.

When the State University of New York at Binghamton relocated to the Vestal Parkway, it forced the Vestal Hill Country Club to move from its original home. The golf course moved to Webb Road in the town of Binghamton.

The former Common School District #7 school building was converted into the Town of Binghamton Town Hall in 1970. The building is located on Park Avenue in the Park Terrace section of the town. (Courtesy Town of Binghamton Historian)

Broome County is unusual in that the Vestal Hill Country Club is in Binghamton, the Binghamton Country Club is in Union, and Binghamton University is in Vestal. The town of Binghamton is also home to the Binghamton Tennis Center for sports enthusiasts.

Ingraham Hill is the location of many of the county's television and radio broadcasting towers because of its excellent location for sending radio and television signals with no impedance from the nearby structures. Ingraham Hill is also home to one of the stranger "urban legends" of Broome County. In recent years, the story has been told of a teacher from the Ingraham Hill School who went berserk and murdered many of the students of the school, burying them in the adjacent Ingraham Hill Cemetery. Although the story works as a tool to scare young students, there is no truth behind the tale.

CHAPTER 17
The Town of
Chenango

This is a postcard of Main Street in Castle Creek in the town of Chenango taken about 1910. Castle Creek retains much of the look it had during the nineteenth century. (Courtesy Broome County Historical Society)

THE TOWN OF CHENANGO was created on February 16, 1791, when Tioga County was split off from Montgomery County. It became one of the original towns of Broome County in 1806. It currently has a population of 11,454 residents (2000 census figure). Through the past two centuries, the boundaries of the town of Chenango have changed completely. At one time, the township encompassed the entire county east of the Chenango River. The evolution of town boundaries eventually moved the entire town to the west of the river. Today, the town of Chenango includes 28.06 square miles of land.

The town was the site of Native American inhabitation for a long period prior to the American Revolution. An Owasco pre-Iroquoian settlement existed there in the thirteenth century. (Other Owasco settlements have been found at Round Top in the town of Union and the Boland site in the town of Fenton.) Various members of the Iroquois Confederacy later inhabited the area. After the end of the American Revolution, a small reservation was located near the Castle Creek area. It is unclear how long this reservation existed, but documentary evidence indicates that it lasted into the early 1800s.

Captain Joseph Leonard settled near what is now Broome Community College in 1787 and attempted to purchase a square mile of land from the local Indian inhabitants. Although the

The Glen Castle Methodist Church is located on Route 12 in the town of Chenango. Its exterior remains similar to its appearance in this photograph taken about 1900. (Courtesy Broome County Historical Society)

agreement was later deemed to be illegal, it was apparent that early settlers had to deal with the Native American residents of the area. Squire Antonio was the Onondaga chief who had great influence over the residents of Otseningo and the "Castle Farm." Squire Antonio's son, Abraham, was fooled into signing away title to the "Castle Farm" for a rifle for which an unscrupulous settler named Patterson traded for the land. Abraham Antonio sought vengeance against Patterson for his deceit and allegedly killed Patterson and his family later in Ohio.

This is the area that was first inhabited by the European-American migration that began shortly after the end of the American Revolution. Broome County's first sawmill was founded in this town in 1788. Either Henry French built it, or Clement and Thomas French may have constructed it. All of the territory of the present township was part of the Boston Purchase, and many of the early settlers came from Massachusetts, Connecticut, and the Hudson River Valley. Many of the families in this area are descended from those early settlers. Much of the township is hilly and rural, and the major areas of settlement are focused along the Chenango River and Creek areas.

The expansion of the suburbs can be seen in this aerial view of Chenango Bridge in the town of Chenango. Kattelville Road is in the foreground, and the area that would become Chenango Commons Golf Course is to the left of the Chenango River. (Courtesy Broome County Historical Society)

There are seven hamlets within the town of Chenango. Castle Creek is the oldest settlement in the town. It is located along Route 11 (also called Castle Creek Road) and is near the site of the Native American reservation of the late 1700s. It is named after the "Castle Farm" where about twenty Native American families resided on approximately 160 acres of land. The Chenango Plaza now occupies the exact site. A post office was established in Castle Creek in 1828, but it was discontinued in 1837. It was revived in 1845 and continues to this day. The hamlet included blacksmiths, several stores, sawmills, gristmills, and two churches.

The hamlet of Chenango Bridge is located along the Chenango River, about four miles north of the city of Binghamton. The New York State government approved the construction of a toll bridge over the river at this point in 1829. The bridge was completed in 1836 and also crossed over the Chenango Canal that ran parallel to the river on its eastern banks. The establishment of the bridge brought in steady revenue for the township and helped establish the growing hamlet. A post office began in 1825 with Charles Jewell as the first postmaster. The post office continues in operation today. Chenango Bridge has developed into a bedroom community with several churches, a golf course, an ice rink, stores, and several other small businesses.

This is a photograph of the Joshua Lewis house in Chenango Forks in the town of Chenango. Joshua Lewis is seen holding the horse in front of the house in this picture from about 1900. (Courtesy Broome County Historical Society)

Glen Castle was originally called Castle Creek Corners. The post office located in this hamlet changed its name in 1857. The settlement is located on the Castle Creek Road between Hinmans Corners and Castle Creek. Today, the area has become more of a crossroads. Nearby, Hinmans Corners was similarly developed after Charles Hinman purchased four hundred acres of land at what is now the juncture of Route 11 and Route 12, at the site of the Chenango Plaza.

The hamlet of Kattelville is named after Elias Kattell, who came from Vermont in 1796 and bought one thousand acres of land. In this area, the large Kattell family operated a tavern, store, hotel, distillery, gristmill, and two sawmills. One of the descendants, Thomas Kattell, was a founding member of the Hinman, Howard and Kattell law firm in Binghamton. Nimmonsburg is located near where the original village of Chenango was once situated. That village evaporated after Joshua Whitney convinced settlers that a new bridge was about to be constructed on the site of present-day Binghamton. Previously known as Goosetown, Colonel William Rose and his brother called the hamlet Rose Settlement because of their original purchase of the land. Burwell Nimmons bought a farm on this site in 1813, and the name was changed to Nimmonsburg. The hamlet of West Chenango was originally called Dimmick Settlement in the early 1800s. It was a stagecoach stop and was once home to a post office. Today, the area is a residential community.

Like all of the rural townships of Broome County, the town of Chenango was home to many farm operations in the nineteenth and twentieth century. Large dairy operations once were common in the town, but only a handful of farms, mainly beef farms, still operate today. The demise of dairy farms has left vacant land that is slowly being developed into tracts of homes with names like Chenango Heights and Maplewood.

The township is also home to one of the earliest airports of the county. Originally called the Binghamton Airport, the Chenango Bridge Airport opened in 1923. Theodore M. Macomber and George Christman started it. During the next eight decades, several different flight schools and operations have been located at the airport. Edwin A. Link operated his flight instruction business there for a short time. Major fires in 1937 and 1953 nearly ended the operation. In the mid-1930s, Harold and Harmon Johnson took over the operation of the field for the next half-century. Today, the airport is home to several local pilots and a large number of model plane enthusiasts.

Lou Rappaport's House of a Thousand Items was a well-known store on Front Street in the town of Chenango in the 1960s. The building has been converted to smaller retail shops today. (Courtesy Broome County Historical Society)

One of the area's oldest cemeteries, Kattelville Cemetery, is the burial place of several Revolutionary War soldiers as well as three men accused of murder. This last fact lends itself to some interesting storytelling during tours of the cemetery. One of the three men, Samuel Miller, was a prominent farmer (and this author's great-great-great-grandfather). His original name was Simeon Mead, and, as a young man, he accidentally killed a wrestling partner during a barn raising. He left Massachusetts after assuming his new name and marrying a young lady in another part of the state. It is unsure how many of his family were even aware of his past.

Another interesting resident of the cemetery is Philemon Beecher Van Trump, the first man to scale Mount Rainier. Although he was born in Lancaster, Ohio, in 1838, he lived most of his life in the West and had worked with General Hazard Stevens on the ascent of the mountain in 1870. A glacier, river, and park on the mountain are named after him. In 1915, he moved to Kattelville to live with his brother, Thomas. He died on December 28, 1916, and his story adds to the continuing sagas of those buried in this town of Chenango cemetery.

CHAPTER 18
The Town of Colesville

This imposing structure is one of the few buildings left from S. Andral Kilmer's sanitarium at Sanitaria Springs. What was once a barn has been converted to a residence. (Courtesy Broome County Historical Society)

The four corners of Harpursville in the town of Colesville retain many of their original buildings, as can be seen in this recent photograph. A fire destroyed the Eldorado Hotel in the early twentieth century, and the site was used for the current fire station. (Courtesy Broome County Historical Society)

THE TOWN OF COLESVILLE was formed on April 2, 1821, when the township was broken off from Windsor. It has a population of 5,441 (2000 census figure) and is one of the largest townships in terms of land size with 68.18 square miles contained within it. It is named after Nathaniel Cole, a Revolutionary War veteran who came to the area in 1795 and settled his family on top of a hill that overlooked Harpursville. The hill is still called Cole's Hill. Although the town is not as old as some in the county, settlement of the area started long before Broome County existed. There were several Tuscarora villages along the Susquehanna River that were destroyed in 1779 by General James Clinton's forces as part of the Sullivan-Clinton Campaign during the American Revolution.

In 1785, John Lamphere and his wife settled in the area that is today Colesville. He began a homestead along the Susquehanna River near present-day Harpursville. The first year, he was alone to clear the land and hunt for wild game on which to survive. The next year, 1786, Lemuel and Nathaniel Badger along with Casper Spring came from New England to settle in the area. They settled near the Lampheres, and the Badgers operated their home as a tavern. During this period, Robert Harpur purchased approximately sixty-one thousand acres of land in present-day Colesville. He sold much of the land to new settlers, and he helped establish the town with his gristmills and sawmills.

There are eleven existing settlements within the town of Colesville. The hamlet of Belden sits atop a steep hill on Route 7. It began with the construction of the Albany & Susquehanna Railroad (Thomas). The workers would stay at Levi Manville's Belden Hotel. The origin of the name Belden is uncertain. There was a post office operation in the settlement from 1870 through 1910. Although much of the settlement has since disappeared, there are several businesses in the area, including the Belden Hill Golf Course.

Center Village is a hamlet whose name explains its location; it is situated between Harpursville and Ouaquaga on Route 79. It was settled in the early 1800s. A hotel was opened in 1832. Lewis Northrup began a tannery operation at the site, and a post office began in 1851. A dam was built across the river at this site; the hydroelectric power was used by many of the residents of the community. The Afton-Windsor Light, Heat & Power Company began its operations in 1913. Although the flood of 1935 destroyed much of the dam, it was rebuilt, and the company continued for many more years.

Doraville is a hamlet that is located two miles south of Center Village on the east side of the Susquehanna River. The settlement was originally called Harmony, and the origin of the present name has been lost. A post office was in operation at the hamlet from 1832 until 1907. In 1994, town historian Minerva Flagg began an effort to save the Doraville Schoolhouse. The building had been constructed in 1830, and it was in danger of being destroyed. Eventually, the schoolhouse was moved to the rear of the Town of Colesville Hall in Harpursville. It has been lovingly restored to its appearance of a mid-nineteenth school and is used as a teaching tool for the students of the Harpursville Central School District and visitors to the area.

Harpursville is the largest hamlet within the town of Colesville. Robert Harpur and his family settled it. In 1790, St. Luke's Episcopal Church was organized. The current church building was erected in 1829 and was in continuous use until 1968. The Old Onaquaga Historical Society, which had begun in 1964, was given permission to use the building as a means to save it from destruction. The society began use of the church as its museum and meeting place in 1970. The Episcopal Church still performs services from the church on rare occasions, making it one of the oldest existing churches in Broome County. Harpursville has been home to many businesses in its history. A post office was established there in 1829 (although using the spelling Harpersville until 1886). The Eldorado Hotel was located at the intersection of Main Street and Route 79. It was destroyed by fire in 1933. Several of the main commercial/business buildings in the hamlet were lost in large fires in 1889 and 1901. Today, the hamlet still has a general store, several businesses, and the Methodist Church.

Nineveh is the only hamlet in the town of Colesville that is shared by both Broome County and Chenango County. Named after the Biblical location, Nineveh was settled before 1830. Located along the Chenango River on Route 7, a post office opened in the hamlet in 1833. J. W. Hobbs and his sons operated a carriage-manufacturing factory. They ran the firm from 1845 until 1920. It was later called the Nineveh Coach & Car Company.

North Colesville is located on the top of Windy Hill on Route 79. Aptly named, the location was

This was the Mumford Store, located in the hamlet of Tunnel. The photograph was taken about 1900. The Gates family now uses the structure as a residence. (Courtesy Town of Colesville Historian)

An oil tank of the New York Transit Oil Company in Osborne Hollow (Sanitaria Springs) exploded in 1917, causing a massive fire. The facility was closed in 1926. A residence is now on the site. (Courtesy Town of Colesville Historian)

CHAPTER 18: THE TOWN OF COLESVILLE

formerly called Watrous Corners for an early family that once inhabited this small hamlet. At one time, a grange and general store were located at this crossroads. Ouaquaga is located in the southern part of the town across the Susquehanna River from the base of Ouaquaga Mountain. The name is derived from one of the many of the many spellings of Onaquaga, the Iroquois settlement. The hamlet was originally called Susquehanna when a post office was established there in 1826. The name was changed in 1859.

Sanitaria Springs is located near Route 7 and Interstate 88. It was originally called Osborne Hollow, but the name was changed when S. Andral Kilmer used its mineral spring water to develop a complex of buildings on the site and promote the water's "medicinal" effects. He built a hotel at the site in 1890 and operated the curative sanitarium until 1914. A post office operated from 1828 until the 1980s. A grange and a railroad station have both ceased operation. The hamlet still has one church and several small businesses that continue to operate. Most of the spa buildings were sold and dismantled. Only the sanitarium's carriage house and springhouse are still standing today.

The Doraville Schoolhouse was moved from its original location to Harpursville where it stands on the ground of the Colesville Town Hall. It is used to educate local students about how schools operated in the 1850s. (Courtesy Town of Colesville Historian)

Tunnel is one of the best known of the hamlets within the town of Colesville. The name is derived from the railroad tunnel carved through the mountain by the Albany & Susquehanna Railroad in 1869. This is the site of the famous fight between robber barons Jay Gould and Jim Fisk, the owners of the New York and Erie Railroad, versus the forces of the Albany & Susquehanna Railroad managed by Joseph Ramsey. On August 10, 1869, the two forces met in the tunnel, and a battle ensued with men with pick handles, shovels, hammers, and other weapons from two trains of opposing workers. Eventually, the men of the Albany railroad won the battle. The event became part of the novel and movie *Saratoga Trunk*. The tunnel is now denoted as a National Engineering Landmark. Tunnel is also home to the Villeco Cheese Factory, a family-operated business that has been a part of the hamlet for over five decades.

Vallonia Springs is a hamlet named after mineral springs that were used to promote the area in the late nineteenth century. A hotel was constructed on the site in 1884. The hotel was a stagecoach stop on the route between New York and Syracuse. A post office opened in 1838 but ceased operations in 1903. The settlement once included a church, store, bar, restaurant, and creamery. Today the hotel building still stands, but many of the other structures are now gone.

West Colesville is the final settlement in the town of Colesville. Old State Road coming from Port Dickinson intersects this crossroads. The area had a post office in operation from 1846 until 1902.

The town of Colesville is one of only two townships in Broome County with no zoning or code ordinances (the other is Nanticoke). Despite its large size, it remains fairly rural and sparsely populated. A new senior citizens center opened in Harpursville in the last five years to aid the growing population of the aged in the township. Colesville has been home to many interesting residents in its history. One of the most compelling was Joseph Smith, the founder of the Church of Jesus Christ of Latter-day Saints (Mormons). Smith was a carpenter who spent time in this region working at several locations, including Nineveh and Windsor, New York, and Susquehanna, Pennsylvania. He lived in the home of Joseph Knight in Nineveh for several years. He preached from that location, and on more than one occasion, he was arrested. Deacon Josiah Stowell and other residents staunchly defended him. He met his future wife, Emma Hale, while in New York and married her in 1827. Smith took her to Manchester, New York, and then he returned to the region, moving to nearby Pennsylvania.

CHAPTER 19
The Town of
Conklin

This is the summer home of H. C. Larrabee of the Sturdevant-Larrabee Wagon Company of Binghamton. Many businessmen and their families enjoyed summer homes along the Susquehanna River in Conklin. (Courtesy Broome County Historical Society)

This is a 1910 photograph of the Conklin railroad station. The area was called Milburn until the early years of the twentieth century. The station has since been taken down. (Courtesy Broome County Historical Society)

THE TOWN OF CONKLIN was formed from the town of Chenango in 1824. It is named for Judge John Conklin, who purchased three hundred acres on the north side of the Susquehanna River in 1817. With an area of 21.55 square miles, it is one of the smaller townships within Broome County. It has a population of 5,940 (2000 census figure) in an area divided between an industrial core and a rural exterior. Located in southern Broome County and bordered by Pennsylvania, the township was originally bisected by the Susquehanna River. The northern portion, including the former John Conklin land, was removed in 1959 to become the town of Kirkwood.

The first settlers came to the Conklin area in 1788. Waples Hance, Jonathan Bennett, and Ralph Lathrop settled on separate farms near the mouth of Big Snake Creek where it meets the Susquehanna River. By the time of the town's creation in 1824, there were 635 people living in the area. In 1844, Turnbull & Company began operations of the first hardwood acid distillation factory in the United States. The town already had several sawmills and tannery operations because of the large number of hardwood trees available in the area and the large agricultural base of the county. The factory was located at the mouth of Little Snake Creek and lasted through several owners. Workers' homes were built near the factory site, and remnants of the factory are still visible.

There are five centers of settlement within the town of Conklin. The hamlet of Conklin was originally called Milburn and is located on Route 7. At this site, a post office was located between 1826 and 1857. In the last thirty years, a small retail operation has formed in this area. The Lawrence Brothers Dairy operation was located near here for much of the twentieth century. Portions of the former dairy operation have been turned into a sports park business.

The town hall is located nearby. The "Castle" was originally constructed as the home of Alpheus B. Corby, in about 1905. It was built to resemble the castles of Europe. By 1920, the structure had been converted to the Universal Spiritualist Church where Carol McKinistry sought to raise the spirit of Rudolph Valentino. George F. Johnson purchased the home in 1930. It was used as a home for undernourished and underprivileged children, run by the Broome County Humane Society and Relief Association. Finally, on June 13, 1944, Johnson donated the home to the town of Conklin to be used as a community center.

The Corbettsville Post Office as it appeared in 1965. Mr. and Mrs. B. Browe Stone kept the facility operating. The Postal Service recently completed construction on a new post office for the hamlet. (Courtesy Broome County Historical Society)

It has been used as the town hall since that date. In 2004, the town government enlarged the town hall. By staying with the original style of architecture, the new addition adds to the grandeur of the building.

The hamlet of Conklin Center is located on the eastern edge of the township. The pioneer settlers of this area began arriving in 1813, and a post office was established here in 1851. More established as a settlement is Conklin Forks, located at the confluence of the Little Snake Creek and the West Fork. A post office was begun here in 1873 but closed in 1902. Conklin Center survived a tornado in August 1924. A barn was destroyed, several cattle

The Conklin Town Hall was originally a residence before George F. Johnson purchased the Castle and gave it to the community. A recent addition has doubled the space for town offices. In this 1954 photograph, Nina Crocker is seen near the flagpole. (Courtesy Broome County Historical Society)

killed and several homes were damaged. Still mainly a farming area, the hamlet includes a store and several small businesses.

Conklin Station was located adjacent to the railroad lines of the Delaware, Lackawanna and Western Railroad. A new bridge between Conklin and Kirkwood now cuts Old Conklin Road into two streets and divides Conklin Station into two small residential areas. John Bayless began a general store here in 1840. The settlement also included a grocery store, a Presbyterian church, and a schoolhouse. The area had its own post office in 1870.

Corbettsville is the oldest settlement within the town of Conklin. It is named after Robert Corbett, who moved here from Milford, Massachusetts (via New Milford, Pennsylvania), in 1801. The Corbett family was involved in many of the early businesses and industries of that area, including sawmills, gristmills, a foundry, a wagon shop, a hotel, and a store (Thomas). The first post office was begun in 1839, in the Corbett store. The hamlet now has a modern post office.

In recent decades, the town of Conklin has evolved toward a more complex role in the county. Still very much of a bedroom community, it includes three churches, the Susquehanna Valley High School, the Middle School, and Francis P. Donnelly Elementary School in Conklin Center. Conklin is also home to many industries. One of the oldest businesses in the town is Eureka Tent & Awning Company, a division of Johnson Worldwide. The tent company began operations in the late nineteenth century. It makes and sells many different lines of tents, including those for the military.

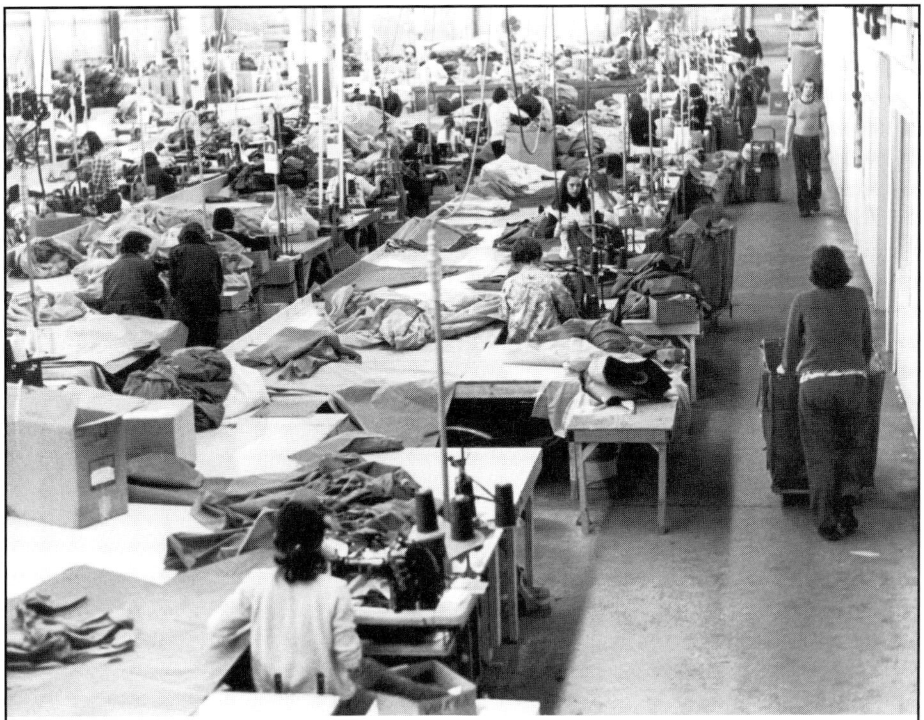

In 1986, the Broome Corporate Park opened in the town of Conklin. It was meant to be a counterpart to the Broome Industrial Park located across from it in the town of Kirkwood. As industries came to require more modern factory space, industrial parks became more popular across the country. The Broome Corporate Park was designed to meet the needs of the newer non-smokestack industries. Today, it houses the corporate offices of firms such as Maines Paper & Food Service, a multibillion-dollar enterprise.

In recent years, Conklin has expanded with the creation of the Broome Industrial Park and Eureka Tent & Awning (seen here) that is part of Johnson Worldwide Associates. (Courtesy Broome County Historical Society)

As an example of the continual development of the town, near the corporate park are Schurbusch Park and a newer executive-style golf course. The town of Conklin continues to thrive as a vital part of Broome County.

CHAPTER 20

The Town of Dickinson

Sawtelle Tavern was a popular stagecoach stop on Chenango Street in Port Dickinson. It was built in the late 1700s and located across from the intersection with Old State Road. It was removed to make way for a two-family home. (Courtesy Broome County Historical Society)

This 1911 photograph shows the town of Dickinson as seen from Mount Prospect. The area in the foreground was developed as Sunrise Terrace in the 1940s and 1950s. (Courtesy Broome County Historical Society)

THE TOWN OF DICKINSON was the last township to be created in Broome County. It was broken off from the town of Binghamton to become an independent town on December 12, 1890, and was named in honor of Daniel S. Dickinson, the area's leading politician. At the time of its creation, Dickinson had a population of 525. Currently, it has a population of 5,325 (2000 census figure) including the population of the village of Port Dickinson and 3,618 excluding the village. There are 3.47 square miles of land in the township. The first post office in Dickinson was started in 1890, shortly after the town was created. While the area may have been the last town to be created in the county, the history of the town of Dickinson dates back to the earliest history of the region.

Situated along the banks of the Chenango River, the area was the site of Otseningo, a Native American village. The stable life of that village ended during the American Revolution when the forces of General James Clinton invaded its territory. The inhabitants chose to burn their own village rather than allow the colonists' forces to destroy what the Iroquois had worked to build. Today, the site is home to Otsiningo Park. The park is part of the Broome County Parks System and has the largest number of visitors each year among county parks.

The area was also the site of the first-known New England settler in the county. Captain Joseph Leonard built his log home near the Chenango River, along what is today Front Street. There was a family story in which members of the Leonard family came downstairs and found several Native Americans sleeping by the fireplace. The home stood from its construction (the chimney had the date 1799 on it) until it was burned down in 1985 by the town's fire department as an exercise. The site is now occupied by the GHS Federal Credit Union building.

Near the Leonard home settled many other early residents of Broome County. By the late eighteenth century, a string of homes and farms could be found on the western side of the Chenango River. The first court in the future Broome County was held in 1791 under the elm trees of the Joshua Whitney farmhouse near present-day Sunrise Terrace. The first school was held in a building at the base of Mount Prospect, bordering the town of Dickinson and the current boundary of the city of Binghamton.

Much of the development of the town of Dickinson was dependent on improving the systems of transportation. Many of the main roads in the town of Dickinson were former routes of the Native Americans living in this region. These include Front Street, Chenango Street, and Old State Road. Along these routes traveled stagecoaches moving people in and out of Binghamton. Taverns and stops for the stagecoaches were built in the town. Sawtelle Tavern was built in the 1790s. The building faced Old State Road, originally the Catskill Turnpike. The French statesman, Talleyrand, was a visitor to Sawtelle Tavern during his visit to the area in 1794–95. The building was

Captain Joseph Leonard's 1799 home was located on Front Street across from Broome Community College. It was removed in the 1980s to make way for the GHS Federal Credit Union building. (Courtesy Broome County Historical Society)

demolished in 1964 for the construction of a two-family home. Farther north along the road at 761 Chenango Street was another tavern and stop that was built in the early 1800s. The home was used at various times as a fruit stand and doll hospital, but today it has been restored to its original appearance.

The Chenango Canal ran through the town of Dickinson along the eastern side of the river. The canal opened up in 1837, and the arrival of packet boats loaded with coal resulted in the development of a coal station in the town. This stop along the canal grew into the village of Port Dickinson. The history of the village will be discussed in a later chapter. As it did in many areas, the canal resulted in an increase in the population, business, and industrial base of the community.

In 1850, John Ward Cutler built a substantial farmhouse along Front Street adjacent to his farmland and the pond that was located on the land. A smokehouse on the rear of the property became the first home of the Cutler Ice Company. Its employees cut large blocks of ice each year from the pond, stored them, and cut them into smaller blocks to be sold to fill the thousands of iceboxes of the area in the late nineteenth and early twentieth centuries. The firm operated in Binghamton for many years and continues under new ownership as Magic City Ice Company.

Cutler's son, Philander Cutler, constructed a Victorian farmhouse in 1875. It was built directly across Front Street from his father's home. In 1954, Frances Cutler left the home and twenty-three acres of land in her will to be used by the Broome County Farm and Home Center and the 4-H Club. Cutler Gardens has been developed at the site and is a popular horticultural experience for both young and old.

Just north of this site, the Broome County government purchased ninety-five acres of the Joshua Whitney estate in 1831. The site was located on both the west and east sides of Front Streets and developed as the Broome County Poorhouse (discussed earlier in the text). The farm operation of the Poorhouse was later used as part of the operation of the Broome County Jail. The Jail Barracks were constructed on the site in 1936 and used until the new jail facility was opened in 1995.

In 1956, the campus of the Broome Community Technical Institute was relocated from the Kalurah Temple in Binghamton to a new facility on Front Street adjacent to the Broome County Infirmary (as the Poorhouse was then called). The name of the school was changed to Broome Community College in 1971 as the liberal arts program increased in importance. The campus now hosts over seven thousand students annually.

Excluding the village of Port Dickinson, the town of Dickinson has three settlements within its borders. Chenango Shores, Forest Hills, and Morningside Heights were planned developments using the lands and resources of Francis "Zip" Boland. He was a New York State Assemblyman whose family had been involved in the construction of many Endicott Johnson homes. His family home on Front Street became the core of the Elizabeth Church Manor, a nursing and retirement facility operated by the United Methodist Church.

Prospect Terrace began its history as the hamlet of Stella. The name came from the daughter of Henry Butman, the first postmaster of the town, who selected the name when the post office began in 1890. The name also was associated with Stella to New Ireland Road, the route connecting the hamlet to an area of Irish farmers near the present-day Greater

Children enjoy the elephant ride during a circus sponsored by the Port Dickinson Fire Department in 1964. Today, children of the area still enjoy the village's park and many recreational facilities. (Courtesy Broome County Historical Society)

From the 1950s until today, the area surrounding the former Broome County Poor Farm has developed into Broome Community College, the Broome County Public Safety Facility, an ice rink, the BAGSAI facility, and other facilities. (Courtesy Broome County Historical Society)

Binghamton Regional Airport. The name has since been shortened to Stella Ireland Road. The Stella School has since closed and is used for offices. In the early 1910s, Ann McNamara constructed a number of homes on land she owned on the north side of Prospect Street. She coined the name Prospect Terrace.

While that name is still used today, many residents used another name—Polish Heaven. It was an area settled by Eastern European immigrants who moved there to work in the nearby factories of Endicott Johnson and Ansco. The Polish Community Center was constructed on Prospect Street. The area had two churches:

St. Stanislaus Kosta Roman Catholic Church was a congregation that was primarily of Polish descent; the congregation of St. Ann's Roman Catholic Church consisted of Slovak immigrants and their families. In 2004, these two churches were merged with St. Mary's Russian Orthodox Church, located on Baxter Street in the city of Binghamton. The combined church is now called the Church of the Holy Trinity.

Sunrise Terrace began near the former lands of the Whitneys and Cutlers in the town of Dickinson. Albert C. Adams and his wife, Edith, owned farmland that faced the east. A visit to a development in Texas called Sunset Terrace inspired the Sunrise Terrace name (Thomas). The development was begun at a time when the suburban areas were experiencing monumental growth. Sunrise Terrace included a community center, a garden club, and other amenities associated with planned suburban life. It was an area close to Binghamton without the hubbub of city life. It is interesting to note that this area was the last to be involved with an annexation of land to the city of Binghamton. The city required land to expand the Ely Park Apartments and made a deal that would allow the students of Sunrise Terrace to attend the city school district in return for the acreage.

In recent years, the town of Dickinson has experienced many of the growth pangs of suburbia with increased traffic and retail growth. The former lands of the Broome County Poorhouse have been turned into parking spaces for Broome Community College; the poorhouse's cemetery was closed, and some of the bodies were removed to Spring Forest Cemetery. The area was first used as the garden plots for the Broome County Parks System and now hosts a Regal Theater complex, a hotel, and a restaurant. The area around the community college now includes the county's dog shelter, the headquarters for the Broome-Tioga Association of Retarded Citizens, an ice rink, and the Broome County Public Safety Facility, which houses Emergency Services, the Sheriff's Department, and the jail.

CHAPTER 21

The Town of Fenton

This is a 1940s look at the intersection of Albany and Canal Streets in Port Crane. Port Crane began developing with the opening of the Chenango Canal and continues to thrive today. (Courtesy Town of Fenton Historian)

This is an 1876 engraving of the home of William Williamson located in North Fenton. Farmsteads such as this one were common in the town. The home, located on Route 369, still stands today. (Courtesy Broome County Historical Society)

THE TOWN OF FENTON was created on December 3, 1855, when two portions of the town of Chenango were split off to form the town of Binghamton and the town of Port Crane. The name of Port Crane referred to the hamlet on a "port" of the Chenango Canal that ran through the township. The name was changed in 1867 to honor Reuben E. Fenton, who was then governor of New York State. The town of Fenton has a population of 6,909 (2000 census figure). It includes 28.5 square miles of land that is split into a highly suburban area and a much larger rural portion.

For much of its existence, the town of Fenton was an area that relied on lumbering and a largely rural area dotted with many family-operated farms. Many of the families who ran these farms moved into Broome County during its first half-century. English, Miller, and Prentice are only a few of the families whose descendants continue to inhabitant this township. While the agricultural aspect of the town's economy was important to its continued success, it was the opening of the Chenango Canal that spurred its economic activity and growth.

The Chenango Canal promised to bring both people and business to the areas that it traversed. This was true for the town of Fenton. The route of the canal passed close to the Chenango River through this area. Also in this area was Lock 107 near Chenango Forks. It was the only guard lock on the entire canal, allowing boats to both leave and enter the canal at this point. This bode well for the town of Fenton because the traffic would increase in this section as the canal approached the growing city of Binghamton. The main product carried on the canal was coal, and the stops along the canal would prosper from the ability to bring this and other products to their communities. This was certainly true of Port Crane.

Port Crane is one of four hamlets in the town of Fenton. While it grew because of its connection to the Chenango Canal, it was an important economic part of the development of the township during the nineteenth century. It was named in honor of Jason Crane, an engineer on the canal. The post office opened here in 1842. The growing hamlet included a variety of businesses and industries, including a blacksmith shop, cooperage, stove factory, grocery store, doctor's office, and hotel. The Van Amburgh Hotel in Port Crane became the spot for canal travelers who enjoyed the company of other travelers and canal workers. Some would take a side trip to nearby Lily Lake. The hotel burned down in the 1870s, and, with the closing of the Chenango Canal by 1878, the growth of Port Crane came to an end. Today, the hamlet still survives. The former Port Crane Elementary School has been converted into both the Town of Fenton offices and a laboratory for the New York State Police.

North Fenton is another hamlet that was created in the early years of Broome County. It was originally known as Ketchum's Corners after Caleb Ketchum, an early settler in the area. Located near Page Brook, it was a convenient location for those involved in both farming and early industry. Isaac Page settled adjacent to the brook in 1807, and others shortly followed him, including the Hull, Lounsberry, and Taber families. Several sawmills were located along the brook, especially near its proximity with the Chenango Canal. North Fenton's business district included churches, a schoolhouse, and a hotel. It also included the Ketchum Corner Chair Factory that began in 1866. Located nearby was a cheese factory that began operating in the 1860s. In the early 1900s, the factory was converted into a creamery. A post office opened there in 1867, but it was closed in 1904. The North Fenton Methodist Church began in 1840 and continues to the present day. The most recent addition to the area is the North Fenton Baptist Chapel that operated from the former Grange building.

The suburban area of Hillcrest is the largest population center in the town of Fenton. It is also the most recent of the residential developments within the town. There were early settlers in the area, including members of the Hotchkiss and Crocker families. Their Federal and Greek Revival homes still adorn parts of Chenango Street, the main thoroughfare through the hamlet. The proximity to the Chenango Canal, as well as to the Delaware and Hudson Railroad lines, aided in attracting residents and businesses to the region.

The Binghamton Art Club enjoys the beauty of Lily Lake in an early 1900s photograph. Now called Chenango Lake, it remains the heart of Chenango Valley State Park in the town of Fenton. Seated at the right is local artist Catherine Bartoo. (Courtesy Broome County Historical Society)

A group of buildings located on Nowlan Road have been home to several firms through the decades. During World War I, evaporated milk was made in cans for the soldiers. Larrabee Deyo Truck Company used the facility to manufacture fire engines, ambulances, and other vehicles. Nestlé's Ice Cream occupied the factory in the 1920s. Link Aviation (later CAE Link) used the buildings as one of its plants, and recently, B. W. Elliott Manufacturing has made the facility its headquarters. Metalworking plants and small stores began to grow around the factory. St. Catherine's Roman Catholic Church, Ogden United Methodist Church, and the Church of the Nazarene service the community. The residents of the town enjoy the Fenton Free Library located in the Moody Memorial Building, the bequest of Mr. and Mrs. Raymond Moody in 1967.

Hillcrest is also home to the Wyoming Conference Children's Home. Operated by the United Methodist Church, the home began in 1922 originally to take care of

The Wyoming Conference Children's Home is a town of Fenton facility that has helped local youth in need for many decades, Operated by the Wyoming Conference of the United Methodist Church, the institution assists hundreds of children each year. (Courtesy Broome County Historical Society)

orphaned children. In recent decades, the home's administration has converted the facility to assist children with special needs who are referred by the Department of Social Services, local school districts, the courts, and the Department of Mental Health. Funding is provided by a number of governmental and private sources.

The town of Fenton is also home to a number of smaller religious organizations. The Pilgrim Holiness Church Camp has operated since 1905 in Hillcrest. During the summer, revival-type meetings are held. The Path of Life Camp is a privately owned summer camp where a special program mingles deaf and hearing children in normal events. Lily Lake Camp, which is an operation of the Churches of Christ in Christian Union, is located near Chenango Valley State Park. It operates both a summer camp and a family camp each year.

The Chenango Valley State Park began as farmland around Round Pond, a spring-fed pond where fishermen found many types of trout, bass, perch, and bullhead. A couple that lived at the lake sold sandwiches to the fishermen. They dammed the lake, increasing its size. Flooded tree stumps gave rise to a new name, Stumpy Pond. In 1890, Charles C. Warner purchased the lake, pulled out the stumps, and built four cottages and a boathouse. He renamed the lake Long Pond. By 1901, the body of water was again renamed, becoming Lily Pond. In 1927, the area was acquired for a state park and opened to the public on Memorial Day, 1930. From 1933 to 1942, the park underwent major construction as part of the Works Progress Administration with the help of two hundred workers from the Civilian Conservation Corps. Many stone buildings were erected, trails were added, and a fish hatchery was added near one of the two lakes of the park. Lily Pond became Chenango Lake, and a smaller pond became Lily Lake. The park originally had a nine-hole golf course that was enlarged to eighteen holes in the late 1940s. Today, the park hosts thousands of campers, golfers, picnickers, and swimmers.

The town of Fenton has been home to several interesting personalities. The Reverend Enos Puffer was a pastor of the North Fenton Methodist Church, but he also invented a bomb that was used during the Civil War. George Hull was a part-time cigar maker and full-time scam artist who spent his time at his home near Port Crane and in Binghamton. He concocted the idea of creating a fake prehistoric giant while living with his sister in Iowa in 1866. Hull contracted with two sculptors in Chicago to create a giant man made out of gypsum. The statue was crated and shipped to the home of his cousin, Stub Newell in Cardiff, New York. There it was buried in 1868 and "accidentally" found in 1869, and the news announcement that a petrified giant had been discovered brought thousands to see the creature. The

The Chenango Canal brought economic growth to Port Crane. This is a 1920s photograph of the remains of one of the canal's locks. Today, only Lock 107, located in Chenango Valley State Park, remains intact in Broome County. (From the *Putnam Collection*, courtesy Broome County Public Library)

scam made a small fortune for Hull, despite the revelation that the Cardiff Giant was a fake. Hull died in 1926.

One of the most infamous inhabitants of Port Crane was Dr. Thomas Tiffany, who was tried and convicted for the attempted murder of a Port Crane storeowner, Charles Carman. Dr. Tiffany was involved with Mrs. Carman and planned Charles Carman's murder. Although the attempt failed, it was revealed that Dr. Tiffany had been involved with mysterious poisonings in Afton, where he had lived before arriving in Port Crane. Charles Jackson was a well-known resident of the Port Crane area. He assisted many of the families in the area by helping to dig basements, ditches, graves, and wells for most of his life. When Jackson was swindled out of his home, the aged and respected African American's care was a concern. He was taken to the Port Crane fire station where a small shed was built next to the facility to be used as a home. The fire company provided for his care until his death.

CHAPTER 22
The Town of Kirkwood

In a departure from the usual residential architecture, Gottlieb Dieke (seen standing) built this unusual home in the 1930s on Old Windsor Road at Five-Mile Point. (Courtesy Broome County Historical Society)

THE TOWN OF KIRKWOOD was created from the town of Conklin on November 23, 1859. It lies on the northern side of the Susquehanna River and was named after James Pugh Kirkwood, the chief engineer of the New York and Erie Railroad, who was instrumental in building the Starrucca Viaduct and bringing the railroad through this area in 1848. It includes 25.7 square miles of land and has a population of 5,651 (2000 census figure).

Haynes Johnson built this Federal-style brick home prior to 1835 in Kirkwood. Haynes was descended from Irish surgeon Jeremiah Johnson, who came to New York before 1750. The home shows the spread of culture and architecture in what was a rural community. (Courtesy Broome County Historical Society)

The first known settler to the area after the conclusion of the American Revolution was Jonathan Fitch. He came to the town in 1789 and settled near the outlet of Fitch's Creek at Five Mile Point. Here he began the first gristmill in the county in 1792. Gerret Snedaker arrived shortly afterward and established residence along the Susquehanna River about one mile from the hamlet of Kirkwood. Many of the new settlers to this region came along what was called the Catskill Turnpike. The route ran through the Catskill Mountains from the Hudson River and continued to its end terminus at the Chenango River. Today, the remaining portion is known as Old State Road. Part of this road runs through the northern portion of the town of Kirkwood. Another early road through the region followed the route of the Susquehanna River from Great Bend, Pennsylvania, and continued through to Binghamton. Today, it is part of U.S. Route 11, and it has helped bring many travelers through the Kirkwood area.

The development of the railroad through the town of Kirkwood aided in its growth and settlement. Although much of the township was rural in nature in its first century of existence, there were pockets of development. The town has six hamlets within its borders. Brookvale is centered on Colesville Road in the town. It has also been called Standley Hollow after Benajah Standley, who came to the area around 1805. A post office was established in 1873

The impressive two-room Kirkwood School educated thousands of children before it closed. The Kirkwood Historical Society restored it for use as a community center. (Courtesy Broome County Historical Society)

and discontinued in 1902. Early families such as Pierce, Randall, and others helped create the community. There was a Universalist Church in that area about 1900. The Brookvale United Methodist Church still operates here. Five Mile Point gets its name from its geographical location; it is five miles from the Broome County Courthouse. The hamlet includes Five Mile Point Speedway, a racing facility that has operated since 1950 and was also the end terminus of the first section of what was originally called the Penn-Can Highway. Now Interstate 81, it opened to the public in 1961, the first of several interstates developed through Broome County.

The hamlet of Kirkwood is the largest of the settlements within the town. It dates to the 1840s and 1850s. A bridge connects residents of the northern side of the Susquehanna River with the inhabitants of the southern side in the town of Conklin. A post office was opened in Kirkwood in 1850 and continues to operate today. The Kirkwood Wagon Works began operations in this hamlet in 1884. Although a redirection of Route 11 has moved much of the traffic away from the hamlet, it continues to thrive. In the 1990s, the Kirkwood Historical Society undertook the restoration of the two-room schoolhouse located here. Today, the building is used for historical meetings and serves as a community center for the local people.

Kirkwood Center is a small hamlet located along the western edge of the township. A

The Kirkwood Wagon Works was one of the early industries in the town. This is a photograph of the business and its employees about 1890. (Courtesy Town of Kirkwood Historian)

The town of Kirkwood was originally the location of the New York State Inebriate Asylum, described earlier in this text. The cornerstone for Isaac Perry's "Castle" building was laid in 1858. It was still part of the town when a major fire in 1864 nearly destroyed the facility. But with the growth and importance of the institution, the property was annexed to the city of Binghamton in 1866. Another fire ruined the Kirkwood railroad depot in 1864.

post office was opened there in 1861, but it was closed in 1910. The hamlet of Langdon was a milk and postal stop for the New York and Erie Railroad and was named for David Moore Langdon, who settled there with his family from Connecticut in 1842. A post office was opened in about 1877. One of the family's descendants, Frank Langdon, was a cousin of Joyce Kilmer, the author of the well-known poem "Trees" (Kilmer's aunt and uncle lived in the city of Binghamton), and he was a distant cousin of Willis Sharpe Kilmer. Riverside is the hamlet closest to the border with the state of Pennsylvania. It had a post office in operation from 1870 to 1911. The riverboat *Ermine* ran excursion rides from this point on the Susquehanna River to the Starrucca Viaduct.

There have been several interesting personalities who have lived in the town of Kirkwood. The journals of Samuel Bayless give interesting insights into the early history of the town. Bayless was a farmer and businessman whose writings cover the period from 1858 to 1865. During this time, Bayless describes going out "west" to Olean, New York, on a cattle drive where the livestock were put on railroad cars to be brought back to Kirkwood. Dr. Beebe was a local physician during the early decades of the twentieth century. His daybook reflects the day-to-day care of his patients. When the Spanish influenza epidemic spread from Europe to the United States in 1918, the seventy-three-year-old doctor was put to the test. Rather than the usual two or three visits each day, he was treating twenty-three patients each day during the height of the disease.

The town is the only one in Broome County where the children of the town are served by four different school districts: Chenango Valley, Harpursville, Susquehanna Valley, and Windsor. Both the Floyd Bell Elementary School of the Windsor Central School District and the Cedarhurst Elementary School of the Susquehanna Valley School District are located in the town.

In the last fifty years, the town of Kirkwood has undergone a tremendous growth in industry and business. In 1965, Link Aviation opened a plant in the town. The facility was close to both the burgeoning interstate highway system and railroad system. It was also on open land with a lower tax base than the city of Binghamton. In the last five decades, the plant has had several owners and is currently operated by L-3 Communications/Link. It continues to develop and make simulators and related software.

The opening of the Link plant paved the way for the development of the Kirkwood Industrial Park. Today, New York State Electric and Gas Corporation, Putnam Publishing, and two dozen other companies are within or adjacent to the industrial park. The increasing truck traffic from the interstate and from local businesses is serviced by two truck stops located within the town. Since 1995, travelers coming north on Interstate 81 have been greeted by the New York State Gateway Center. Thousands of tourists stop in Kirkwood and refresh themselves while learning about the wonders of New York State.

The construction of Interstate 81 marked a turning point for Kirkwood. The Kirkwood Industrial Park near Five-Mile Point helped to spur growth in the area. The Singer-Link building can be seen in lower right. (Courtesy Broome County Historical Society)

CHAPTER 23

The Town of Lisle

The Stoddards were among the early settlers of Lisle. The left side of this home was the original portion; the right side was added in the late 1800s and included a dance hall on the top floor. The house still stands today. (Courtesy Broome County Historical Society)

This early 1900s postcard shows Center Lisle. The original name of the settlement was Yorkshire but was changed in the late 1800s. (Courtesy Town of Lisle Historian)

This is an aerial view of the hamlet of Killiwog in the town of Lisle. Many of the original buildings remain standing today. The origin of the community's name continues as a matter of debate. (Courtesy Town of Lisle Historian)

THE TOWN OF LISLE is one of the oldest towns in Broome County. Split off from the town of Union on April 7, 1801, it was one of the original townships when Broome County was created in 1806. The name of the area was originally Mudlick, but it was later named Lisle after Lisle, France. General Lafayette, the hero of the Revolutionary War, toured the new nation after the war. He was acquainted with Broome County residents General Hyde and John Patterson. The region was said to have reminded Lafayette of his estate in Lisle, France. The town was sometimes called the Old State of Lisle before it was reduced in size in 1831. The towns of Nanticoke, Barker, and Triangle and a small piece of Union were split off from the town of Lisle. The current configuration contains 40.03 square miles of land (or 39.31 square miles without the village of Lisle). The population is 2,405 (2000 census figure).

The Tioughnioga River bisects the town, creating a rich river valley. There are also many low hills that are well suited for agriculture. All of Lisle was part of the Boston Purchase that encompassed northern Broome County. The first settlers in the town were Josiah Patterson, Ebenezer Tracy, Edward Edwards, David Manning, Eliphalet Parsons, and Whittlesey Gleason, who arrived as early as 1791. The waterpower provided by the Tioughnioga River and nearby creeks made the area ripe for the development of a number of mills. Jacob Hill built the first gristmill in 1800. By 1810, several sawmills and a carding mill also existed in the town. A quarter century later, in 1835, the town had three gristmills, twenty sawmills, one oilcloth mill, three fulling mills, three carding mills, one triphammer (forging) mill, three tanneries, and one potash manufacturing facility.

The first free library in Broome County opened in the town of Lisle in 1814. The Union Free Library evolved out of the town residents' interest in having a library. The hamlet of

Chenango Point (Binghamton) had opened the county's first library in the county in 1801, but it was a subscription library with members paying for the privilege of borrowing books. The Union Free Library published a catalogue of its holdings, with a total monetary value of just over three hundred dollars. The library received operating funds from the taxes of property owners. It remained in operation until 1839.

As in most of the townships in Broome County, the children of the town were served by a number of small, local school districts until school consolidation occurred in the twentieth century. At one time, the town of Lisle had ten school districts within its borders. The first school was held in the corn barn of Alpheus Hanks. The most famous teacher in Lisle's history was Abigail Powers, who taught school at Lisle in 1824. Two years later, she married Millard Fillmore of Moravia, New York, who would later become the thirteenth president of the United States.

The town of Lisle expanded faster than any other town in the early history of Broome County. Its population was 660 in 1800, but it had grown to 2,144 only ten years later. By 1830, the population had grown to 4,393. The town appeared to be on its way to being a center of population and industry until two things happened to change the course of its development. As previously mentioned, the town was split into four parts in 1831, reducing the size and population of the remaining portion that is today the town of Lisle. In 1834, construction began on the Chenango Canal. Its opening in 1837 took water traffic away from Lisle. Both goods and people now moved along the route of the canal, several miles away. The town had reached its height of growth before 1850.

The importance of agriculture is still evident in Lisle today. Clearing the forests for the lumber used in the various mill operations and in the construction of homes and barns left the land ripe for use by farmers. Sizable farms were located among the hills surrounding the various hamlets of the town. Although the number of farm operations has declined in recent decades, farming is still an important part of the landscape in the town of Lisle.

There are eleven areas of settlement within the town's boundaries. The village of Lisle is the only incorporated municipality within the town and will be discussed in a later chapter. Caldwell (sometimes spelled Cadwell) Settlement was named after one of the early families in the vicinity. Caldwell Road remains today and ends at Route 79 near Center Lisle. Center Lisle was originally called Yorkshire and developed in the early 1800s along the banks of Yorkshire Creek and Dudley Creek near the center of the township. The hamlet included a post office by 1828, a church, an Odd Fellows Hall, and several small stores. Cook Hill was named after Colonel William Cook who moved

to the area in 1798. The area has also been known as West Hill.

Killawog is probably one of the oddest names for a hamlet in the United States. The original name for the hamlet was Union Village. Although the exact reason for the name change is unknown, the apocryphal story is that postmaster Gideon Messenger had difficulty sorting the mail for Union Village and another Union settlement within the town of Union. Around this time, a small boy named Abel Hartshorn was run down by a team of runaway horses in front of the school where he was playing with his friends. The driver of the team of horses never stopped. Messenger coined the phrase *kill a wog* (*wog* was an Indian expression meaning boy). The difficulty with the story is that the Native American language using the word is unknown, and the only other uses of the word are as an older English slang term for homosexual and a derogatory term for Middle Eastern people in the United Kingdom. Nevertheless, Killawog slowly became accepted as the name of the community. The hamlet has included flour and feed mills, several stores, a creamery, two churches, and several small industries. Many of these facilities have disappeared in recent years. The residents of this small hamlet enjoy the benefits of the Marathon Municipal Electric District because of their proximity to that Cortland County village.

Manningville was a hamlet named after Major David Manning, who came to this area in 1795. He settled on land to the east of Center Lisle and was buried in the Center Lisle Cemetery. Millville is the area between the village of Lisle and the village of Whitney Point where a number of the mills previously mentioned were located along the banks of the Tioughnioga River. Mount Hunger is located on the hills to the west of Center Lisle near the center of the town. It is an area of rich farmland and large agricultural ventures.

Ortonville was located near Route 79 and Clute Hill Road where the Rev. Dr. Azariah G. Orton and his family settled in the early 1800s. Many of the family members are buried on a family plot on the family's former farm. Azariah's son was the prominent physician Dr. John G. Orton of Binghamton. Owen Hill was named after Major Solomon Owen who moved to Lisle from Stockbridge, Massachusetts, in 1798. Wattles District was named after Mason Wattles who served as Broome County Sheriff in 1851.

The residents of the town of Lisle have experienced a number of floods in the two hundred plus years of its existence. As in

> Above: Dr. Saphronius French built this Greek Revival home in Lisle in the 1850s. His office can be seen on the left of the engraving. The home was the residence of other doctors in the area and is still standing on Main Street (Route 79) in the village of Lisle. (Courtesy Broome County Historical Society)

The 1935 flood devastated parts of the town of Lisle. In this photograph, some household items of local residents have been salvaged and placed on the lawns of one of the surviving homes. Dudley Creek was later rerouted away from the village of Lisle. (Courtesy Broome County Historical Society)

many areas of the county, flooding was not uncommon along the rivers and creeks that constitute much of the town. Yet, none of the residents could be ready for the deadliness of the raging Dudley Creek and Tioughnioga River during the flood of 1935. As previously mentioned, the flood was the worst natural disaster in county history. Dudley Creek nearly ripped the village of Lisle in two as homes, barns, and factory buildings were destroyed when the floodwaters swept through the region. Entire families were wiped out as residents clung to rooftops and trees for hours while the flood persisted. When the disaster finally came to an end, much of Dudley Creek was rerouted away from the remaining homes, and levees and dikes were put in place to protect the village residents from the Tioughnioga River.

The town of Lisle has had its share of interesting personalities. Lyman Cornelius Smith came from Center Lisle. He was the founder of the Smith typewriter industry, which later evolved into the Smith-Corona Typewriter Company. His father was Lewis Stevens Smith, who had run a tannery and sawmill operation in the area. The family also became involved in the manufacture of guns. Another resident of Center Lisle was Herbert H. Franklin. He was born there in 1866 and later became known as one of pioneering creators of the American automobile. The Franklin automobile made him a very wealthy industrialist. He endowed the residents of the community with the Lisle Free Library as a memorial to his father. The library still operates off the endowed trust that Franklin established in 1925.

CHAPTER 24

The Town of
Maine

Inah and Inas Pitcher arrive at Hanile's Creamery in the town of Maine in this early 1900s photograph. The Pitcher family operated Pitcher's Mill for many decades. (Courtesy Broome County Historical Society)

THE TOWN OF MAINE was originally part of the Boston Purchase. It was formed from the town of Union on March 27, 1848. In 1856, a small part of the northeastern part of the town was relegated to the town of Chenango, giving the town its current configuration. The name, as with the town of Lisle, is attributed to General Lafayette, who commented upon its resemblance to an area in his native country, France. The town includes 41.76 square miles of land and has a population of 5,459 (2000 census figure).

Andrew Taylor built this home in 1822 in Maine. Taylor was the great-grandfather of Dr. Clement Bowers. The home has had several owners, including Dr. Seymour Pitcher of Binghamton University who resided there when this photograph was taken in 1958. (Courtesy Broome County Historical Society)

The settlement of the region started as early as 1794 with the arrival of Benjamin Norton, who came from Stockbridge, Massachusetts. In 1797, Alfred and Russell Gates moved to the town from Chenango Point (Binghamton) where they had settled in 1793. The two brothers had originally come from Connecticut. To reach their new lands, they cut timber and built the first road leading from Centerville (Union Center) to their lands just north of the hamlet of Maine.

Many of the early settlers moving into the area were Revolutionary War veterans who returned to farming after the conclusion of the war. The area was well suited for the pursuit of agriculture. A wide valley allowed for fertile fields, and the hills surrounding the valley were gentle, permitting the spread of farms up the hillsides. Other early settlers who came to this blossoming area include Jedediah Dudley, who moved just south of the Gates brothers, and Amos Howard. The first child born in the town was Cynthia Rose, who was born in July 1797.

In 1802, the first school began operations with Betsey Ward as the instructor. This is a bit unusual, as it was the custom of the early nineteenth century that all educators should be men. The first school building was constructed in 1815 and was located near the present-day Maine Cemetery. As the town grew in population, so did the types of businesses and industries located within its boundaries. Daniel Howard, brother of Amos Howard, began the first sawmill in 1810. John Payne settled in the town in 1816, and his son, Peter, was the first physician to practice there. His practice was short-lived, however, and he moved to Illinois after only six years.

Two brothers, Daniel and Belden Slosson, built a gristmill in 1830. For much of its history, it was known as Pitcher's Mill, and it remained in operation for nearly 150 years, turning out between two and three tons of flour each day. The building has now been restored and is part of the holdings of the Nanticoke Valley Historical Society. In the early 1830s, members of the McIntyre family began a sawmill and rake factory operation that continued to manufacture rakes until 1928. In 1832, E. H. Clark began a tannery operation that relied on the abundant timber in the town. The timber would be used to produce acids to soften the hides into pliable leather. The tannery eventually employed twenty-five men who turned out thirty thousand sides of sole leather each year that were used in the making of shoes.

The area that is now the town of Maine was one of the many stops of the Reverend Seth Williston, the itinerant Baptist minister who began his preaching there in 1797. The first organized church in town was the Congregational Church that began in 1819 as a Presbyterian church. The first church structure was built in 1840. In the same year, the Baptist Church built a new structure, having organized in 1835. Both of those church buildings are still in use today. The Methodist Episcopal Church was formed in the hamlet of Maine in 1833, and its first building was completed in 1850. This structure was destroyed by fire in 1928. The members of the Methodist Church then joined those of the Congregational Church to form the Federated Church of Maine. The Methodist Church in Union Center (Union Center actually borders both the towns of Union and Maine) was formed in 1825, and the current church building was constructed in 1852. The newest church in the town of Maine is Most Holy Rosary Roman Catholic Church, opened in 1968.

In *Naming the Hills and Hollows of Broome County*, author Carol Thomas identifies twenty hamlets or settlements within the town, more than any other township in Broome County. Allentown is an area that was home to Ebenezer Allen, who came to the area in 1836. Arbutus was named for the wildflower that was found in the area, although it was also called Craftville after Dr. Edward S. Craft,

who settled there in 1875. Bowers Corners is near the meeting of Nanticoke Road and Tiona Road and was named after Gardiner S. Bowers, who settled in the region in 1822 after leaving his home in New Hampshire. The Bowers family continued to be a prominent force in this area for 180 years. Lamont Bowers also became involved as an advisor to John D. Rockefeller, who was born nearby at Richford in Tioga County. Bowers worked closely with Rockefeller, especially with his coal mining operation in Colorado, before returning to rebuild the family home that stands today. When the Bowers Corners school building was closed, his son, Dr. Clement Bowers, had the school building moved and attached to the home. His brother, Franck Taylor Bowers, was a well-known local artist. The home was the residence for many years of Janet Bowers Bothwell and her husband, former Broome County Historian Lawrence Bothwell.

Brockett Hollow was named after the family of Dwight Brockett, who came to the town from Connecticut. Broughamtown, sometimes called Dutchtown, was named after John Brougham. The settlement called Canada received its name from incidents of robbery attributed to certain local residents. When the legal authorities questioned others about their whereabouts, they were told the robbers had "gone to Canada." Chauncey Hollow was named after Russell Chauncey, who came to the area about 1850 and began a sawmill operation on Bradley Creek.

Near Chauncey Hollow, Death Valley Road is associated with many apocryphal stories. Legends describe a family murdered in a log cabin. There is the tale of a man killed by a Native American with a knife, while another version of this legend has two men moving into a log cabin and robbing the neighbors. One story tells of a horse thief hanged from a tree on the road. What is known is that the Ludington family operated a slaughterhouse and that some of the bones of the slaughtered animals were dragged out to the fields and roadways by wild animals.

Delano Corners was named after Moses Delano, who moved there in 1812. East Maine was formerly called Stone Settlement for Samuel Stone, who came there in 1816. It was also called Hogg Settlement before the post office opened there in 1849 using the name East Maine. The post office closed in 1904. Finch Hollow was the site of the home of Nathaniel Finch, who came there in 1840. The former Finch Hollow school building has been converted into a Nature Center that is operated by the Broome County Parks Department.

> This is an 1876 engraving of the F. H. Marean & Son store in Maine. The Mareans were early settlers in the community. The site of the store is now the parking lot of the Most Holy Rosary Church. (Courtesy Broome County Historical Society)

Gates Settlement is named after the Gates family, one of the most active and historically important families in the town. Cyrus Gates, son of Russell Gates, was involved in the Underground Railroad. The Cyrus Gates home is now on the National Register of Historic Places because of its probable involvement in this activity. The escaped slaves were said to be hidden in a secret room before making their way farther northward. Margaret Cruzer, the daughter of a slave who lived in Broome County, became the domestic servant of the family in the late 1830s. "Black Madge" became part of the family, and she is buried in the family plot. She was one of the wives of Thomas "Old Bay Tom" Crocker, another former Broome County slave. In a bit of irony, Cyrus Gates' brother, William, was the minister of the Baptist Church and preached that the Bible condoned slavery. The Reverend William Gates later began the Maine Academy. Another member of the family, Frederick Taylor Gates (1853–1929), became an advisor to John D. Rockefeller, specializing in his philanthropies. He helped to found the Rockefeller Foundation. Ketchumville is named for James Ketchum, who came from Connecticut in 1802, and for Ithamer Ketchum, who arrived there in the 1820s.

Cyrus Gates built this home on Nanticoke Road in Maine in 1848. The family acted as conductors on the Underground Railroad. The house remained in the family until 1994. It is now on the National Register of Historic Places. (Courtesy Broome County Historical Society)

The hamlet of Maine is the largest settlement within the town. The post office began there in 1828 and continues to operate today. Home to the majority of the town's churches, stores, and businesses, it is also home to the Maine Memorial Elementary School. The former Ralph J. Ingalls School, which was constructed in 1940, is now home to several businesses. Many of the historic homes along Main Street, Church Street, MacGregor Street, and others have been carefully restored. The hamlet is home to the town park and the Nanticoke Valley Historical Society. Little is known about the settlement called Mayor. A post office was opened there in 1885, but it was discontinued a year later.

Mount Ettrick has had an interesting history. It is named for the Scottish poet, James Hogg, who was called "the Ettrick Shepherd." James Hogg's nephew, William Hogg, arrived in 1836 and settled on top of Mount Ettrick. Soon after his family's arrival, the region's other immigrants from Scotland reached the area, including William Paisley, Alexander and George Ross, Hugh Young, the Forresters, the Gillespies, and the Olivers. The area was selected as the home of a new airport that formally opened in 1951 as the Broome County Airport. The name of the facility was later changed to Edwin A. Link Field, after the inventor of the flight simulator. In recent years, the facility was again renamed, this time as the Greater Binghamton Regional Airport.

New Ireland is mostly within the town of Maine, but some of its inhabitants live in the town of Chenango. The area has also been called Penders Corners for the Daniel Pender family, who arrived from Ireland in 1854. Immigrants from Ireland who farmed the stony hillsides of the region largely settled this area. A post office opened in 1894 but closed in 1897.

This home is located at 2563 Main Street and is owned by Edward and Genevieve Bernhauer. It replaced an early structure that was destroyed by fire as they were purchasing the home. (Courtesy Broome County Historical Society)

Norton's Corners was named after Isaac Norton, who settled in that area. Oak Hill is an area near Oak Tree Lane that was once part of the Farm to Market Road.

Tiona has also been known as North Maine or McIntyre Settlement. Marsena McIntyre arrived there from Otsego County in 1829. The current name was derived from the Tiona Kerosene Company that delivered fuel to a local store in the area. Apparently, the store received a free barrel of kerosene for having the post office named after the company (Thomas).

CHAPTER 25

The Town of Nanticoke

This is a 1963 photograph of the Nanticoke United Methodist Church, located in Glen Aubrey in the town of Nanticoke. Lightning struck the church, and it burned down in 1965. (Courtesy Broome County Historical Society)

George W. Smith built the Octagon Inn as a residence in 1857. It was one of the few octagon-shaped buildings in Broome County. The structure was later a dance hall and tavern before it was destroyed by fire in the 1990s. (From the *Putnam Collection*, courtesy Broome County Public Library)

THE TOWN OF NANTICOKE was part of the Boston Purchase area, with early settlement beginning about 1793. The name is derived from the Nanticoke Creek that runs through much of the township and after the Nanticokes, a Native American tribe that traveled through this region. The area was split off from the town of Lisle on April 18, 1831. The town includes an area of 22.15 square miles, and it has a population of 1,790 residents (2000 census figure).

Philip Councilman was the first known settler of the area. He arrived in Chenango Point in 1793 from Luzerne County, Pennsylvania. He brought his family from his previous home by using a Native American dugout canoe. Once he arrived at the future Binghamton, he purchased a two-wheel wagon and a team of oxen to move the family and its possessions to their new land. The Councilman family became prominent in the new area. Philip Councilman, along with his sons, Philip Jr., John, Henry, and Peter, were avid hunters, and the new town provided ample wildlife to feed the incoming new settlers. Within a short time after the arrival of the Councilman family, James Ames arrived from Luzerne County, James Stoddard came from Connecticut, and John Beachtle, also from Luzerne County, moved here. Betsey Stoddard, daughter of James Stoddard, was born in the township in 1794.

Much of the activity of the early history of the town of Nanticoke revolved around lumbering, sawmills, and flourmills. The ample variety of trees allowed for several mills producing lumber for the new settlers to construct homes, barns, and outbuildings. Other small industries and businesses flourished during the first half of the nineteenth century. George W. Smith came to the town from Delaware County and began the Glen Aubrey Tannery, which was in full operation by the mid-1850s. From 1831 to 1860, the town was home to a small resort community at Nanticoke Springs. The facility was built around two sulfur springs. It included a hotel, a post office, and several homes. Stagecoaches brought visitors from Binghamton, New York City, and elsewhere to enjoy the "benefits" that the springs offered. Nanticoke Springs grew at the same time as other mineral spring operations developed across New York State, such as Saratoga Springs and Ballston Spa. Within Broome County were Valonia Springs, the Mount Prospect Water Cure, and Sanitaria Springs (Osborne Hollow). The demise of interest in the alleged "curative" waters also led to a decline in the growth of the town of Nanticoke. The hotel burned down in 1865.

When the first town of Nanticoke meeting was held in 1832, a number of town officers were selected but not in a calm and pleasant manner.

In 1966, in honor of the centennial of the Pony Express, this rider took cards from the Glen Aubrey Post Office in the town of Nanticoke to Maryland. (Courtesy Broome County Historical Society)

A dispute over the need for taxes to support the local schools and the poor resulted in the failure of that effort, but the meeting still culminated in the selection of two people as overseers of the poor. The meeting degenerated into a free-for-all fight with several attempts to stuff the ballot box or to set it on fire.

Despite this ignominious beginning, the town of Nanticoke developed as a calm, rural area with a stable population. In the midst of this agricultural setting, there are five areas of settlement. Butler's Corners was named after Elijah Butler, an early settler from Massachusetts. Glen Aubrey is the largest of the five hamlets in the town of Nanticoke. The settlement was originally called Councilman Settlement after the Philip Councilman family previously mentioned. The name Glen Aubrey was selected in honor of the wife of early tanner George Smith. Smith also built the area's most famous landmark, the Octagon Hotel. The building was one of the few eight-sided structures in Broome County. In later years, the building became the Octagon Inn, a bar and dance hall. Unfortunately, the Inn burned down in 1996.

Linwood is a hamlet that was originally called Japhet Hollow after its early resident, Stephen Japhet, who came to the area in 1822 from Massachusetts. Nanticoke is the second largest of the five hamlets in the township. It was originally called Lamb's Corners, named for Isaac Lamb, who settled on the western side of the Nanticoke Creek. He arrived in 1804 and built a log cabin on the site. A post office was moved there from Nanticoke Springs in 1860, and the hamlet was officially named after the Lamb family. The

This turn-of-the-century postcard shows Main Street (now Route 26) in the hamlet of Glen Aubrey. The hamlet was home to several businesses, including a tannery in the 1800s. (Courtesy Town of Nanticoke Historian)

name was changed to Nanticoke in 1891. The post office was closed in 1954. The Lamb's Corners (Nanticoke) area was home to a number of stores, homes, a hotel, a cheese factory, and a newspaper—the *Lamb's Corner Eagle*.

The Tinker & Wells Creamery was located in the town of Nanticoke. It was one of several creameries that operated in the township during the late 1800s and early 1900s and relied on the dairy farms of the area for its business. (Courtesy Town of Nanticoke Historian)

The hamlet of Nanticoke was also the home of a large annual fair operated by the Nanticoke Valley Agricultural Society from 1871 to 1885. Despite the popularity of the event, the buildings were dismantled, and the land was used for the expansion of the adjoining Lamb's Corners Cemetery. Nanticoke Springs was the site of the home of Nathan Caldwell. The operation of the Nanticoke Springs has been previously mentioned. It had its own post office operation from 1831 until 1862 when the facility was moved to Lamb's Corners.

Today, the township can boast of several sport and recreational facilities. The Broome County Parks Department established Greenwood Park on 439 acres of land that offer a full range of activities, including boating, hiking, camping, swimming, and picnicking. Ford Hill Country Club offers twenty-seven holes of golf overlooking the Whitney Point area. Recently, Foxfire Golf Course opened, adding another opportunity for golfing enthusiasts in Broome County. Between 1950 and 1962, the Glen Aubrey raceway ran stock car races every Friday evening. The site is now a mobile home park.

Like all other parts of Broome County, the issues of everyday life do not escape the residents of the town of Nanticoke. The Broome County Landfill is located partly in Nanticoke and partly in the town of Maine. The operation continues to thrive, especially after the county's extensive recycling operation lengthened the life of the landfill by several decades.

CHAPTER 26

The Town of Sanford

Oquaga Lake is located in the town of Sanford, set amidst a thick forest as can been seen in this aerial photograph. The lake is popular with both tourists and local families. (Courtesy Broome County Historical Society)

THE TOWN OF SANFORD is located on the eastern border of Broome County. It was split off from the town of Windsor on April 2, 1821. The eastern border of the township follows the line of the 1768 Fort Stanwix Treaty that separated the colony of New York into the eastern half for colonial settlers and the western half (including the future Broome County) for Native Americans. The origin of the name of the town has remained in some doubt since its creation. There was no known family or early settler with the last name of Sanford (or Sandford, as some maps have spelled it). It is highly possible that the name was chosen to honor Judge Nathan Sanford, a member of the New York State Senate and Assembly and a chancellor of the state. The town includes 78.37 square miles of land, making it the largest of the sixteen townships in Broome County. It has a population of 2,477 residents, or 1,642 if the village of Deposit is excluded (2000 census figure).

The "Black Bridge" was one of the many covered bridges that were once located in the area. It spanned the Delaware River in the village of Deposit on the Delaware County side. There are no public covered bridges remaining in Broome County. (Courtesy Broome County Historical Society)

The first settler in the region was William MacClure. He was hired as a surveyor for the Fisher and Norton tract, one of several large parcels that made up the town of Sanford after the conclusion of the American Revolution. He reached the area in 1787 and established his surveyor's business at the mouth of the Oquaga Creek on the site that is now part of the village of Deposit. He purchased a number of parcels of land around the area and moved five miles west to build a log home that he called "Castle William." His wife joined him at the "Castle" in 1791. In an interesting note, in his journals, MacClure describes having the census takers of the first federal census in 1790 as guests in his home. However, in the official census, MacClure is not listed among the residents of the area.

In 1791, Nathan Dean built the first sawmill on Oquaga Creek. He added the first gristmill on the Broome County side of Deposit three years later, in 1794. Dean had been a captain during the Revolutionary War and had moved to the area with his family from Massachusetts. Dean also established the first blacksmith operation in the town. Benjamin and Peter Gardner moved to the area from New York City in 1796 and brought eight sleigh loads of goods to establish the first store on what is now Front Street in the village of Deposit.

Settlers continued to flow into the region in increasing numbers in the first four decades of the nineteenth century. Many had been Revolutionary War veterans. Some were moving in from neighboring Delaware County while others were arriving from northern New Jersey and New England. In 1811, the village of Deposit was incorporated within Delaware County, but the Broome County portion of that municipality had not yet been added. A complete discussion of this village is found later in the book.

The first official town meeting was held in 1822, and Squire William MacClure was selected as the first town supervisor. At the time of creation, the official spelling of the township's name was Sandford, and that spelling was used until approximately 1868. The development of the town increased dramatically in 1835 when the groundbreaking for the creation of the New York and Erie Railroad took place near Deposit. The development of the railroad helped to bring economic growth and population increase as workers toiled on the four hundred miles of the first long railroad in the country's history. In Sanford, it meant the building of the first railroad station, which was located on the Broome County side of the village of Deposit, helping to move the business development of that municipality from Delaware County into Broome County.

In one of the tragic incidents of the railroad's history, three people were killed on February 17, 1852, when an out–of–control freight train crashed into a passenger train. One of those killed was

Borden's Condensed Milk plant was located at Deposit in the town of Sanford. It began as New York Condensed Milk in the early part of the twentieth century. Agway later used the facility. (Courtesy Broome County Historical Society)

One of the well-known destinations at Oquaga Lake is Scott's Oquaga Lake House. This resort has been providing a relaxing environment for visitors for over 125 years. (Courtesy Broome County Historical Society)

This is an early photograph of the Deposit area showing the Central House hotel on the left and the former Oquaga House on the right side of the picture. The Central House was lost to fire in 1903. (From the *Putnam Collection*, courtesy Broome County Public Library)

Sa-Sa-Na Loft, a Canadian Mohawk who had performed along with her family the previous night at the Oquaga House in Deposit. Judge Charles P. Avery of Owego had housed the family before their performance and felt so compelled at the loss of her life that he had her body brought to Owego for burial. The judge sued the railroad and received a $2,000 settlement that was used to publish books in the Mohawk language. A large monument overlooking Owego in Evergreen Cemetery marks the final resting place of this woman.

The heavily forested areas in the town of Sanford led to the development of a large lumbering industry, the creation of tanneries that used the bark of hemlock and oak as part of the tanning process, and the building of acid factories. During the nineteenth century, fortunes were made from the area's forests. But as that century progressed, the number of these facilities dwindled along with the fresh supply of wood. The number of dairy farm operations grew, especially in the outlying areas of the town.

There are nine settlements within the town of Sanford. As stated earlier, the village of Deposit will be discussed in a later chapter in this book. Danville, also called Danville Corners, was named after Phillip Dan and his family. Dan served in the War of 1812 and settled in the town at the conclusion of that war. Phillip Dan's son, Wellington, was a veteran of the Civil War. Gulf Summit was a stop on the New York and Erie Railroad. It cost the railroad $200,000 to cut through the rock to reach the point. A post office was opened in 1856, and for a short time, the area was called Underwood (1859). But the name returned to Gulf Summit by 1865.

Hale Eddy (sometimes referred to as Hale's Eddy) was named for Oliver Hale who came to the area in 1787 but only remained for a few years before moving away. The settlement is located five miles east of Deposit on the west branch of the Delaware River. A post office was established in the hamlet in 1850. Howes was a stagecoach stop during the nineteenth century that was named after Philo P. Howe. A post office that opened there in 1898 was closed in 1914. MacClure was named for William MacClure, who was previously discussed in this chapter. A post office operated in the hamlet from 1865 to 1921.

North Sanford was originally called Potter's Settlement after General James Potter, a member of General George Washington's army. Potter County in Pennsylvania is also named for him. Potter was a resident of Pennsylvania, and it is unclear why the settlement received his name. However, a post office opened in 1856 using that name before the name North Sanford came into common use. The vacation community of Oquaga Lake began after 1868 when Elwyn J. Scott and his wife purchased a 98-acre farm on what was then called Sand Pond. They began a resort business that is still operated under the name Scott's Oquaga Lake House. Several other resorts later flourished on the lake. Samuel Retzer constructed the Chestnut Inn on the former site of the Monoquaga Cottage in 1928. The new resort, originally called the Hotel Monoquaga, was later called the Chestnut Lodge. After renovations in the early 1990s, it reopened as the Chestnut Inn. At least one hundred families still have cottages on the 140-acre lake.

Sanford was first called Creek Settlement. Four years later, in 1800, James Applington established residency at Creek Settlement. A post office opened there in 1825 (which closed in 1925), but the name was changed to Sanford around 1830. Sanford also had a blacksmith shop, several stores, a wagon shop, a small tannery, and a small Methodist church. It was through this area that the "Old Plank Road" ran between Deposit and Afton.

In recent years, the bucolic rural life of Sanford has been marred by a series of disasters. On July 3, 1970, a heavy rainstorm caused flash flooding that rushed over Bone Creek and caused the loss of the dam on Palmer Pond, bringing deep waters through the village of Deposit. On May 31, 1998, a tornado that had originally struck the Binghamton area made its way through the town of Sanford, destroying several homes. On June 2, 2004, another tornado cut a path through the town, destroying several barns. Only three months later, on September 18, 2004, the remnants of Hurricane Ivan caused Oquaga Creek to overflow and cause serious damage in the Deposit area. A year later, on April 6, 2005, floods comparable to those of 1936 caused the flash flooding of Oquaga Creek. Two men and a dog were killed while trying to drive down a flooded street in Deposit. The storm also caused serious damage at MacClure and other locations around the town.

CHAPTER 27

The Town of
Triangle

This is the Dorchester School building in 1910. The students are waiting for the teacher to raise the American flag before entering the building. The area is now part of Broome County's Dorchester Park and under the lake created by the Whitney Point Dam. (Courtesy Broome County Historical Society)

This is a 1906 photograph of Tabor's Bridge in the town of Triangle. Covered bridges provide a romantic view of life long ago, but they did not withstand the forces of nature. (Courtesy Town of Triangle Historian)

THE TOWN OF TRIANGLE was split off from the town of Lisle on April 18, 1831. However, early settlers had begun to arrive in this area as early as 1790. The name of the town is derived from the Chenango Triangle, a land grant of which a portion of the town was once part. The township encompasses 30.48 square miles of land, and it has a population of 3,032 including the village of Whitney Point or 2,067 if the village is excluded (2000 census figures).

General James Patterson is the first known settler to the area. He arrived from Lenox, Massachusetts, in 1791 as one of the sixty proprietors of the Boston Purchase. Patterson had been raised in Connecticut, and he was a graduate of Yale. He served in the Revolutionary War where he was part of the forces under General Montgomery that invaded Canada. He lived in the area until his death in 1808. He served as a state legislator, a representative in the United States Congress, and the first judge in Broome County. Patterson's in-laws, Deacon Josiah and Hann Lee, came with Patterson or immediately followed him.

In 1792, David Seymour and his sons, David and Ira, moved into the area. Other settlers made their way into the town within a few years. Timothy Shepard, Asa Rodgers, Benjamin and Hendrick Smith, and John Landers settled into the Upper Lisle area between 1794 and 1797. In 1802, Thomas Whitney moved into the area that would later bear his name. He was the brother of Joshua Whitney, the land agent for William Bingham and major force behind the development of Binghamton. His younger brother, William, came with Thomas Whitney to the area. Deacon Josiah Lee performed the first religious service in the town, but the

Reverend Seth Williston, who has been previously mentioned in this book, closely followed him.

One of the reasons for the quick development of the area was that the route of the Catskill and Ithaca Turnpike ran through the center of the town. The turnpike made travel much easier into the region. Before it opened in 1796, settlers had been required to take boats from the Bainbridge area into the Binghamton area and then go up the Chenango and Tioughnioga Rivers to reach the new settlements. Today, the road is known as Route 206.

Dr. Danial A. Wheeler arrived in the area of Whitney Point in 1796 or 1797. Isaiah Chapman was the first physician in the Upper Lisle area. He arrived about 1799 or 1800 and continued to practice there until his death in 1812. The first church was a Baptist church constructed in Upper Lisle under the auspices of Reverend Timothy Shepard in 1802 (although one history mentions an earlier church built before 1800 in Whitney Point, there is no certain evidence to confirm its existence). Jacob Coburn began the first sawmill operation in the area. David Smith, who also added a gristmill and carding department for the manufacture of wool and woolen cloth, later operated the mill. Benjamin Gibbs began the first blacksmith operation in the hamlet of Triangle. Timothy and David Clark also began a tannery operation in this area and built the first tavern in that part of the township.

Like many of the other communities in the county, Whitney Point used the waterpower from the rivers to produce electric power. This is a 1908 photograph of the electric company plant at Whitney Point on the Otselic River. (Courtesy Town of Triangle Historian)

The number of mill operations continued to grow through the mid-nineteenth century. By 1835, there were ten sawmills, two gristmills, two fulling mills, two cotton mills, and four tanneries operating in the town of Triangle. The area was manufacturing 1,400 yards of fulled cloth, 3,118 yards of flannel, and 2,100 yards of cotton and linen goods. The remaining part of the town was heavily rural with many large farm operations with sheep, hogs, and cattle numbering over sixteen thousand head.

This is the Dr. E. H. Porter house located in Upper Lisle in the town of Triangle. The main portion of the home was built about 1860, and the portico and wings were added at a later date. This photograph dates from about 1912. (Courtesy Broome County Historical Society)

In 1854, the Syracuse and Binghamton Railroad was opened through the Triangle area. The opening of the railroad was met with great fanfare in those areas where the line ran, including the town of Triangle. The railroad ran into financial problems and was foreclosed by 1856. It was reopened under the name of the Syracuse and Southern Railroad and later became part of the Delaware, Lackawanna and Western Railroad. The importance of the railroad in the expansion of the business and industrial growth in the town of Triangle, especially in the village of Whitney Point, is immeasurable.

During the period just prior to the Civil War, multimillionaire and abolitionist Gerrit Smith purchased a number of acres of land in the Upper Lisle area. Smith owned thousands of acres across the state. It was his intention to create new communities for the settlement of African Americans, especially former slaves who had escaped via the Underground Railroad. A few African American families settled on his property during this period, but little is known about the settlement. Most, if not all, of the families moved away from the township within a few years of their arrival. Nevertheless, there is some evidence that they farmed the land and worked with some of the white families who lived nearby.

There are eight hamlets or settlements within the boundaries of the town of Triangle. Clark's Settlement was named after Timothy and David Clark, who were previously mentioned in this chapter. They arrived in the region in 1805. Connecticut Hill included an exchange stable for the daily stagecoach on the turnpike, a tavern, and a schoolhouse. Nearby was an early distillery. Hays Settlement was named after Nathaniel Hays who had purchased a tannery that had been begun by David Clark. He built his residence two miles east of the hamlet of Triangle. Hazard Corners was named after Edmund Hazard, who was once the supervisor of the town of Triangle. A Baptist church was formerly at the Corners.

Penelope is located in the northeastern part of the township and very close to the boundary of Broome County and Cortland County. It was once called the North Woods. A local resident, Minnie Yarnes, did not like the name and requested a name change from the postmaster of the United States, who suggested the name

Penelope, after his daughter. At one time, a cheese factory and a creamery operated near this crossroads, but little is left there today.

The hamlet of Triangle is located five miles to the east of Whitney Point, along the former Catskill and Ithaca Turnpike. It grew around a tollgate of the turnpike. A post office was opened there in 1818. Today, the hamlet supports two churches and several stores and has one of the more interesting road names in the county with Wheel Barrel Alley. Upper Lisle was originally called Sharp's Mills after Conrad Sharp, who operated sawmills and gristmills. A plow factory was later located at this site, and a post office was established there in 1826. Upper Lisle also included a cloth dressing factory, a distillery, blacksmith shops, taverns, and several stores. The first church was the Universalist, built in 1830. There was also a cheese factory, tannery, sawmill, and wagon shop. The earlier First Baptist Church apparently did not put up a building until 1842. The village of Whitney Point, the largest of the settlements within the town of Triangle, will be discussed in a later chapter in this book.

The area was prone to floods such as those that occurred in 1865 and 1878. But like many other parts of the region, the ravaging effects of the floods of 1935 and 1936 were felt throughout Broome County. Besides causing millions of dollars of damage to the homes, businesses, and industries of the county, the floods also caused the deaths of eighteen people. The call for flood control came swiftly, but action took much longer. Beginning in 1938, plans for controlling the waters of the Otselic River were developed. Eventually, under the auspices of the United States Army Corps of Engineers, an earthen dam was constructed just north of the village of Whitney Point. The construction of the dam caused the removal of several farms and homes in that area, but the dam prevented much damage from occurring in subsequent floods of the river valley. The resultant man-made lake created new recreational opportunities for local residents. The Broome County Parks Department has created three park areas around the lake, including Dorchester Park. The town of Triangle continues to thrive on agriculture and recreational usage of the lake and rivers.

Everyone was waiting for the stagecoach in Upper Lisle in the town of Triangle in this photograph taken about 1917. Louis Dunham was the mail carrier with news for everyone. (Courtesy Broome County Historical Society)

CHAPTER 28

The Town of Union

This is the LaTourette farmhouse located on West Main Street in the town of Union. The picture was taken about 1910. The home is still standing and is located across the street from the En-Joie Golf Course. (Courtesy Broome County Historical Society)

THE TOWN OF UNION was created on February 16, 1791. It was one of the original townships when Tioga County formed from Montgomery County and became one of the original townships of Broome County when it was split off from Tioga in 1806. It was within the boundaries of this township that the union of the two armies of Generals Sullivan and Clinton took place in 1779 during the American Revolution. A historic marker donates the presumed site of the meeting of the armies. Union has two incorporated municipalities within its area: the villages of Endicott and Johnson City. The town has an area of 26.63 square miles. Its population of 56,298 includes the population of the two villages. This is the largest populated area within Broome County. It has a population of 27,725 if Endicott and Johnson City are excluded (2000 census figures).

This 1963 aerial photograph shows the Union district of the village of Endicott. The old village of Union was settled in the early 1800s and was focused around the intersection of Main Street and Nanticoke Avenue. (Courtesy Broome County Historical Society)

The history of the town of Union starts long before the American Revolution. This area was a relatively populated region of inhabitation by Native Americans. The Nanticoke, Chugnut, and others occupied villages near the Susquehanna River and its tributaries. The archaeological excavations and discoveries of early agriculture at Round Top Hill in the town of Union have been previously discussed in this book. Missionaries and traders traveled through this area, long before any permanent settlement by transplanted New Englanders.

By 1785, however, new settlers were arriving. General Orange Stoddard, one of the

As IBM grew in size and suburbia expanded in the river valley, places like Endwell sprang literally out of farmland. This 1963 aerial view shows how quickly the suburbs spread across the hills surrounding Endicott. (Courtesy Broome County Historical Society)

commissioners appointed to negotiate with the Indians for the Boston Purchase, settled at Hooper in 1785. By 1791, there were already 177 landowners who were required to maintain the newly developed roads of the township. The original area of the town of Union at that time included over seven hundred square miles, and major portions were broken off in subsequent years. It included parts of Chenango and Tioga Counties as well as present-day Vestal, Conklin, Chenango, Lisle, Triangle, Nanticoke, Barker, Maine, the town of Binghamton, and parts of Dickinson and the city of Binghamton. Settlers such as William Brink, Ezekial Crocker, Nehemiah Crawford, Nathan Howard, Jabesh Winship, and Caleb Merriman had all settled there before the town's creation in 1791. The Dutch Reformed Church was established in 1789, and the first church building was constructed in 1791, near the current Riverside Cemetery.

By 1791, there were already three settlements situated within the town's boundaries. One was a settlement called Hooper, the area now known as Endwell. It was named after Robert Hooper, one of the three men (William Bingham and James Wilson being the other two) who had vied for the area in the 1790s. Nanticoke was a settlement near the meeting of Nanticoke Creek and the Susquehanna River. This area did not long survive. Union Corners began to the west of the Dutch Reformed Church location. As more families came to this location, the hamlet eventually grew to form the village of Union.

Amos Patterson, one of the proprietors of the Boston Purchase, arrived in the area in

1793 along with his family. In 1799, he built a magnificent Federal-style home that still stands today. It is probably the oldest structure in Broome County and is on the National Register of Historic Places. It came to be called Washingtonian Hall because of its later use by the Washingtonian Society, a temperance organization. Patterson's sister, Esther, and her husband, Thomas Marean, settled north of Patterson in what would later become the town of Maine after it was split off from the town of Union. They built their home there in 1818.

Joshua Mersereau moved here from Staten Island in 1789. His brother arrived in 1792. Their careers during the American Revolution were previously mentioned in this book. The Mersereau, LaTourette, LaGrange, and other French Huguenot families were prominent in the early development of Union. Joshua Mersereau was the first judge of the Broome County's eastern district. The Mersereau family was instrumental in the successful development of many of the early businesses and farming enterprises in that area.

Throughout the nineteenth century, the major economic activity in the town of Union was farming. The open valleys surrounding the Susquehanna River and the adjoining creeks made this an ideal location for sizable agricultural ventures. The arrival of the New York and Erie Railroad by 1851 helped to spur further business growth, especially in the fledgling village of Union. The Major House opened in that hamlet in 1852. It was constructed by Major David Mersereau to house the visitors traveling by railroad or roadway.

The hamlet of Union continued to grow and was finally incorporated as an official village in 1871. This village's growth did not go unnoticed by the business leaders closer to Binghamton. Harvey Lester was attracted to Union because the land was cheap and he could avoid the city's taxes. The area was still close to Binghamton, and it was accessible by rail. The Lester Brothers Boot and Shoe Company moved out of Binghamton and into the open lands of the town of Union to create a company town to be called Lestershire. Today, that area is Johnson City, and its history will be discussed in a later chapter in this book. The success of Lester Brothers was well established by 1900, especially after its takeover by shoemaker and creditor, Henry B. Endicott, and former Lester Brothers supervisor, George F. Johnson. The success of the Endicott Johnson Shoe Company at Lestershire brought the attention of a group of investors. They saw the farmlands to the west of Lestershire as an ideal place for the creation of another company town. Calling themselves the Endicott Land Company, they persuaded Henry B. Endicott to construct a factory in the town and promised to name the new area after him. The complete history of the village of Endicott will be discussed in a later chapter of this book.

The Union Fire Station was constructed in 1876. Members of the department can be seen in this early 1900s view. (Courtesy Broome County Historical Society)

The first school in the town of Union was begun in 1795. By 1800, one school was operating near the homes of the Mersereaus and another near the home of Amos Patterson. This school system continued to develop with separate schools located in the many hamlets and settlements of the town. In 1886, a formal school district was formed. Eventually, the Union-Endicott School District included students from both Endicott and Union villages. The sharing of electrical systems, trolley car systems, parks, and other enterprises made the line between the two villages more unclear. Finally, in 1921, the village of Union merged with the village of Endicott, and the Union District of Endicott came into being.

Outside of Endicott and Johnson City, there are seven hamlets or settlements within the town. Bible School Park is the home of Davis College. This site along the banks of the Susquehanna River was once Wagener's Park, an amusement park that included a Ferris wheel, carousel, and a number of midway games. It changed its name to White City Amusement Park, promoting family fun. The area became anything but family-oriented, however. Gamblers, prostitutes, and crooks frequented the area so much that the park had

CHAPTER 28: THE TOWN OF UNION 343

its own jail cell. In 1911, the Reverend John A. Davis purchased the park. He transformed what he called "the den of iniquity" into the Practical Bible Training School. It has operated quietly from those grounds and includes its own post office. The school changed its name to Davis College in 2003.

Endicott Johnson laid out many of the homes and streets that formed West Endicott. Over four thousand homes, such as this one on South Street in West Endicott, were built in the area between 1913 and 1952. (Courtesy Broome County Historical Society)

Choconut Center is situated on the Little Choconut Creek. Its named is derived from a corruption of the name of the native settlement of Chugnut. A post office opened there in 1869. The Choconut Center United Methodist Church was built in 1854. It was moved four hundred yards in 1973 to remove it from the path of the new Airport Road. In 1980, the Savin Corporation built a new copier plant nearby. Several firms now occupy the building.

Endwell is the current name for the hamlet of Hooper. A post office was established there in 1853, but it ceased operation in 1917. When the area grew as a suburb of Endicott, it became necessary to reopen the post office in 1921, but there were several already using the name Hooper. It was decided to use the name Endwell. Endwell was a line of shoes from the Endicott Johnson Shoe Company that had in turn been an adaptation of the name of Henry B. Endicott's son, Wendell. This area was formerly the home of Carmel Grove, a Methodist encampment that would house hundreds to hear revivalist sermons and lectures during the early twentieth century.

Oakdale, today part of the village of Johnson City, began as an area rich with large virgin oak trees. Simon Bigler built a steam sawmill operation at this location. The mill was very successful, and several workers' homes were built near the mill. During the Civil War, Bigler and his brother received a contract from the War Department to produce a keel for a new type of ship. The keel was to be sixty feet long and constructed of one piece of white oak. The piece was so long that it took two wagons hitched together to bring the piece to the Chenango Canal where it was floated up to Utica and the Erie Canal. From there, it was floated down to New York City where it became the keel of the Union's first ironclad ship, the *Monitor*. A marble marker denotes the location of the Bigler mill. Oakdale became the location of the first enclosed mall in Broome County in 1975.

Union Center is an unusual hamlet in that part of it is located in the town of Union and part of it in the town of Maine. It was originally called Centerville because it was the halfway stop between the two towns. A post office opened there in 1848. There have been several churches, an early tavern, sawmills, a gristmill, and a cheese factory at Union Center. West Corners is named after Orman West. West arrived here in 1817 from Schoharie County, and his farm operation was located at the heart of what is now a heavily trafficked area. Westover is located just to the west of the village of Johnson City. It shows on the Plat Book of Broome County for 1908 as one of two planned developments located on former farmland. The other, Westunder, never really took, but Westover was located on the main road, and in 1942, Remington Rand built a large factory on the site. It was built on land owned by the Defense Department, and the factory made airplane propellers during World War II. After the war, General Electric Company used the facility. It was sold to Martin Marietta, which became Lockheed Martin. It is now operated by BAE Systems.

In recent decades, the town of Union has grown as a bedroom community for IBM. Large residential neighborhoods, such as Lyndhurst in the Endwell area, made this area attractive to many of the professional employees of area firms. Parks such as Highland Park helped to make the area more attractive. Although the downsizing of IBM and the loss of Endicott Johnson have hurt the property values in this area, resurgence has begun with the expansion of Lockheed Martin in Owego (a former plant of IBM). The company has recently hired seven hundred workers to help build a new fleet of helicopters to be used by the president of the United States.

CHAPTER 29

The Town of Vestal

A familiar landmark for several decades was the large bull atop the entrance to the Vestal Steak House. In 2005, the bull was relocated to the Discovery Center in Binghamton and given a fresh coat of paint. The restaurant was removed for new development. (Courtesy Broome County Historical Society)

In 1901, a Delaware, Lackawanna and Western Railroad train carrying dynamite exploded when another train hit it. The accident caused the deaths of several railroad workers and left a large crater at the site. (Courtesy Broome County Historical Society)

THE TOWN OF VESTAL was split off from the town of Union on January 22, 1823. Although the origin of Vestal's name is uncertain, Carol Thomas describes three possibilities in her book on the name derivation in Broome County. The most likely explanation is that it is one of the classical names that are attributed to Robert Harpur who, as Deputy Secretary of State and Secretary of the State Land Board, gave many places names based on Roman and Greek history and mythology. Its area includes 49.94 square miles of land, and the town has a population of 26,535 (2000 census figure).

Like its parent township, Union, Vestal has a history that predates the American Revolution. Native American groups, including the Tuscarora, settled near the large village of Chugnut in an area now known as Willow Point. Colonial forces under the command of General Poor destroyed this settlement in 1779. The army of Generals Clinton and Poor encamped on the south side of Susquehanna during this time, before moving back across the river to meet at Union with the forces under the command of General Sullivan.

Amos Draper was the first known European American to remain in the area. He came to the region in 1782 and established the area's first trading post. He had dealings with many of the Native Americans as well as with the early settlers, including Samuel and Daniel Seymour who arrived in 1785. Major David Barney also arrived during that year. Joshua and John Mersereau originally lived on the south side of the Susquehanna before moving across the river to the town of Union. Jonathan Crane ran a ferry operation on the Susquehanna River, as well as a tavern and store operation. Before the official name of Vestal was selected, the area was called Crane's Ferry. The ferry continued to operate for a number of years, with Jacob Rounds taking over the business from Crane.

In 1793, Bethias DuBois purchased 821 acres of land from the Robert Hooper patent and built that area's first gristmill. It was during the building of that mill that DuBois' son, Lewis, was killed. Thomas Eldridge moved from Connecticut to the Vestal area in 1794. In 1799, he purchased land on which he had squatted near the former Chugnut site. The tract included 205 acres of land along the Susquehanna River. Other early arrivals to the town of Vestal included a number of Huguenots from New Jersey and Staten Island, including the LaGrange and LaTourette families.

The expansion of population into places like the town of Vestal resulted in the need for the construction of new schools. The Clayton Avenue Elementary School educates hundreds of children each year as part of the Vestal Central School District. (Courtesy Broome County Historical Society)

Lumbering, like it had in many other areas of Broome County, became a major industry in the town of Vestal in the first half of the nineteenth century. By the 1830s, there were fifteen sawmills, two gristmills, one cotton mill, one distillery, an oilcloth factory, and two tanneries.

The arrival of the Delaware, Lackawanna and Western Railroad helped continue the steady growth and increasing traffic in the town of Vestal. Despite this improvement in the transportation system, Vestal remained a basically rural and agricultural area until the mid-twentieth century.

One major event that brought attention to the town of Vestal occurred on June 8, 1901, when two westbound trains collided. The first train was carrying a carload of dynamite in the car immediately ahead of the caboose. When the second train slammed into the caboose, the collision caused the dynamite to explode. The explosion was so loud that it was heard in Binghamton, nearly eight miles away. It blew out all of the windows of many of the stores and one side of the Vestal Methodist Episcopal Church. The explosion lifted both engines far into the air. It moved the rear engine up onto the embankment. The first engine was torn into pieces and strewn around the tracks. Five railroad employees were killed and seven others were injured. Over ten thousand curiosity seekers traveled to the site, and the railroad ran trains every fifteen minutes to handle the number of onlookers.

In the 1950s, construction began on a new campus for Harpur College. What had started in 1946 as Triple Cities College in Endicott had grown to such an extent that a new campus was needed. The open lands of the town of Vestal were chosen for the new school. The construction required the Vestal Hills Golf Course to relocate to the town of Binghamton. By 1960, the new campus of Harpur College was open to new students. In 1965, it became the State University of New York at Binghamton and is now called Binghamton University. It was selected as one of the four university centers in the state, and its growth continues to this day. The influxes of students, faculty, and staff have made the area around the campus desirable for development.

The Vestal Parkway originated as part of New York Route 17 in 1941. Later designated Route 434, the parkway has carried an ever-increasing traffic load along the burgeoning commercial corridor that has developed since the 1960s. New restaurants and businesses began to spread farther west along the Vestal Parkway. The opening of strip plazas like the Vestal Plaza, Campus Plaza, Town Square Mall, and others have moved the center of retail business away from the traditional centers like Binghamton, Johnson City, and Endicott and into the town of Vestal. During the period from 1940 to the early 1980s, the town of Vestal experienced some industrial growth with plants built for both Link Aviation and the Ozalid Division of GAF. Although the demise of those industries has left the town without any heavy manufacturing facilities, several smaller, high technology firms are headquartered in Vestal.

In the 1960s, the Jewish Community Center left its Binghamton headquarters and built this new facility on Clubhouse Road in the town of Vestal. The Center provides classes, recreational facilities, and camaraderie for thousands each year. (Courtesy Broome County Historical Society)

On Old Vestal Road, the Binghamton-Johnson City Joint Sewage Treatment Plant was built to handle the increasing problem of solid waste management in the county. In recent years, the problem of odors and overuse of the facility has caused considerable consternation by residents in the community. The plant is currently being rebuilt.

There are eight hamlets within the town of Vestal. Castle Gardens was the site of a Native American settlement prior to the American Revolution. In the early twentieth century, this region became a suburban development and home to a retirement facility. Choconut derived its name from the meeting of the Choconut Creek and the Susquehanna River. This was the site of the Native American area called Chugnut (alternatively spelled Chugnutt). The origin of the name could have been one of several Native American words. Ross Corners was named for David Ross. He operated a large-scale lumbering business beginning in 1835. Ross floated much of the lumber from his mill down the Susquehanna River, using as many as twenty rafts in a season. Ross Corners

Another landmark that has gone is Taylor's Tiny Town in the town of Vestal. For many years, the miniature golf course provided entertainment for everyone. The site is now used by the Serafini automobile dealership. (Courtesy Broome County Historical Society)

is the location of the Ross Corners Christian Academy.

South Vestal is located very close to the border of the town of Vestal with Pennsylvania. A post office opened there in 1839, but it lasted only three years, closing in 1842. Tracy Creek is named for the body of water that flows through this hamlet. The name comes from the Thomas Tracy family who settled in that region in 1790. Tracy Creek was the most prominent settlement in the town by 1885. It included a sawmill, a blacksmith shop, two churches, and one store. A post office began there in 1850 but was closed in 1911. Twin Orchards was named for two orchards on either side of the road. The area became famous as the training camp of German heavyweight champion Max Schmeling for his bout with Binghamton boxer Jack Sharkey. Sharkey lost that bout but regained his title two years later, in 1932.

Vestal Center is located adjacent to Big Choconut Creek in the southern portion of the township. A post office began operations there in 1851, but the office was closed in 1924. Vestal Center had a hotel before the Civil War, but it was later converted to a store. There were other stores, two sawmills, a gristmill and a planing mill, two wagon shops, two or three blacksmiths, and a Baptist church and a Methodist church. Willow Point was named for the large number of willow trees that grew on a point of land along the Susquehanna River. A post office was opened there in 1890 but ceased operations in 1918. The former Willow Point Elementary School has been transformed into the headquarters for WSKG, the public broadcasting television station of the region. Broome County also operates the Willow Point Nursing Home at this location. The nursing home has been in operation by Broome County for three decades, and the county government is now looking to replace the aging facility, although a location is yet to be determined.

One of the more interesting personalities to come from Vestal was David Ross Locke. Although most people may not have heard of him using his original name, historians of the Civil War period know him under his penname, Petroleum V. Nasby. Locke, born in 1833, was the grandson of John Locke, an early Vestal resident and Revolutionary War veteran. Locke, writing as Nasby, wrote a series of humorous papers that appeared in many American newspapers at the time of the Civil War. Abraham Lincoln was a fan of Nasby, and after the war, Nasby appeared on a speaking tour with Mark Twain and Josh Billings.

The town of Vestal has spawned other well-known writers, including Laurence A. Leamer, author of many books on the Kennedy family. He is the son of former Binghamton University professor and Town of Vestal Historian Laurence Leamer. John Gardner, also a faculty member on the staff of Binghamton University, wrote a number of best-selling books, including *Mickelsson's Ghosts*, based on this area. He was killed in a motorcycle accident in 1982 at age forty-nine.

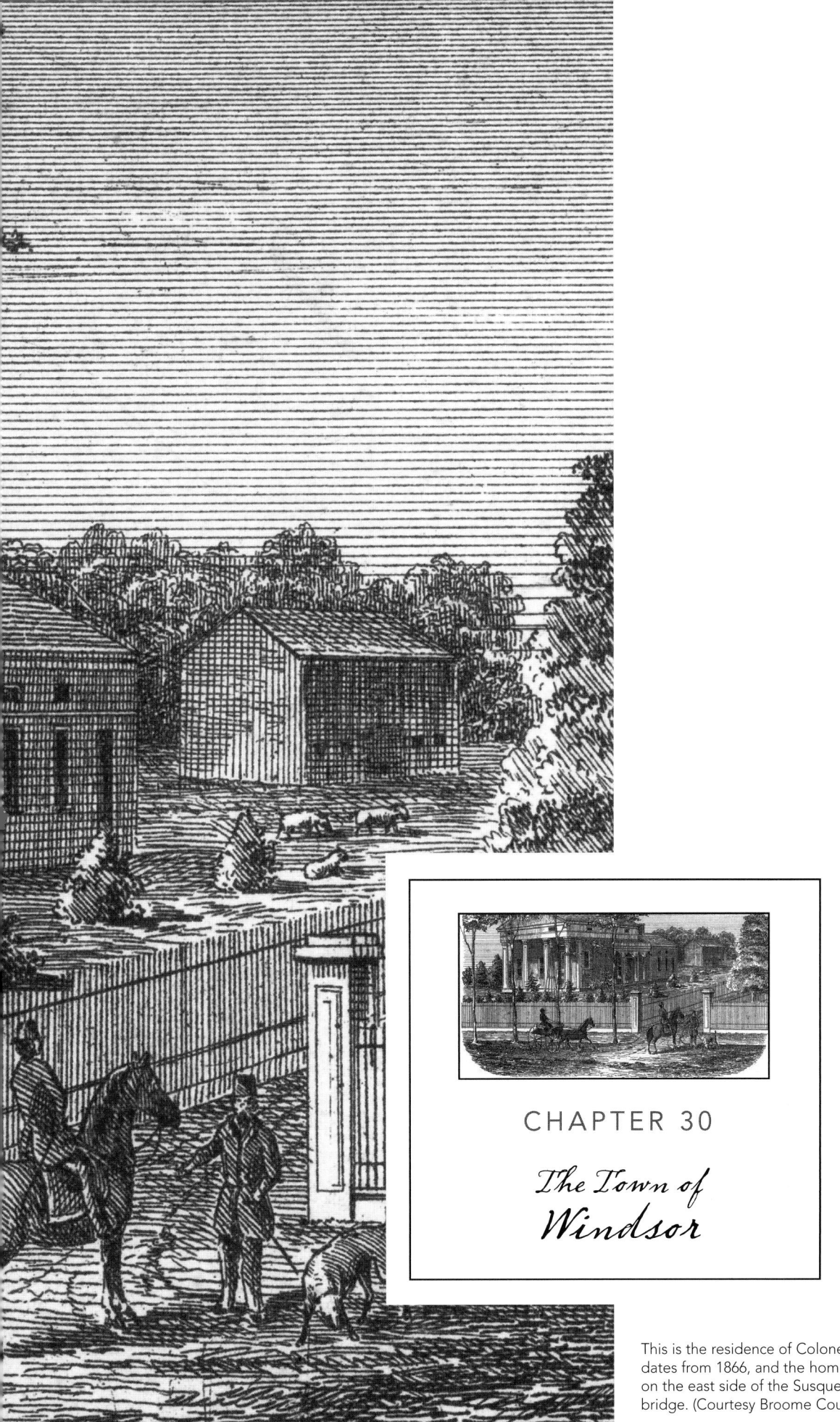

CHAPTER 30

The Town of Windsor

This is the residence of Colonel Ira Knox. The engraving dates from 1866, and the home was located in Ouaquaga on the east side of the Susquehanna River near the old bridge. (Courtesy Broome County Historical Society)

Levi Shaw built the Shaker barn that still stands on Route 79 in the town of Windsor, although a Shaker community never developed there. The two cupolas have been removed. (Courtesy Broome County Historical Society)

THE TOWN OF WINDSOR was formed from the town of Chenango on March 7, 1807. It originally included the present towns of Colesville and Sanford. The name may be derived from Windsor, England, or from Windsor, Connecticut. Many New Englanders settled in this area after the conclusion of the American Revolution. There are 79.56 square miles of land within the boundaries of the township and a population of 6,421 including the village of Windsor, or 5,520 if the village is excluded (2000 census figures).

The history of Windsor predates the history of Broome County. As has been previously discussed in this book, the town of Windsor was the location of Onaquaga, the "southern longhouse of the Iroquois Confederacy." This important Native American settlement was home to several groups, including the Oneida, Nanticoke, Delaware, and Tuscarora. The settlement existed by 1712, and missionaries arrived in the area by 1748. During the Revolution, Joseph Brant, the Mohawk who was the last powerful leader of the Iroquois Confederacy, used the village as his base of operations. His actions made Onaquaga the target of reprisals by the American Revolutionary forces. Those forces destroyed it in 1778.

After the conclusion of the American Revolution, the land was open for settlement, and by 1786, new residents began to arrive. John Doolittle was the first permanent settler, making his home near Sage Creek. Jesse Doolittle settled near him in that same year. In the next year, 1787, Captain James Knox moved across the river from the Doolittles. David Hotchkiss followed him to the area within a short time. Hotchkiss came with his sons, Amraphael, Gilead, Cyrus, and Charles, and moved close to the present-day village of Windsor. His residence was situated on two thousand acres of land.

John Garnsey arrived in the area in 1788 and settled on a thousand-acre tract near present-day South Windsor, along with several members of his family. Many of his daughters intermarried with the families of early settlers. In 1791, Frederick Goodell, a Revolutionary War veteran, moved to an area farther north up the river that would later become Flowers. Roswell Higley came to the town of Windsor area in 1788 and moved near the fort that had originally been constructed under the auspices of Sir William Johnson. By 1796, he was living in the area that would become Occanum and built a sawmill at that location.

In 1790, Major Josiah Stow arrived in the area, followed by Samuel Stow in 1793. The Stows settled near present-day North Windsor close to the former site of Onaquaga. William Moore, John and Jacob Springsteen, and Isaac Churcher lived across the river from them. By 1800, dozens of other settlers were living up and down the Susquehanna River. In 1797, Nathan Lane built the first gristmill operation. John Doolittle began the first sawmill, and Amraphael Hotchkiss built a series of mills near the present-day village.

The town of Windsor experienced its largest growth in population in its first few decades of existence. It grew from approximately 1,000 in 1805 to 3,354 by 1820. The next year, in 1821, the towns of Sanford and Colesville were excised from Windsor, and the population plummeted. It would take several more decades to regain that loss of residents. As in many of the towns of Broome County, lumbering was an early important industry in Windsor. Many of the mills were built prior to the Civil War. There was also a distillery that was operated by Stiles Hotchkiss.

Transportation played an important role in the development of the town of Windsor. The area's pioneers improved the roads that began as Native American trails. Ferry operations commenced by 1815, but in 1823, the Windsor Bridge Company was started. The company built a toll bridge across the Susquehanna River near the ferry operation in 1825. By 1835, the town included fifteen sawmills, two gristmills, one fulling mill, one carding machine, one distillery, one rope works, and two tanneries. Other businesses included blacksmiths, farms, and wagon shops.

Much of the development of the township revolved around the increasing growth of the village of Windsor, which will be discussed in a later chapter in this book. The growth of the area was spurred by the opening of the Delaware and Hudson Railroad that came through Windsor in 1872. The railroad helped to make the town's whip manufacturing industry grow in importance.

Adin Coburn opened the area's first whip factory in 1854. Coburn had begun as a shoemaker and then moved into selling whips to residents of the area. After learning how whips were made, he began to manufacture the product. Soon, he moved to the village of Windsor and built a larger shop. In 1872, he sold the shop to I. G. Owen and began building another factory the following year. Coburn died in 1877, and the business was sold to United States Whip Company of Westfield. The factory was destroyed by fire in 1907. The Empire Whip Company operated from the I. G. Owen Company factory until the 1930s. James C. Elliott began another whip company that would operate in Windsor until 1950.

Religious beliefs played an important role in the history of Windsor. The first church was the Windsor Presbyterian Church, which began in 1793. The church continued to grow in strength until a dispute over slavery in 1840 led to a schism. In 1842, two new church buildings were built next to the existing church. The two factions met in the separate buildings for ten years. In 1852, they were reunited. The "North Church" was sold to the Free Methodists in 1872. Both churches are still standing at the village green and the original church was moved to Academy Street. Churches of other denominations followed, and a large number of religious organizations graces the township. Levi Shaw, a Shaker, moved into the area and acted as an agent for other Shakers during the mid-nineteenth century. A Shaker-style barn that was constructed by him still stands on Route 79 in the township.

Excluding the village of Windsor, the town has fourteen hamlets or settlements within its borders. Blatchley was once called Hazardville after the Hazard Brothers who lived in that area. A Hazardville post office was established in 1859 but closed after six months. The current name honors Daniel Blatchley Jr., who came to the region in 1816. A Blatchley post office opened in 1859 and closed in 1904. Cascade Valley is an area very close to Pennsylvania and is adjacent to Cascade Creek. The waters of its many streams run into a deep basin called the "Devil's Punchbowl." A post office operated in this hamlet from 1862 until 1914.

Damascus was originally called Baldwinsville and then Crandallsville. It was later called Tuscarora for a Tuscarora Indian settlement formerly at this location. The post office settled on the name Damascus in 1899 because another town was already using Tuscarora. It had been settled by 1815 and included mills and a tannery. Damascus is now a busy exit off Route 17. Dunbar was originally called Peasetown, but the origin of the name is unclear. A post office operated only from 1892 to 1894. East Windsor developed near the base of Ouaguaga Mountain, and the name was selected when the post office opened in 1875. It closed in 1954. Edson was once called Barton Hollow and Bartonville after Hiram Barton, who came to that region in 1843.

Many of the smaller settlements formerly had their own churches. Quite a few of these churches have closed, and this particular former Methodist church is now a residence. (From the *Putnam Collection*, courtesy Broome County Public Library)

The name was changed in honor of Dr. Isaac Edson, the president of the Broome County Medical Society. A post office operated there from 1892 to 1905.

Flowers was so called after John J. Bell began a wildflower seed company there. Much of the early business was handled by mail order, and when the post office opened in 1886, the name Flowers was selected. The Bell Seed Company eventually moved to Binghamton and then to Deposit. Hoadley Hill was named after Daniel Hoadley, who came to that area in 1795 from Connecticut. Lester was originally called Griggs Settlement after Noah and Amos Griggs. Samuel Rexford first settled it, before 1790. It has also been called Randolph Center after the Randolph Township land patent of which it was once part. The name was later changed to possibly honor Horace Lester, one of the two brothers who began the Lester Brothers Boot and Shoe Company.

North Windsor, as was previously discussed, was near the site of Onaquaga. The original settlers of the hamlet called it Oquago before the present name was adopted. Oquago was the first center of population in the town, before the development of the village of Windsor. It included a tannery, a tavern, stores, a school, a blacksmith shop, and three mills with at least one dam on the Susquehanna. Occanum is named after the creek that runs through this area. Occanum Creek's name may have been derived from that of Samson Occum, a Native American missionary who preached at Onaquaga and Otsiningo. Occum died in 1792. An Occanum post office operated from 1893 until 1907.

South Windsor was once called Wallersville after postmaster Nathan Waller. A post office opened with that name in 1825, but the name was changed to Wake in 1899 after another postmaster, Thomas Wake Benedict. The office was closed in 1905. George Catlin (1796–1872), famous for his portraits of Native Americans, spent his boyhood years at South Windsor.

A dusty ride for many a traveler was had on the old stagecoaches that once were a common site in Broome County. This is the Windsor to Binghamton stagecoach. The last stagecoach run ended about 1915. (Courtesy Broome County Historical Society)

Stateline was a hamlet located on the east side of the Susquehanna River. It had a post office from 1891 until 1908. West Windsor was once called Stillson Hollow after Lyman Stillson, who ran a tavern there. A post office was in operation from 1832 until 1910. It also included several stores and blacksmith shops, a cheese factory, taverns, and a church. In the 1920s, the Sukver Fox and Fur Company operated a fox fur farm near the hamlet. Ansco Lake, a recreation area owned by a Binghamton photographic company, was also nearby.

There have been many notable personalities from the town of Windsor. Rebecca Kellogg Ashley was the daughter of Martin and Sarah Kellogg of Deerfield, Massachusetts. Native Americans kidnapped her in 1704 at the age of eight. She was taken to Canada until the age of thirty-three when she was recaptured by her brother and brought back to Massachusetts. She married Benjamin Ashley, an aide to the Rev. Gideon Hawley, who came as a missionary to Onaquaga. Her services as an interpreter were considered essential to the mission. She arrived there in 1753 and died four years later, in 1757. She is buried at the site of the old village of Onaquaga.

Jedediah Hotchkiss was born in Windsor in 1828. He moved to Virginia in 1847 and worked as a schoolteacher. Hotchkiss supplemented his income with work as a geologist and as

One of the wilder spots in the county is Devil's Punchbowl. It is an area near the Pennsylvania border that is part of what is called Cascade Valley in the town of Windsor. (Courtesy Broome County Historical Society)

a cartographer. In 1859, he and his brother opened a school for boys at Churchville, Virginia. When the Civil War broke out, Hotchkiss sided with the Confederacy and later served with General Stonewall Jackson until Jackson's death. Hotchkiss' maps were so detailed that many are now in the collection of the Library of Congress. Many of Hotchkiss' relatives fought on the side on the Union. After the conclusion of the war, Hotchkiss helped form a group called the Army Corps of Engineers. Charles English, the historian for the village of Windsor, now occupies Jedediah's father's sturdy stone house. He operates the Stone House Museum at the site, specializing in Civil War memorabilia and local history.

CHAPTER 30: THE TOWN OF WINDSOR   361

CHAPTER 31

The Village of
Deposit

Front Street in the village of Deposit remains close to its nineteenth-century appearance. Several fires in the last few years have destroyed some of the historic buildings of the area, but many others remain. (Courtesy Broome County Historical Society)

This Italianate structure dates from 1901 and is located on Church Street in the village. They are called the Wickwire Cottages after the man who built them. Unfortunately, some of the peaks and detail work have been removed from the façade. (Courtesy Broome County Historical Society)

THE VILLAGE OF DEPOSIT is located in both Broome County and Delaware County. The original settlement was located on the Delaware County side of the boundary and was incorporated as a village in 1811. The name of the village is derived from the deposits of lumber gathered there for floating down the Delaware River to markets at Philadelphia. The western portion located in Broome County merged with that village in 1851. The village has only .53 square mile of land and a population of 835 (2000 census figure).

The site was originally a Leni-Lenape village called Koo-koose. The anglicized version of this name, Cookhouse, is sometimes seen on old maps and documents. Deposit is located on the west branch of the Delaware River, and the abundance of lumber around the river valley provided ample opportunity for many adventurous newcomers to make small fortunes after the conclusion of the American Revolution. During the first half of the nineteenth century, the Delaware County side of the village grew steadily while the Broome County side grew much more slowly.

As was previously mentioned, the groundbreaking for the construction of the New York & Erie Railroad Company took place at Deposit in 1835. Because of financial difficulties, leadership changes, and problems in laying hundreds of miles of track over varying terrain, the railroad did not officially reach Deposit until 1848. Once the railroad opened, it brought much new economic development to the village. By 1850, three hotels had been constructed to handle the increasing business traffic of the growing village.

Beginning about 1859, Sheldon Hyde built "Hyde's Castle" on Second Street in Deposit. It combines several architectural elements and may have been built in sections. (Courtesy Broome County Historical Society)

Many of the new businesses opened closer to the railroad depot, which meant increased growth on the Broome County side of the village in an area that was once called Deansville. New York State recognized the need to recharter the village to include the growing Broome County portion. The new village, created in 1851, included the original 426 acres on the Delaware County side and 400 acres on the Broome County side. These boundaries still exist today.

During the second half of the nineteenth century, a number of industries and businesses prospered in the village. Lumberman Charles Knapp, among others, founded the Deposit National Bank in 1856. Under the control of the Knapp family, the bank became a dominant force in the economic life of the village. During the bank's operations, the village added a pearl button factory, a sled factory, a glove factory, an overall factory, a cigar factory, the Borden's Milk Plant #4, and the Outing Publishing Company. This company published *Outing*, the nation's leading outdoors magazine, as well as many others. Despite the healthy growth of many of these companies, the bank had made some poor investments. The Knapp bank failed in 1909, and its closure hurt many of the companies that had relied upon it. Today, the original Knapp bank building is the home of the Deposit Historical Society. Its later building is now a bank branch office.

Many of the county's most historic homes are located in this Victorian village, and many have kept close to their original appearance. The village acquired its own library in 1929 when the Deposit Civic Club formed the Deposit Free Library. The library was located over Smith's Pharmacy, now the site of Katie's Kafe on Front Street, until 1937. In that year, a Deposit native, Clark H. Minor, president of International General Electric, provided the funds necessary to build the first freestanding library building in the community. In the 1960s, a library addition was constructed, again the gift of Clark H. Minor.

In one of the more unusual events of this area, the village of Deposit was the victim of the Pumpkin Freshet. On October 3, 1903, three days of steady rain caused most of the area's ground to be so saturated that it could no longer hold any more water. The continued rains washed away the plank sidewalks that were located on Front Street and flooded the village as far as the Wickwire building on Mill Street. The railroad bridge was saved from being washed away because a loaded freight train was put on top of it. The Devereaux suspension footbridge that was across the Delaware River was taken out by the storm. The name of the flood came from the large number of pumpkins that were washed out of the fields and taken down the main streets of the village.

The original Knapp Bank building is located on Second Street in the village. Charles Knapp operated the bank for many years. It is now the home of the Deposit Community Historical Society and Museum. (Courtesy Broome County Historical Society)

A large number of fires have brought devastation to parts of the village of Deposit. On May 17, 1964, a fire destroyed the Delaware Mills feed mill located on Front Street. Another fire, on December 6, 1983, caused the death of firefighter Dale Linkroum, who was struggling to extinguish the fire in the Video Shack on Front Street. On August 5, 1995, a fire consumed the huge Indian Country Industries plant. The building had begun as New York Condensed Milk before Borden's had taken over the facility in the early 1900s. Later, it had been an Agway warehouse. The building was 90,000 square feet in size and had housed Indian Country's trophy and awards division.

Another fire on December 28, 2002, destroyed a restaurant and bar named ET's located on Front Street. Fires continued to ravage the village. On January 13, 2003, an arsonist set fire and destroyed another building on Front Street that housed several businesses and families. Another arsonist-set fire occurred on October 8, 2003. It destroyed the Panda Restaurant, also on Front Street, and a building adjacent to that structure. A fire on January 28, 2005, burned two buildings and damaged a third after a cat tipped over a lit candle.

C. J. Knapp, a wealthy banker, built this beautiful Second Empire home on Second Street about 1878, next to the family-owned bank. The home was demolished in the 1950s to make way for an automobile dealership. (Courtesy Broome County Historical Society)

In one disaster that was eventually redressed, the State Theatre suffered major damage when its roof collapsed under heavy snows. The residents of the village were not to be defeated by another disaster and raised funds to restore the theater to its original appearance. Today, the theater operates with a new roof and a new lease on life.

The village of Deposit continues to thrive despite some severe setbacks. Its annual Lumberjack Festival draws thousands to enjoy demonstrations of the skills and crafts of the area's early industries. The weekly newspaper, the *Deposit Courier*, continues to publish well into its second century and has branched out into the publishing of books and other items. The historic nature of Deposit and its placement in two counties helps to make it unique.

CHAPTER 32

The Village of Endicott

This aerial view shows the Union-Endicott High School with a portion of En-Joie Park in the foreground. The park was removed in the late 1960s to make way for the connecting bridge to Vestal. In the background can be seen the factories of EJ and IBM. (Courtesy Broome County Historical Society)

The village of Endicott grew around the factories and its retail area located on Washington Avenue. This 1916 photograph of that street shows the old village hall on the right and the smokestacks of the Endicott Johnson factory in the distance. (Courtesy Broome County Historical Society)

THE VILLAGE OF ENDICOTT was incorporated on August 28, 1906. Endicott is part of the town of Union, as is its sister village—Johnson City. It has an area of 2.57 square miles and a population of 13,038 (2000 census figure). Endicott is located on the north side of the Susquehanna River, and its growth was based on the growth of the industries that helped the village form in the first years of the twentieth century.

The village has been called "The Magic City." This nickname was well earned. The area was very little but farmland before 1900 when a group of investors formed the Endicott Land Company and began its rapid development. But the earlier history of this part of the town of Union mirrors that township's history. Native Americans hunted, fished, and lived along its riverbanks prior to the outbreak of the American Revolution.

Early settlers made way to the area to use the level river valley as farmland during the nineteenth century. The growing village of Union to the west of this area provided all of the amenities the new settlers could ask for—stores, railroad transportation, a post office, hotels for visitors, and schools. But as the years of the 1800s dwindled down toward a new century, the growth of nearby Lestershire brought increasing interest to the flatlands near the Susquehanna.

In 1899, George F. Johnson purchased a half-interest in the former Lester Brothers Boot and Shoe Company from Henry B. Endicott. Endicott loaned him the funds to complete the purchase, and the Endicott Johnson Shoe Company was formed. Johnson had already eyed the lands to the west of Lestershire as a possible area for expansion. But it was G. Tracy Rogers, the president of the Binghamton Railway Company, who first saw the land as an ideal location for an industrial community. His street railroad's trolley lines had already helped develop the outskirts of Binghamton. He and others formed the Endicott Land Company in 1900 to purchase large tracts of land in the area. It was also he who had discussed the creation of another village with Henry B. Endicott. Endicott was enticed to build a factory in the new area with the promise the area would be named for him. George F. Johnson persuaded Endicott to purchase two hundred acres of land for the construction of a new shoe factory.

The new factory was constructed in 1901 at what would become the intersection of North Street and Washington Avenue. The plan for the new village was fairly simple: Washington Avenue would serve as the main commercial street. At the north end of this street, North Street would be the location of the new factories. Residents would live on either side of Washington Avenue, near to their workplaces. Main Street would mark the southern boundary of the early Endicott and help connect it with the nearby villages of Lestershire and Union.

Many of the streets on either side of Washington Avenue were laid out at nearly the same time. It was originally thought that McKinley Avenue would develop as a main commercial street, and it was designed to be wider than neighboring streets for this reason. However, Washington Avenue's proximity to the factories kept the center of development near that roadway.

Word of the planned community spread quickly, and developers and contractors worked

The Mattoon Building on Washington Avenue in Endicott contained the Washington Hotel, doctors' offices, a drug store, and a barbershop in this 1937 photograph. The building still stands and is now being renovated. (Courtesy Broome County Historical Society)

CHAPTER 32: THE VILLAGE OF ENDICOTT   371

feverishly to meet the demands of building a new town. By 1902, over four hundred new structures were under construction or were planned for construction. A new home for George F. Johnson was planned for Endicott to show his commitment to the importance of the new town. In 1904, lots were selected for his new home on Broad Street. He would later build an even larger home on Park Street.

The new Endicott Johnson factory town provided the company with an opportunity to develop a new operation. Johnson had long wanted to control all aspects of shoe production, and the new land allowed room for a tannery. Within a few years, several tanneries were constructed along North Street. Endicott Johnson also erected other buildings to support the growing shoe company. A diner building opened to feed the thousands of workers in the community; medical offices handled the illnesses and injuries of the company's employees.

In addition to EJ, another firm planned to expand into the new village. In 1904, the Bundy Time Recording Company plant began construction. By 1906, Bundy had evolved into the International Time Recording Company. In that year, ITR began construction of what would become known as IBM Plant Number 1. At that same time, other companies started up in Endicott. Forging operations commenced at Union Forging and Endicott Forging. Union Forging had been formed from Union Hardware Company in 1848, and Endicott Forging followed in 1915. The LaMotte Enterprise Box Factory opened in 1904.

New enterprises opened in response to increasing activity in Endicott. The Frederick Hotel was built on Washington Avenue in 1906 to house visiting businessmen and travelers to the area. Churches sprang up throughout the community. Endicott Johnson began building homes for the workers of the company when its housing program started up in 1913. The Endicott Land Company was already developing tracts of homes on several streets in the village. Burt's Department Store began operation in the 1920s on Washington Avenue. Well-known bakeries such as Elks opened to the delight of workers while movie theaters such as the Regis and the Lyric entertained the families of the community.

Nearby, Union-Endicott High School was constructed in 1915 to replace an earlier school on Loder Avenue. The Loder Avenue School then became an elementary school. In the 1970s, a large complementary-looking addition was built onto the original structure. In addition to these two schools, the village also had the Broad Street School, the George F. Johnson School, and the George H. Nichols School. Nearby, Seton Catholic High School opened to handle the increasing parochial student population.

As thousands of immigrants flooded Broome County, many settled in the new village of Endicott to work in the factories and tanneries of Endicott Johnson. While some resided in the neighborhoods on either side of Washington Avenue, many more moved toward the hills at the north end of Endicott. The North Side of Endicott became an enclave of newly arrived future citizens of the county as well as others who came to this area from the coalfields of Pennsylvania. This was especially true of Italians who helped to settle a large portion of the "Nob." It was here that foods such as spiedies and hot pies (pizza) were introduced to the residents of the county for the first time.

By 1921, it was clear that the expansion of Endicott was encroaching upon the village of Union. The merger of the two villages in that year nearly doubled the geographical size of Endicott. In 1920, the employees of the Endicott Johnson Shoe Company had gathered nickels, dimes, and quarters to erect two arches to denote the boundaries of Johnson City and Endicott. With the merger of Union and Endicott, the westernmost arch was no longer at the village line.

Tri-Cities Airport was founded in Endicott in 1933 and moved to its present location in 1936. It had the first scheduled passenger flights to New York City in 1945. With the opening of the Broome County Airport in 1951, Tri-Cities Airport became more focused on private and

The village of Endicott is host to one of the six carousels in the county. Located at the George W. Johnson Park on Oak Hill Avenue, the carousel has been restored to its original appearance. (Courtesy Broome County Historical Society)

corporate air transport. In 2004, consideration was given by village officials to selling the airport to ease financial burdens on the municipality.

As the health program of the Endicott Johnson Shoe Company expanded, so did the need for adequate medical facilities. Dr. Roger Mead operated the first hospital in the village of Endicott, beginning in 1915. But the facility quickly became too small to handle the growing needs of the community. An emergency facility was opened in 1922 to handle maternity requirements and the minor injuries of Endicott Johnson employees and their families. In 1927, Endicott Johnson opened Ideal Hospital. A year after it was opened, a nurses' quarters building was donated by Mrs. George F. Johnson.

In 1894, the owners of the Binghamton Railway Company had developed a park at the end of

The George F. Johnson Memorial Library stands on the site of the home of the local industrialist. Many residents hated to see his beautiful home destroyed, but the new building provided much-needed room for the library's collection. (Courtesy Broome County Historical Society)

their trolley car lines, near where the village of Endicott later sprang up. Casino Park was created atop some previous bicycle trails and relied on the beauty of the walks along lagoons and bridges as the people in the park made their way to the Casino building. The company charged an admission to the park. Meanwhile, George F. Johnson had begun to promote the development of parks as a means of free recreation for the residents of the community.

Endicott Johnson purchased Casino Park and opened it as a free facility, renaming it Ideal Park. Residents could watch a boxing match in the Casino building or enjoy roller-skating inside of the structure. A horseracing track and stable complex was added to the eastern end of the park, and one of the area's six carousels was installed nearby. The park was later called En-Joie Park, like the golf course that the company built to the western edge of the village of Endicott. In 1948, the Casino building was destroyed by fire and replaced with the Endicott Johnson Recreation Building.

En-Joie Golf Course was intentionally built nearly flat to avoid tiring out the workers who played the course for a greens fee of twenty-five cents. The golf course was part of the En-Joie Health Club, a facility that was one of the first corporate-operated health facilities in the country. George F. Johnson was aware that the physical and mental health of the workers was important to their level of productivity. The recreational benefits bestowed by Endicott Johnson became a very important part of the company's efforts to keep a contented workforce.

After World War II, the village of Endicott seemed at the height of success. The stability of Endicott Johnson was complemented by the growth of IBM in the town. When the strength of EJ later waned in the 1950s and 1960s, IBM grew into the area's leading employer and kept up the vitality of Endicott. Changes in the environment of the village began as early as 1968 when the owners of the Endicott Johnson Corporation divested itself of the many parks and extraneous operations of the company. En-Joie Park was sold, and a portion was used to build a connector bridge to Vestal. The carousel was moved to Highland Park in Endwell. The former Endicott Johnson Recreation building was sold to the Union-Endicott School District for use as its administrative office. The decline and eventual loss of Endicott Johnson in the 1980s had a serious effect on the village of Endicott.

The loss of EJ was significant, but the near loss of IBM was catastrophic for the village. The end of the Cold War meant the loss of contracts for a number of local defense industries, including IBM. Added to this were the changes in the computer market that spread the revenues from that industry over a larger number of competitors and took funds away from the rather stale IBM of the 1980s. By 1994, IBM had begun to lay off large numbers of workers, and many others were forced to move to company positions in other states. The population and tax base of the village began to erode quickly during the 1980s and the 1990s.

The 1980s purchase by IBM of many of the parking lots used formerly by EJ and the leveling of homes and businesses now seemed, at best, premature. Endicott was left with a large number of empty lots and little prospects for future development. The site of an EJ tannery, factory, and medical building was used for the construction of a strip plaza containing a Price Chopper supermarket and other stores.

In 2000, a major change occurred when a group of local investors formed Endicott Innovation Technologies. Using industrial development funds, they purchased the IBM campus and brought in the Huron Company to manage the real estate. IBM continues to lease space for operations that now employ about one thousand workers, compared to its height of fourteen thousand in the early 1980s.

There is still hope for the future of the village of Endicott. A redevelopment effort is taking place on the North Side to revive the Oak Hill Avenue area as a Little Italy–type neighborhood. The village has entered a partnership with Broome County to stabilize the management of the En-Joie Golf Course and maintain the B.C. Open, an annual PGA golf event since 1971. A new taxing district is in place to stabilize funding for both the George F. Johnson Memorial Library and Your Home Public Library in Johnson City. United Health Services closed the former Ideal Hospital, but it has been converted into a retirement facility. Nevertheless, the village of Endicott is in a state of flux that may not end in the near future.

CHAPTER 33

The Village of Johnson City

The rise of Lestershire, now Johnson City, was dependent on the growth of Endicott Johnson. The factories provided employment to thousands for about a century. This is a view of the factories near Corliss Avenue. (Courtesy Broome County Historical Society)

Main Street in Johnson City looks much as it did at the beginning of the 1900s. Although the store names have changed since this 1960s photograph, many of the façades have been carefully maintained. (Courtesy Broome County Historical Society)

THE VILLAGE OF JOHNSON CITY was incorporated on September 15, 1892. It was originally called Lester Shire, but a post office name change at another town required the change to Lestershire on October 17, 1893. It is the central component of the Triple Cities, with the city of Binghamton to its east and the village of Endicott to its west. It has a land area of 3.53 square miles and a population of 15,535 (2000 census figure).

Although the formal birth date of Johnson City is 1892, its history dates long before then. Located on the north side of the Susquehanna River, Johnson City was also the site of Native American habitation as well as an early settlement after the close of the American Revolution. Settlement began to occur about 1790 when Samuel Allen became the first resident of that section of the town of Union. He purchased four hundred acres of land, much of which constitutes the modern-day Johnson City.

The more recent development of the village began when George Harry Lester saw the area as an ideal location for the expansion of the Lester Brothers Boot and Shoe Company. His father, Harry Lester, had begun the company in 1854 in Binghamton. But the labor unrest of the cigar industry had marred his perception of Binghamton's economy. Also, he felt that if the company was to expand, it needed land outside of the city where the taxes were lower.

In 1888, he purchased eleven acres from Francis Allen, the son of early settler Samuel Allen. From others in the area he acquired most of the original Allen tract. By 1889, surveys and maps had been produced that laid out the planned village of Lestershire. In March 1890, the Lestershire Boot and Shoe Manufacturing Company was incorporated. A new factory was constructed along Corliss Avenue. The Pioneer factory was a wooden structure that was four hundred feet long and fifty feet wide. The four-story building was the most prominent structure in the fledgling village.

The Lestershire Boot and Shoe Company sold home lots to new residents. The company also opened up several shops along Main Street and strongly encouraged workers to purchase from the company's stores. Despite these efforts to create a company town, the business ran into serious financial difficulties by 1892. A downturn in the country's economy had followed Lester's overextending the company's assets into too many ventures. In January 1892, the company was taken over by the newly incorporated Lestershire Manufacturing Company, with former creditor Henry B.

Endicott of Massachusetts as its president. Former factory foreman George F. Johnson became superintendent.

Endicott and Johnson brought a level of stability that was needed for growth. Johnson had been one of the workers, and he had the type of touch that made both workers and managers feel comfortable with his decisions. Endicott quickly realized that Johnson's leadership inspired loyalty among company employees. In 1899, he loaned Johnson the money to purchase a partnership in the firm, and Endicott Johnson was born. By this time, the village of Lestershire had three thousand residents.

Johnson worked quickly to promote his Square Deal program in both Lestershire and the newly created village of Endicott. The popular policies of the company drew thousands of new workers, and the number of factories being built in Lestershire kept pace with the number of new residents who were arriving in the village. Main Street in Lestershire was the focus of most of the commercial development. A municipal building that housed the village offices and police and fire departments was constructed on Willow Street. Factories were located to the north and south of Main Street. Most of the factories were located along the tracks of the Delaware, Lackawanna and Western Railroad line on the southern side of the village and the New York & Erie Railroad on the north side of Lestershire.

By 1910, three of the four Johnson brothers were in command at Endicott Johnson. George F. Johnson was in charge of the overall operations of the company while C. Fred Johnson operated the company fire department. Harry L. Johnson was in charge of many of Endicott Johnson's benefit programs. It was said that he cared too much for the welfare of the worker. Harry constructed an elegant Colonial Revival home on Main Street, now the site of Barber Funeral Home. When he was worried that some workers and their families did not have enough to eat, he planted potatoes on his front lawn and gave them away to the needy. Harry L. Drive is named for him.

Harry L. Johnson also helped to develop the workers housing program. The housing plan began in earnest in 1913 when the company purchased one hundred acres to the north of Main Street and adjacent

The former Village Hall on Willow Street in Johnson City also housed the fire department and the village police. A new facility has been constructed to hold the police department, and the village offices are now located on Main Street. (Courtesy Broome County Historical Society)

Construction on the steelwork for the Oakdale Mall can be seen in this 1970s photograph. The mall was the first enclosed mall structure in the county. It altered the retail market of the community forever. (Courtesy Broome County Historical Society)

to Broad Avenue. The illness and death of Harry L. Johnson in 1921 put the housing program in the hands of C. Fred Johnson and, later, Charles F. Johnson. Roberson Lumber was contracted to provide the lumber for the homes while Boland Construction built the structures. Workers were charged only the cost of their homes and mortgage costs were taken directly out of their wages. In an interesting note, C. Fred Johnson incorrectly calculated the cost of homes by one hundred dollars per home. Instead of charging the extra cost to the workers, the company took a loss on the first one hundred homes.

Several streets to both the north and south side of the village were lined with Endicott Johnson workers' homes. The new village continued to grow with a new high school on Main Street, built in two stages. The section to the east was built first in 1914–1915, and the western half was built thirteen years later. Elementary schools such as C. Fred Johnson, Harry L. Johnson, and the Lincoln School brought twentieth-century elementary education to the younger students of the village.

Other companies were also part of Lestershire's early development. The Alonzo Roberson & Son Lumber Company had moved out of downtown Binghamton to the western edge of the city. It built a new lumberyard and headquarters that straddled the line between the village and the city. Although most of the company was in Lestershire, it used Binghamton as its mailing address. The Faatz Felting Company located in the 1890s near Corliss Avenue and the Pioneer factory. The Vulcan Corporation built a factory on Grand Avenue making rubber products, many of which were sold to Endicott Johnson.

Fair Play Caramel Company also built a new plant on Grand Avenue. The firm had started out as the E. F. Hopton Candy Company in Binghamton but moved to Lestershire within a few years. It was sold in 1920 and became the Ideal Candy Company. Finally, in 1924, the name was changed to Fair Play Caramels. It produced a variety of well-known candies such as B. B. Bats until it closed in the early 1980s. Today, the Islamic Organization of the Southern Tier has rebuilt the structure as a mosque. Ansco opened a camera factory in 1910. The site was later expanded with a complex of streamlined Art Deco–style industrial buildings, occupied by the Ozalid Company in 1938. The company would employ hundreds of workers at this site until the 1980s. The village also was home to firms such as the Marshall Furniture Company and the Wells & Brigham Brickyard, which had originated here in 1856, long before the birth of Lestershire.

In 1916, George F. Johnson did something that no other shoe company employer in the United States had done before: he lowered the workday from nine and a half hours a day to eight hours a day. The workers kept the same daily pay rate but had to work fewer hours for their pay. Johnson had determined that the more tired a worker, was the less productive he or she became. Both the workers and the community met his decision with vigorous approval. A large parade honoring the change was held throughout the Triple Cities. Two months later, it was suggested that the name of the community be changed to honor the man who had done so much for the area, and the village of Johnson City became a reality.

As Endicott Johnson became an industrial giant, the benefits to the residents of Johnson City increased. In 1913, George F. Johnson purchased the Bingos baseball team and built Johnson Field adjacent to the first section of EJ homes near Broad Avenue. As previously discussed in this book, the team would later become a farm team associated with the New York Yankees organization. On Willow Street, near the municipal building, the Goodwill Theater was constructed. It could operate as both a performing arts center and as a movie theater. In later years, the complex became the En-Joy Theatre, part of the Comerford Theater chain.

C. Fred Johnson was put in charge of reclaiming the brick pond of the Wells & Brigham Brickyard when that firm went out of business. Beginning in the early 1910s and continuing over the next decade, C. Fred worked to make the pond an attractive recreational area and park setting. The pond gradually became smaller until it was completely filled. The area was developed as both a park and a factory site. CFJ Park included a carousel, playgrounds, and a huge Binty aboveground swimming pool that was added in 1927. The pool could hold two thousand swimmers at once. Adjacent to the park was the George F. Johnson Pavilion. The pavilion could entertain two thousand people inside and several thousand more outside on the lawn. Each week, local bands would play on Friday evenings at the cost of twenty-five cents per person. On Saturdays, residents could enjoy the strains of swing music with performers like Benny Goodman, Glenn Miller, Guy Lombardo, Ella Fitzgerald, and many others for only fifty cents.

In the midst of the factories adjacent to the park was the Public Market building. Starting in the 1920s, Endicott Johnson began to offer farmers a direct market to sell their produce to local residents. Public markets were built in both Johnson City and Endicott. Thousands enjoyed the opportunity to save by buying from the source, and the farmers enjoyed the opportunity to maximize their return on their products. No one thought it odd to have the market located in the middle of factories, parks, and houses.

As previously discussed in this book, EJ helped to develop Charles S. Wilson Memorial Hospital as part of its medical program. The hospital also developed a nursing school that operated from the former Frank M. Smith School. Endicott Johnson also operated its own Medical Department. The department provided basic medical care for many of the workers and their families. When the company began to downsize in the 1960s, the hospital became part of the United Health Services and the Medical Department was closed. Today, the hospital offers a wide range of medical services, and the area around the hospital now has a wide array of doctors' offices.

As happened in the village of Endicott, Johnson City saw rapid change in the 1960s. The sale of Endicott Johnson to an outside firm brought an end to many company benefits. The company turned over the operation of CFJ Park to the village while the George F. Johnson Pavilion was converted to a roller-skating rink and eventually became the Fountains Pavilion. The facility has recently closed, and

A former A&P grocery store on Harry L. Drive in Johnson City was converted to the "Small Mall" in the 1970s. Later, one building was converted to a Chuck E. Cheese's, then the Touch of Texas dance hall, and, currently, Magic City Music Hall. (Courtesy Broome County Historical Society)

its future is uncertain. Operations of Your Home Library were made independent of any funding from EJ. In the same time period that Endicott Johnson was closing factories in rapid succession in Johnson City, Anitec closed the Johnson City site that had been created by Ansco. Eventually, the only EJ factory still making shoes was the Paracord factory next to the CFJ Park. Finally, this factory was closed in 1995.

By 1980, the Johnson City government was faced with aging factory buildings, a diminished tax base, and a declining population. In an underhanded move in 1982 that outraged many residents, the pool at CFJ Park was demolished in the middle of the night. It was a sign of many changes to come for the village. The Paracord factory complex was sold, originally for the development of a factory outlet shopping center. Instead, it is under the ownership of the Newman Development Group. Gannett Corporation is constructing a new building on the site for the production of the *Press & Sun-Bulletin* newspaper and three other newspapers.

Some of the factories such as the Victory Factory have had limited usage as storage malls and retail space. Others have been demolished. The former C.F.K. factory complex on Lester Avenue was replaced with a much smaller plant operated by Country Valley Industries for the Broome Tioga ARC. A new police station has been constructed in a former industrial area to replace the dilapidated Willow Street building. The old Lestershire Spool Company was refurbished and reopened as a large art space called Spool MFG [*sic*] in 2002.

Parts of Main Street in Johnson City have preserved the appearance of Johnson City in its heyday. A stainless steel 1950s diner, the Red Robin Restaurant, was moved from Binghamton in 1959. It is set among rows of brick buildings and storefronts that harken back to the late nineteenth century origins of the village. After the annexation of Oakdale in 1964, much of the residential and commercial development shifted to the north, away from downtown.

The Oakdale Mall (1975) and surrounding area have become among the busiest commercial centers of the county. On the hill to the north, the new Johnson City High School and Johnson City Elementary School overlook the mall, the rush of traffic on Route 17, and a once busy industrial valley.

CHAPTER 34

The Village of Lisle

This is a look down Main Street in the village of Lisle about 1910. Much of the village remains as it was at the turn of the last century, and some of the buildings date back to 1840. (From the *Putnam Collection*, courtesy Broome County Public Library)

The Leader Store was built in the 1860s. The building is currently empty. (From the *Putnam Collection*, courtesy Broome County Public Library)

THE VILLAGE OF LISLE was incorporated in 1866. Located on the west bank of the Tioughnioga River, it has .71 square mile of land within its borders and a population of 302 (2000 census figure). The original name of the area was Mudlick, apparently for a muddy creek, possibly after one of the many floods that formerly plagued the village. An early local historian and humorist, "Nat Odd," attributed the name to the "low marshy soil and the almost unfathomable depth of mud in the streets, rendering it at times quite impassable." Its current name, like that of the town, is taken from the town of Lisle, France. The post office began operations in 1802 and continues to this day.

The earliest families settled the region long before its incorporation. Settlement began in the early 1790s with the arrival of Ebenezer Tracy, Colonel William Cook, and Dr. Hunt, among others. Unlike many other communities in Broome County, the appearance of the village is remarkably unchanged since its growth ended in the mid-nineteenth century. The area quickly became industrial with a number of mills and factories prior to the outbreak of the Civil War. Gunsmithing became a prominent feature of the 1850s and 1860s, and many of those who went on to fame in that industry had beginnings in this small community.

The arrival of the Syracuse, Binghamton and New York Railroad (later the Delaware and Hudson Railroad) in the 1850s assisted in the village's growth to only a small degree. The operations of the Chenango Canal, the New York and Erie Railroad, and the Delaware, Lackawanna and Western Railroad all diverted growth away from the village. Many of the structures along Main Street date from as early as 1840. The area was serviced by a number

This is Elliott Hall Conference Center. It was constructed in 1959 to match the architecture of the Pigs Ear Tavern located nearby on High Street and maintains the historic look of the village. (Courtesy Broome County Historical Society)

of physicians, including Dr. Salphronious French, whose home still stands in the village. He arrived in Lisle about 1834 and, except for one brief time, practiced there until his death in 1877. His impressive home was later occupied by another doctor and also used as a convalescent home.

In 1912, Mr. and Mrs. Richard H. Edwards began Happy Valley Home as an institution to assist children with special needs. Both private and public funds helped bring in children from many parts of the state. The facility used several buildings in the village, including a former hotel that was constructed in 1831 and located on the corners of Main Street, River Street, and High Street. They also used the former "Pigs Ear," an 1860s tavern on High Street. The home operated for several decades. The facilities were sold for use as a Congregational conference center in 1942.

The Congregational Church building was erected on River Street in 1824, replacing an 1822 structure. The original congregation began in 1797 under the leadership of the Reverend Seth Williston, whose diaries and letters give a picture of a frontier town being carved out of the abundant timber that once played such an important role in the region. The Methodist Church of Lisle was organized in 1815, and the church building that still stands was constructed in 1857. In the 1930s, the congregation of this church gradually

CHAPTER 34: THE VILLAGE OF LISLE   389

merged with that of the Congregational Church to form the Lisle Associated Church. The Congregational Church was closed in 1937. The building was later converted to a private residence.

In the 1860s, the Leader Store was constructed on Main Street and operated by J. C. Lewis. In the later part of the nineteenth century, a former schoolhouse was moved to the east of the store, and a false façade was added to match the original store. Charles Corcoran, husband of former town historian Tressa Corcoran, later operated the twin stores. It is a shining example of the adaptive reuse of mid-nineteenth-century storefronts.

Until a few years ago, the village post office was housed in a small storefront on Main Street. The structure was most probably originally a lawyer's office and dated from about 1840. Since the post office moved to a

The former post office on Main Street in Lisle dates to the mid-nineteenth century. (Courtesy Broome County Historical Society)

new facility across the street, the Greek Revival building has been used to sell antiques. A public park is located on River Street and includes a play area and swimming pool.

Herbert Franklin, the automobile industrialist, donated the funds for the construction of the village's public library. An addition on the rear of the building allowed for the housing of its local history collection. (From the *Putnam Collection,* courtesy Broome County Public Library)

The devastating effects of the flood of 1935 caused a tremendous amount of damage to the village of Lisle. A number of homes, barns, and other outbuildings were either destroyed or severely damaged by the raging Dudley Creek. After the flood, the end of Cortland Street was closed, and other streets were extended. Dudley Creek was diverted away from the village and into a new channel. Today, the last portion of the old creek bed has been filled, removing much of the flood danger from the village.

The former Lisle Academy was demolished, and students in the village now attend Whitney Point schools. Likewise, the *Lisle Gleaner,* the weekly newspaper that began publication in 1871, ended its run in 1928. While the history and importance of Lisle is evident in its architecture, many of the promising business and industrial interests that once made this a thriving community are now gone.

CHAPTER 35

The Village of Port Dickinson

A speeding car turns the corner from Dickinson Avenue onto Chenango Street about 1930 in this photograph of Port Dickinson. (Courtesy Broome County Historical Society)

This is a photograph of the original Port Dickinson School. The building was first used as a church before being converted to educational use. It was replaced with the current elementary school. (Courtesy Broome County Historical Society)

THE VILLAGE OF PORT DICKINSON was incorporated on January 22, 1876. It was formerly called Carmansville in honor of Joseph C. Carman, a contractor on the New York and Erie Railroad. He was also the first postmaster when the office opened there in 1865. When it was incorporated, the village was named in honor of Daniel S. Dickinson. It was called "port" because of its location on the Chenango Canal, which formerly had a dry dock and boathouse in the village. It is the smallest incorporated entity in Broome County with only .45 square mile of land within it. It has a population of 1,697 (2000 census figure).

Old State Road, part of the Catskill Turnpike, ran into the center of Port Dickinson and ended at Chenango Street. The road followed an early trail and was the main route followed by the early settlers as they migrated from the Hudson Valley. Sawtelle's Tavern was located at the end of this road. Founded as early as 1787, it was the oldest tavern or inn in the area and was demolished in 1964. The opening of the Chenango Canal in 1837 was the basis for the formation of the community. A coal station was constructed adjacent to the canal. Coal was the major freight being transported on the packet boats, and the stop made Port Dickinson a vital link on the canal. The village grew quickly as an industrial area, with the Chenango River providing waterpower. A dam was built across the river, and a raceway was used to power several industries. By 1865, the village included the Cary, Nash, and Ogden paper mills, the broom factory of C. Bevier, and a flour mill operated by George Q. Moon. Russell & Hunt ran a whip factory from this vicinity. Nelson Stow began the manufacture of flexible shafts at Port Dickinson until he moved the company to the city of Binghamton in 1884.

The commercial summit of the village of Port Dickinson was between 1880 and 1884 when the aforementioned industries were operating at their height. Two hotels operated in the village to handle the visitors to the community and its many businesses. But a series of fires changed the outlook for the village. Over a period of ten years, flames destroyed many of the factories. Fires destroyed the paper mill and the flour mill

A large skating pond was constructed under the WPA program at the rear of the Port Dickinson Elementary School in the 1930s. The facility is still used for educational purposes today. (Courtesy Broome County Historical Society)

during 1884. A later fire destroyed the National Hotel. The loss of Stow Manufacturing and the closure of the whip factory brought an effective end of Port Dickinson as an industrial center.

The same year that Port Dickinson was incorporated, the Chenango Canal closed in this area. Despite the closeness of Port Dickinson to two railroad lines, the rapid growth of nearby Binghamton seems to have effectively closed off the village from further industrial growth. It became one of the first "bedroom communities" in the area. Many of the residents lived in the village but used trolleys and their own vehicles to go to work in the city of Binghamton.

The Port Dickinson Elementary School is part of the Chenango Valley School System. The school building was constructed in 1921. An addition in 1930 and a large addition in the 1980s expanded the structure. In the rear part of the school lot, the Broome County Emergency Work Bureau (a local division of the WPA) added a skating rink in 1935. The water-filled area is still used both as an educational tool and for recreational purposes.

The former site of the S. N. Carman Pickle factory, mentioned earlier in this book, was vacant for many years, especially after the construction of the Interstate 88 connector to Interstate 81. The area was developed as Port Dickinson's park in the late 1980s. It has been an extremely successful example of reuse of the area, and many area residents enjoy the beauty of this park along the banks of the Chenango River.

Port Dickinson is blessed with beautiful Victorian homes that retain much of their original character, such as this home at 795 Chenango Street. (Courtesy Broome County Historical Society)

The village of Port Dickinson was home to several taverns. Sawtelle Tavern has been previously discussed in this book. Another tavern was also located on Chenango Street at the corner of Perkins Street. The structure dates from approximately 1825. It was later used as an antique store, a flower shop, and a doll hospital before it was restored as a residence. A number of structures in this section of the community show the strong influence of the Victorian period. Large turrets, elaborate inserts into the porch pediments, and graceful Queen Anne and other styles are evident in this area. Many have been lovingly restored, helping to keep the historic nature of the village intact.

The Community Baptist Church is located on Chenango Street. The original structure was built in 1884 (previously, services had been held in a schoolhouse) and was replaced by the current brick building in 1922. The old church building was moved to the town of Chenango and used in the hamlet of Nimmonsburg before it was destroyed by fire a few months later. In the 1940s, a modern-day connector called the Brandywine Highway intersected the village, leaving a small portion of the village on the north side of the roadway. The Brandywine was redirected in the 1980s to better connect with the new Interstate 88. The village of Port Dickinson continues to operate a police department, a fire department, and other offices. The village remains one of the more desirable bedroom communities around the city of Binghamton.

Architect Norman Davies designed these buildings on Chenango Street in Port Dickinson. A variety of stores and businesses are housed in this unique facility. (Courtesy Broome County Historical Society)

CHAPTER 36

The Village of Whitney Point

Victorian-garbed girls cross the street, perhaps on the way to the drugstore to buy candy in this 1896 photograph of Whitney Point. In 1897, a fire would destroy much of the village seen in this picture. (Courtesy Broome County Historical Society)

Snook, Collins and Company operated the sash, door and blind factory that was located in Whitney Point depicted in this 1876 engraving. It was one of the thriving businesses that helped build the village. (Courtesy Broome County Historical Society)

THE VILLAGE OF WHITNEY POINT

was incorporated in March 1871. Located at the confluence of the Otselic and Tioughnioga Rivers, the village is a part of the town of Triangle. It includes a landmass of .79 square mile and has a population of 956 (2000 census figure). It was named after Thomas Whitney, an early settler in the area and a brother of Joshua Whitney.

As previously described, General John Patterson arrived in 1791 to begin the settlement of the area. His home was located where the Hess gas station now sits on New York Route 11. The original name of the area was Patterson's Point, but it was also called Tinker's Point before the arrival of Thomas and William, another Whitney brother. They came to the vicinity in 1802. By that time, the first religious service had already been held (1792), and the first school had been opened (1793). Thomas Whitney operated the first store and tavern and also served as the first postmaster in 1824. It was with the opening of the post office that the settlement became known as Whitney's Point.

In 1858, the village's first newspaper was founded. It was called the *Broome Gazette* published by G. A. Dodge. The name was later changed to the *Whitney Point Reporter,* and this weekly newspaper is still being published. It was during this period that George Seymour and his family assisted in the operation of the

Underground Railroad. The Seymour home was located on the corner of Collins Street and Seymour Street. The family was among the oldest in the village, having arrived just after John Patterson. Slaves were brought into the home and hidden in the attic. One of George Seymour's daughters, Mary, once saw some slaves hidden behind the attic planks. She was told by her mother never to speak of what she had seen. Mary did not mention the incident until very late in life, but most of the neighbors had been aware of the family's involvement in the activity and said nothing to authorities. The home was later used as an antiques store called Underground Antiques. It is now a private residence.

In 1871, the same year that the village was incorporated, the Broome County Agricultural Fair was relocated to Whitney Point. Today, the Broome County Fair continues this tradition after 134 years, mostly at the same location.

The village organized its fire department in 1873. This small group of firefighters was not prepared to stop the village's worst disaster. On the evening of April 23, 1897, a fire broke out in the Griffin Block, a building located on the corner of Main Street and Collins Street. The fire was not noticed until it had spread throughout the structure. Flames swept across the street, and additional buildings were set aflame. The fire spread from block to block, and fire companies from Binghamton,

After the fire destroyed much of the center of Whitney Point, a shantytown was constructed to temporarily replace the ruined businesses. Within a few years, much of the town had returned. (Courtesy Broome County Historical Society)

Marathon, and Hallstead, Pennsylvania, arrived to assist the Whitney Point firefighters. When the fire was finally out, fifty-four buildings had been destroyed. Much of the center of Whitney Point lay in ruins. Amazingly, the three churches in the village were undamaged by the fire.

Within a few weeks, a shantytown was built to replace many of the destroyed commercial buildings. A year after the fire, many new buildings had been erected, giving Whitney Point its Victorian appearance. In 1904, the First Bank of Whitney Point was organized. Electricity was finally introduced to the village in 1922 although it had been used in Binghamton for forty years.

The floods of 1935 and 1936 hit the village of Whitney Point with severity. After visits by Governor Herbert Lehman and President Franklin Delano Roosevelt, it was finally decided to construct a dam across the Otselic River and to build floodwalls along the river behind Main Street. A federally sponsored program completed the Whitney Point Dam in 1942. The dam continues to protect the river valley from the dangers of flooding and to provide recreational opportunities on the Whitney Point Reservoir.

The original Whitney Point Academy was established in 1866. In 1936, the Whitney Point Board of Education resolved to construct a new school. The former facility was located on Academy Street, but it had grown too small to hold an increasing number of students. The new brick school building was located along Route 11 and had separate boys' and girls' entrances. An addition was erected in the 1950s, but there was a need to separate the lower grades. The Caryl Adams Elementary School was built in 1961 on Keibel Road. Six years later, in 1967, a new senior high school was built next to the elementary school. An addition was built onto the high school in 1991. Today, discussions are still underway about replacing the 1967 high school building.

In 1959, the Mary Wilcox Library was opened. Mary Wilcox, a former school librarian, had bequeathed her home to be used as a library. It continues to operate at its Main Street location. An arsonist set fire to the Whitney Point Village Hall and Fire Station in 1967 and destroyed the structure. Today, the village offices are located in the Town of Triangle Office Building, which opened to the public in 2001. The structure is located on Liberty Street and also houses offices of the New York State Police.

In 1974, a nutrition program began in the Grace Episcopal Church Parish Hall. It soon became affiliated with the Broome County Office for the Aging. In 2003, the Northern Broome County Senior Center was opened at Strongs Place on Liberty Street. The center provides meals, meeting facilities, and other opportunities for the older citizens of the area to remain active and share memories.

Daycare is an issue of much importance for families with young children in the area. A preschool was started in the village in 1978, and a daycare center opened in the Methodist Church in 1989, but there was still a need for a larger facility. In 1992, the Whitney Point Preschool and Daycare Center opened on

The Oakland Hotel is located on Main Street in Whitney Point and retains much of its late-nineteenth-century flavor. (Courtesy Broome County Historical Society)

These are the "Big Four" storefronts that were built after the 1897 fire. They are located on the north side of Main Street in Whitney Point. Allan Lee took the pictures in 1987. (Courtesy Broome County Historical Society)

West Main Street. A new building was added a few years later, and the facility now offers a universal Pre-K program. Today, the village is constructing a new sewer system. The system had been under discussion for over forty years.

The village of Whitney Point has had its share of interesting personalities. Milo B. Eldredge was born in 1834 in the town of Barker. He began a teaching career at the age of fifteen at the Mount Hunger School in the town of Lisle. He eventually became the principal of two schools in the city of Binghamton. He began to study for the law, but the outbreak of the Civil War drew him to enlist. He became a captain of Company E of the 137th New York Volunteers. He was made a brevet colonel of the regiment in 1865.

He participated in several important battles, including Chancellorsville, Gettysburg, Lookout Mountain, and Atlanta. A local historian declared in 1885: "A braver officer never drew his sword…in our great struggle for national existence." In 1866, he was elected to the state legislature. He married Alice Hyde in 1870. In 1876, he purchased the *Broome Gazette* and built the Nioga Block the same year. He sold the newspaper after four years, but by then his health had begun to seriously deteriorate. He suffered from a mental disorder as a result of the war, was placed in the Utica Insane Asylum in 1880, and died there in 1881.

Ethel Newcomb was born in 1875 to Willis and Mary Seymour. At an early age she began to play the piano and was taught by her aunt, who was a gifted pianist. In 1897, she traveled to Vienna to study with Theodore Leschetizky. She stayed in Europe until 1907 and then came back to the United States to begin a concert tour. She was a close friend of Clara Clemens, the daughter of Mark Twain, and she played at Clara's wedding.

Ethel came back to Whitney Point in 1926 and played at many local concerts. She taught piano for many years at her studio on Pendell Hill Road. She died in 1959 and is buried in the Riverside Cemetery in Whitney Point. Her memorabilia can still be seen on display in the Ethel Newcomb Room at the Mary Wilcox Library.

CHAPTER 37

The Village of Windsor

The third Coburn Whip Company factory building is seen in this 1870 photograph. The company was one of several whip companies that helped boost the economy in the village of Windsor. (Courtesy Broome County Historical Society)

This is the Stiles Hotchkiss house in Windsor. The stone home was the residence of one of the most prominent families in the village. It is now the home of Charles English, who operates the Stone House Museum dealing with the Civil War. (Courtesy Broome County Historical Society)

THE VILLAGE OF WINDSOR was incorporated on January 18, 1897. It is located on the northern and western banks of the Susquehanna River, which flows north to south past the village. It includes .79 square mile of land within its borders and has a population of 901 (2000 census figure). Although its incorporation took place shortly before the arrival of the twentieth century, the history of the village of Windsor begins over a century before.

David Hotchkiss came to the area in 1787 or 1788. He purchased ten lots of the Allison Classright patent in 1789, each lot containing approximately two hundred acres. This land included the southern portion of the current village. At a later date, he acquired parts of the Moore, Springsteen, and Hotchkiss tracts that make up the northern part of the village of Windsor.

Hotchkiss brought his sons, Amraphael, Cyrus, Charles, and Gilead, with him from Connecticut.

The Windsor Glove & Mitten Company operated from this building from 1910 until 1915. Other companies also used this building during the early 1900s. (Courtesy Broome County Historical Society)

After David's death, his eldest son, Frederick, also relocated to Windsor. Each of the sons contributed to the development of the village. David Hotchkiss donated a lot to be used as a village green, and he, along with his sons, constructed a Presbyterian church.

About this same time, Elias Whitmore moved to the new village, where he began buying land from the Hotchkiss family in 1804. He had been an established merchant at the older settlement of Oquago. He purchased several lots and can only be described as a wheeler-dealer. It was Whitmore who convinced the post office to relocate there in 1818; he also changed the name from Oquago to Windsor, presumably for Windsor, Connecticut. Whitmore served as a representative in Congress in 1827.

The village green was the center of much activity after 1840. The issue of slavery split the Presbyterian Church, and each faction built a new church. The former church was moved to Academy Street and used as a school. In 1880, a band pagoda was constructed while a cast-iron drinking fountain was added in 1899. To this day, the village green is still used to hold concerts and other community events. The nearby Community House is used to hold meetings of many groups and organizations from throughout the area.

The first Windsor Academy was built in 1845 using the lumber from the former Presbyterian Church. The building was used until 1884 when the second Windsor Academy was constructed on the same site. The old school was moved across the street and used as a roller-skating rink until it was demolished in 1906. A new section was added to the 1884 two-story brick school building in 1893. It was used until 1933 when it was replaced with the Alice Freeman Palmer School building. The new high school was built with the assistance of the federal WPA (Works Progress Administration) program. An addition was constructed in 1938. The increasing number of students in the consolidated Windsor School System eventually required a new high school. The present high school opened in September 1974; the former high school building is used as the middle school.

In the 1970s, a movement began to document and preserve many of the historic structures found in the village of Windsor. Some of the homes date back to the first half of the nineteenth century. After a thorough study by Marjory Hinman, Holly Gardiner, and others, the Windsor Historic District was created, the first such district in Broome County. The pride of the village property owners is apparent in the beautiful and graceful lines of the homes and business buildings of the community.

The Windsor Inn building is located on Route 79 in the village. The structure dates back to the 1880s. It began as the Hotel Windsor and was converted to an apartment house in 1967. (Courtesy Broome County Historical Society)

The *Windsor Standard* weekly newspaper continues to operate after a century of reporting the region's news. Main Street is the home to many interesting shops and businesses that reflect the historic

This is the interior of the Eagle Hotel on Main Street as it appeared in 1951. The building was later known as Turner's. (Courtesy Broome County Historical Society)

nature of the village. Several churches continue to thrive in the vicinity of the village green. Modern medical offices have been constructed nearby, offering doctors to the community's residents. The Stone House Museum, previously mentioned in this book, promotes the history of this area's participation in the Civil War while preserving the home of Stiles Hotchkiss. The industrial history of the Windsor area has been documented in the chapter on the town of Windsor. The various whip companies made up much of the industrial sector of Windsor's economy well into the twentieth century.

One of the most interesting personalities of the village has already been mentioned in this chapter. Alice Freeman was born in 1855 in the town of Colesville. Her father was a physician who moved into the village of Windsor within a few years of her birth. She graduated from Windsor Academy and then continued her education at the University of Michigan, one of the best-regarded colleges that would accept female students. She graduated with honors from the university and went on to become the head of the history department of Wellesley College. At the age of twenty-six, she became president of the college. She held that title for five years and then married Harvard University professor George H. Palmer. Alice Freeman Palmer also assisted in starting the College for Women at the University of Chicago. She became a member of the Massachusetts State Board of Education. Her career ended suddenly with her death in 1902 at the age of forty-seven while visiting Paris. She is listed on the New York State Governor's list of significant women of the state, and a historic marker located on the lawn of the Alice Freeman Palmer School denotes her contributions.

BIBLIOGRAPHY

Alberts, Robert C. *The Golden Voyage: The Life and Times of William Bingham, 1752–1804*. Boston: Houghton-Mifflin Company, 1969.

Avery, Grace F. *The Town of Vestal, 1823–1973*. Vestal, NY: Vestal Sesquicentennial Corporation, 1973.

Bothwell, Lawrence. *Broome County Heritage: An Illustrated History*. Woodland Hills, CA: Windsor Publications, 1983.

Ellis, David M., et al. *A History of New York State*. Ithaca, NY: Cornell University Press, 1957.

Fiori, James V. *Between the Arches: A History of the Town of Union*. Endicott, NY: Town of Union, 1990.

_____. *A History of Endicott*. 1982.

Hartzell, Karl Drew, comp. *The Empire State at War: World War II*. Albany, NY: State of New York, 1949.

Hinman, Marjory Barnum. *Bingham's Land, Whitney's Town: A Documentary History of the First Half Century in the Development of Binghamton, New York and Vicinity, 1794–1845*. Binghamton, NY: Broome County Historical Society, 1996.

_____. *Court House Square: A Social History*. Windsor, NY: Marjory Hinman, 1984.

_____. *The Creation of Broome County, New York*. Windsor, NY: Marjory Hinman, 1981.

_____. *Onaquaga, Hub of the Border Wars of the American Revolution in New York State*. Windsor, NY: Marjory Hinman, 1975.

Hinman, Marjory B. and Bernard Osborne. *Historical Essays of Windsor: Township and Village, Broome, New York*. Windsor, NY: Town of Windsor, 1976.

Historical Essays on the Sixteen Towns of Broome County. Broome County American Bicentennial Commission, 1976.

Inglis, William. *George F. Johnson and His Industrial Democracy*. New York: Huntington Press, 1935.

Irving, Walter V. *A History of Ross Park*. Binghamton, NY: Broome County Historical Society, 1985.

Jacob, R. Leone. *Famines, Fire & Festivals: A History of Colesville, 1785–1978*. Town of Colesville, 1978.

Jogo, Ellen and Kay Hoban. *Strolling Through Time: An Architectural Walking Guide of Historic Deposit, New York*. Deposit, NY: Deposit Community Historical Society, 2002.

Jones, Maldwyn Allen. *American Immigration*. Chicago: University of Chicago Press, 1960.

Keeler, Wesley B., comp. *Keeler Family: Ralph Keeler of Norwalk, CT, and Some of His Descendants*. Baltimore: Gateway Press, 1985.

Lawyer, William S. *Binghamton: Its Settlement, Growth and Development and the Factors in Its History, 1800–1900*. Binghamton, NY: Century Memorial Publishing Company, 1900.

McFee, Michele A. *Limestone Locks and Overgrowth: The Rise and Descent of the Chenango Canal*. Fleischmanns, NY: Purple Mountain Press, 1993.

McGuire, Ross and Nancy Grey Osterud. *Working Lives: Broome County, New York, 1800–1930*. Binghamton, NY: Roberson Center for the Arts & Sciences, 1980.

Rodgers, William. *THINK: A Biography of the Watsons and IBM*. New York: Stein and Day, 1969.

Seward, William Foote. *Binghamton and Broome County, New York: A History*. 3 vols. New York: Lewis Historical Publishing Company, 1924.

Smith, Gerald R. *The Valley of Opportunity: A Pictorial History of the Greater Binghamton Area*. Norfolk, VA: Donning Company, 1988.

Smith, H. P. *History of Broome County*. Syracuse, NY: D. Mason & Co., 1885.

Stevens, Marcia Wade Reed and Malcolm Peter Stevens. *Fire! The Story of the Binghamton Clothing Company Fire of July 22, 1913*. Binghamton, NY: Broome County Historical Society, 1988.

Sussman, Lance. *Beyond the Catskills: Jewish Life in Binghamton, New York, 1850–1975*. Vestal, NY: State University of New York at Binghamton, 1975.

Swan, Eleanor Brown. *Story of the Valleys: Town of Nanticoke*. Glen Aubrey, NY: Town of Nanticoke, 1981.

Thomas, Carol LeVan. *Naming the Hills and Hollows of Broome County*. Deposit, NY: Carol LeVan Thomas, 1999.

Versaggi, Nina. *Hunter to Farmer: 10,000 Years of Susquehanna Valley Prehistory*. Binghamton, NY: Roberson Center for the Arts & Sciences, 1986.

Watson, Thomas J. Jr. and Peter Petre. *Father, Son & Co.: My Life at IBM and Beyond*. New York: Bantam Books, 1990.

Wilkinson, J. B. *The Annals of Binghamton of 1840*. Binghamton, NY: Broome County Historical Society, 1992.

Zahavi, Gerald. *Workers, Managers, and Welfare Capitalism: The Shoeworkers and Tanners of Endicott Johnson, 1890–1950*. Urbana, IL: University of Illinois Press, 1988.

List of Sources

African Americans, 59, 60, 74, 85, 90, 91, 110, 158, 164, 169, 179, 187, 206, 212

Agriculture, 19, 39, 56, 58, 159, 166, 218, 219, 220, 268, 294

Airports, 182, 183, 196, 197, 269, 319, 373

American Revolution, 30–35, 38

Anitec, 164, 222, 384

Ansco, 164, 181, 187, 188, 205, 222, 350, 384

Arches, Endicott Johnson, 156

Barker, town of, 252–257, 308

Bennett, Abel, 101, 102

Bigler Mill, *See* Civil War

Bingham, William, 39–46, 65, 70, 75, 246, 260

Binghamton, city of, 46, 53, 54, 64, 68, 70, 71, 88, 100, 101, 244–251, 260

Binghamton Clothing Company, 168, 169, 171, 174

Binghamton, town of, 258–263

Binghamton University, 202, 238, 239, 350

Boscov's, 228

Boston Purchase, 38, 42, 256, 308, 322, 334, 341, 342

Brant, Joseph, 28, 35

Broome Community College, 42, 112, 192, 202, 204, 239, 288, 290, 291

Broome County Historical Society, 204

Broome, John, 52, 53, 138

Bundy Time Recording Company, 128, 131, 144, 157

Carousels, 154, 155, 373, 374

Castle Creek, 20, 58, 264, 265, 266

Catholic Church, 73, 76, 77, 85, 170, 171, 179

Chenango Canal, 65–73, 81, 88, 95, 98, 103, 104, 105, 246, 255, 288, 294, 295, 299, 388, 394

Chenango Forks, 254, 255, 256, 268

Chenango Point, 44, 45, 54, 55, 70, 246

Chenango River, 22, 39, 42, 45, 64, 68, 246, 286, 302

Chenango, town of, 52, 58, 195, 264–269, 314

Children, 112, 114, 142, 143, 144, 296, 297, 389

Christ Church, 62, 76, 86, 87, 94

Chugnut, 22, 237, 351

Cigars, 122–129

Civil Rights, 211, 212, 214

Civil War, 92, 93, 345, 406

Clinton, General James, *See Sullivan-Clinton Campaign*

Colesville, town of, 47, 48, 55, 82, 83, 133, 270–277

Conklin, town of, 93, 278–283, 302

Courthouses, 63, 101, 104, 105, 135, 136, 137, 138, 161, 192, 240, 241, 250

Crocker, Thomas "Old Bay", 116, 117, 119, 318

Delaware River, 24, 25, 328, 364

Deposit, village of, 31, 64, 80, 88, 89, 131, 328, 329, 330, 360, 362–367

Dickinson, town of, 203, 260, 284–291

Dickinson, Daniel S., 70, 85, 91, 92, 286, 394

Draper, Amos, 42, 348, 349

Dwight Block, 115, 116

Dwight, Walton, 115, 116, 117, 118

Education, 74, 75, 83, 84, 85, 114, 142, 143, 189, 202, 203, 207, 248, 257, 261, 263, 276, 282, 287, 304, 332, 333, 343, 344, 349, 368–369, 372, 394, 395, 396, 402, 408

Endicott, Henry B., 141, 148, 342, 371, 379

Endicott, village of, 143, 144, 176, 177, 230, 237, 340, 343, 368–375

Endicott Johnson, 106, 146–157, 160, 167, 186, 191, 199, 206, 207, 211, 214, 220, 222, 234, 345, 372, 375, 376, 377, 382

Endicott Land Company, 143, 370, 371

Exterminator, 134, 135

Fenton, town of, 71, 77, 292–299

Fire protection, 101, 102, 103, 138, 139, 168, 194, 195, 401

Floods, 171, 173, 174, 175, 310, 311, 331, 337, 366, 391, 401, 402

Fowler's, 157, 226, 244, 245

GAF, 187, 205, 350

Gates, Cyrus, 91, 318

General Electric, 198, 199, 235, 345

George F. Pavilion, 151, 152, 383

Germans, 87, 89

Great Depression, 162, 166, 167, 168, 178

Hand, Dr. Stephen, 85, 90

Harpur, Robert, 47, 48, 55, 202, 272, 273, 348

Hawley, Reverend Gideon, 21, 24, 361

Historic preservation, 136, 228, 231, 236, 237, 238, 408

Hooper, Robert, 39, 49

Hospitals, 136, 150, 163, 229, 373, 383

Hotels, 69, 120, 121, 130, 145, 211, 216, 217, 224, 365

Hughes Training, 222

Ice Age, 16, 17

Immigration, 56, 74, 87, 88, 89, 90, 108, 109, 110, 124, 148, 164, 225, 235, 290

Industry, 98, 99, 100, 105, 106, 107, 108, 122, 246, 249, 283, 305

Index

International Business Machines, 167, 176–181, 186, 204, 207, 230, 231, 246, 345, 372, 375

Interstates, 213, 214, 303, 305, 397

Ireland, David, 94

Irish, 74, 87, 88, 89, 289

Iroquois, 18–35, 58, 266, 348

Iroquois Confederacy, 18–35, 58, 266

Jewish, 88, 89, 90, 109, 179, 351

Johnson City, village of, 150, 340, 376–385

Johnson Field, 152

Johnson, C. Fred, 151, 154, 155, 381, 383

Johnson, George F., 128, 141, 143, 144, 148, 149, 154, 165, 192, 281, 342, 370, 371, 379, 382

Johnson, Harry L., 145, 154, 155, 380, 381

Johnson, Sir William, 23, 24, 28, 357

Jones, General Edward F., 98, 99, 100

Keeler, Lewis, 44, 54, 62

Kilmer, S. Andral, 132, 133, 270, 271

Kilmer, Willis Sharpe, 132, 133, 159

Kinyon, Nathaniel, 90

Kirkwood, town of, 201, 222, 280, 300–305

Korean War, 198

Ku Klux Klan, 164, 165, 166, 168

L-3 Communications, 201

Leonard, Joseph, 42, 286, 287

Lestershire, 130, 141, 150, 378

Libraries, 139, 140, 141, 152, 153, 220, 308, 309, 391

Link, Edwin A., 158, 181, 182, 184, 186, 198, 205, 222, 296, 305, 350

Lisle, town of, 52, 55, 60, 306–311, 334

Lisle, village of, 55, 386–391

Lockheed Martin, 231, 235, 345

Lumbering, 39, 50, 51, 56, 70, 72, 257, 349, 364

Mafia, 205, 206

Maine, town of, 91, 312–319

Mastodons, 17

McLean's, 226

Mersereau, Joshua, 48, 342, 349

Nanticoke, 22, 308, 320–325, 341

Native Americans, 18–35, 39, 58, 266, 340, 348, 364, 370, 378

New York State Inebriate Asylum, 110, 111, 304

New York State Institute for Applied Arts and Sciences, 192, 202, 203, 204. *See also* Broome Community College

Oakdale Mall, 215, 224, 381

Onaquaga, 22, 28, 33, 55, 62, 276

Otseningo, 22, 33, 237

Parks, 129, 140, 141, 150, 151, 152, 153, 154, 168, 190, 220, 298, 325, 337, 368, 369, 374, 383, 384, 397

Patterson, Amos, 49, 55, 61

Perry, Isaac, 110, 111, 112, 113, 116, 138, 140, 238

Phelps, Sherman, 117, 119

Police protection, 102, 103, 137

Poorhouse, 112, 115, 116, 203, 288, 291

Port Dickinson, village of, 71, 288, 392–397

Press Building, 133, 139, 140

Radios, 193, 263

Railroads, 73, 78, 79, 80, 81, 82, 98, 126, 214, 277, 302, 329, 336, 350, 379, 388

Religion, 62, 74, 75, 76, 86, 87, 88, 126, 153, 154, 169, 170, 262, 296, 297, 298, 315, 320, 321, 341, 348, 359, 364, 389

Roberson Museum, 134, 202

Robinson, General John C., 93, 94

Rose, William, 42

Ross Park, 129, 140, 141, 211

Round Top, 19, 340

Route 17, 152, 213, 215, 385

Rulloff, Edward, 118, 119

Sanford, town of, 326–331

Security Mutual Life Insurance Company, 138, 139, 140

Sisson, Benjamin, 72, 225

Slavery, 59, 60, 61, 90, 91

Smith, Gerrit, 91, 336

Square Deal, 143, 149, 379

Starrucca Viaduct, 78, 79, 81

State Office Building, 223, 224, 229

Stephens Square, 228

Sullivan-Clinton Campaign, 26, 27, 30, 32, 33, 34, 40, 58, 340, 348

Susquehanna River, 22 23, 32, 39, 49, 223, 246, 276, 280, 342, 406

Television, 195, 204, 207, 263, 353

Tioughnioga River, 55, 254, 308, 388, 400

Triangle, town of, 308, 332–337

Triple Cities College, 190, 191, 202, 350

Triplets, 152, 193

Trolleys, 127, 135, 143, 250

Turner, Dr. Frederick, 111, 112

Turnpikes, 45, 261, 287, 302, 335, 394

Twin Elms episode, 45

Union, town of, 34, 52, 55, 62, 95, 308, 314, 338–345, 348

Union, village of, 130, 341, 342

Urban renewal, 208, 209, 210, 216–221, 227

Vestal, town of, 22, 46, 105, 215, 346–353

Vietnam, 212, 213

Wagon manufacture, 96, 97, 99, 278, 279, 303, 304

Watson, Thomas J., 155, 157, 158, 167, 178, 180, 182, 192, 207

Weed's Tannery, 106, 130, 211

Whitney, Joshua, 42, 44, 54, 55, 60, 61, 62, 65, 70, 75, 76, 77, 84, 246, 287, 334

Whitney Point, village of, 55, 61, 91, 333, 334, 398–403

Williston, Reverend Seth, 62, 315, 389

Windsor, town of, 52, 60, 328, 354–361

Windsor, village of, 131, 405–409

Women, 58, 116, 124, 127, 160, 186

Woodland Period, 18, 19, 20

World War I, 160, 161, 164, 172, 173, 296

World War II, 182–189

ABOUT THE AUTHOR

Gerald R. Smith is a native of Broome County. He attended local schools, receiving degrees from Broome Community College and Binghamton University where he received his Master of Arts degree in history in 1981. He has served as City of Binghamton Historian since 1984 and Broome County Historian since 1988. He is a member of boards of directors of the Broome County Historical Society and the Southern Tier Underground Railroad Historical Society, a former president and board member of the Association of Public Historians of New York State, and a member of the All-Wars Memorial Committee and the Broome County Bicentennial Committee.

Gerry is the author of *The Valley of Opportunity: A Pictorial History of the Greater Binghamton Area* (Donning, 1988) and editor of *Odgen's Observations: Sketches of Life in Binghamton and Broome County* by William H. Ogden (Broome County Historical Society, 2002). He has authored over two hundred articles for local newspapers and statewide newsletters. He is the recipient of the Edmund J. Winslow Local Government Historian's Award for Excellence from the New York State Museum. He has participated in local documentaries and news broadcasts and has had his own segment, the "Remember When Scrapbook," on the Bill Parker radio show for seven years.

Since 2000, Gerry has been the head of the Broome County Local History & Genealogy Center in the Broome County Public Library where he has been an employee since 1978. The Center receives over forty thousand researchers each year. Gerry lives in Binghamton with his wife, Kathleen, and two daughters, Amelia and Abigail.